HIKING THE
HOLY MOUNTAIN

HIKING THE HOLY MOUNTAIN

Tales of Monks and Miracles
On the Trails of Mount Athos, Greece

JOHN MCKINNEY

OLYMPUS PRESS

Olympus Press,
A division of The Trailmaster, Inc.

Cover photo: Travis Dove
Interior Design by Lisa DeSpain

The Map of Mt. Athos on p. 16 is reprinted from the online Pilgrim's Guide of the Friends of Mount Athos (AthosFriends.org) with permission from cartographer Peter Howorth, The Friends of Mount Athos, and Filathonites.org.

Portions of this book previously appeared (in different form) in the *Los Angeles Times*.

The events in this story are true. Some names and identifying details of individuals have been changed to protect their privacy.

To learn more about *Hiking the Holy Mountain* and author John McKinney, visit TheTrailmaster.com

GRATITUDES

I feel an enormous sense of gratitude to those who helped make this book possible. A resonating *Efharisto* to Spiro Deligiannis for sharing his strong faith and his always uplifting company on and off the Holy Mountain. The author greatly appreciates John M. Daniel for his strong storytelling skills, deft editorial hand, and for making this book a much better one. I am very grateful to my godmother, Fotine (the Light) O'Connor, who has always believed in me, and has been a lifelong example to me of faith, courage, and generosity of spirit.

My companions on the first journey to the Holy Mountain, Mike Pahos and Ernest Kolendrianos, were unflagging in their support for my hikes around Mt. Athos, and continued their encouragement of me, and my literary wanderings, long after we returned to Santa Barbara. As for the late Jack Guerrier, our fellow pilgrim, we miss you. On my second journey to the Holy Mountain, I was thankful for the company of fellow eagle scout, Zachary Deligiannis.

Many friends, old and new, were supportive of me as I lived—and wrote—this story, including Voula Aldrich, Ken Atchity, Penny and Terry Davies, the Rev. Hans Kistner, Randy Langel, Shelly Lowenkopf, Bob McDermott, Tim McFadden, Gloria and George Menedes, Nadya Penoff, Susan Petty, Patti Stathis, Jonathan Toste, Alex Trigonis, and David Werk.

Another big thanks goes to George Mamalakis and Greg Pantages for generously sharing their time and talents to help create a warm and wonderful Hiking the Holy Mountain Book Trailer. For his considerable help in improving the phonetic spelling of the Greek words in this printing of the book, I am grateful to longtime Friend of Mount Athos, Bob Allison, Professor Emeritus of Religion and Classical & Medieval Studies, Bates College.

Many thanks to rock-of-faith parish priests Father Simon Thomas and Father Bob Fox, as well as to the many kind and encouraging parishioners at St. Barbara Greek Orthodox Church. I am also thankful for the wise counsel and calm support in moments of crisis of Father Nicholas Speier, dean of St. Athanasius Antiochian Orthodox Church.

It is perhaps true that Athos is out of touch with our times, far more than any monastery in the Western world. But precisely because of this it has much to teach us, since our salvation consists not in keeping up with the times but in transcending them.

—Thomas Merton
Disputed Questions

For you did not receive a spirit that makes you a slave again to fear, but you received the Spirit of adoption.

—Romans 8:15

CONTENTS

Part III Return To The Holy Mountain

CHAPTER 1

EVERY ICON TELLS A STORY

Every icon tells a story.
Or more than one story.

Today all eyes are on the icon of St. Barbara. On the fourth day of December, St. Barbara Day, my son and I gather with fellow parishioners for a special liturgy at St. Barbara Greek Orthodox Church to recall her story, remember her sacrifice, and honor her name.

Ringed with pine boughs and topped with a bright red ribbon, the larger-than-life-sized icon of St. Barbara looks festive indeed, and stands out from the five other, unadorned icons on the altar screen. St. Barbara Day is a big deal for us in Santa Barbara, California. Our parish priest, Father Simon, is joined by guest clergy—Father Gary from St. Demetrios in Camarillo and Metropolitan Gerasimos of San Francisco— making a powerful trio of voices combining to lead our congregation in what surely must be one of the world's most remarkable observances of the saint's day.

"Let us honor St. Barbara, for she broke the snares of the enemy; and like a sparrow, she, the all-modest maiden, was delivered out of them by the help and weapon of the cross."

Barbara is our hometown saint. When explorer Sebastian Vizcaino's crewmen found their tiny ship tossed about by a nasty storm, complete with epic thunder and lightning, along the California coast on the eve of St. Barbara's Day in 1602, they prayed for her to intervene and save them from a cruel death at sea. When the day dawned, the ship found safe harbor, and the grateful sailors named this coastal refuge for the saint. Mission Santa Barbara was consecrated on its present site on December 4, 1786, coinciding with the feast day of St. Barbara.

St. Barbara is known as protector of those who travel in thunder and lightning storms. On several occasions while out hiking and caught in thunderstorms, I have asked St. Barbara for her protection. Whether it was St. Barbara's intercession on my behalf or sheer dumb luck, I was not struck by lightning and lived to hike another day. As a hiking expert, it's my job to offer the very best trail-tested advice; I am of a mind to add my appreciation for St. Barbara's assistance in inclement weather in the next revised edition of my book, *The Hiker's Way*:

The Trailmaster's Tips to Lower Lightning Risk
- Avoid tall or isolated trees.
- Assume the recommended "lightning position."
- Ask St. Barbara for protection.

Silly? Maybe, but a lot of macho guys believe in her. Barbara is the patron saint of artillerymen and those in the armed forces who work with high explosives. St. Barbara's Day is celebrated by the British Royal Artillery, the Royal Canadian Artillery, the United States Marine Corps Explosive Ordnance Disposal Technicians, and the Artillery Corps of the Greek Army.

But there's no annual ceremony quite like the one at St. Barbara Greek Orthodox Church. After an hour or so of the special liturgy, with prayers and chanting as old as Byzantium, all of sudden—and unaccountably—light will shine through the east windows of the church and illuminate the icon of St. Barbara. Only on St. Barbara's Day, and only for a few moments, does the icon of St. Barbara receive such light.

I wonder what my son thinks of icons. When he was a little guy, I explained that icons are paintings that tell the story of Christian faith through events that really happened and people who really lived. At the same time, icons are not painted in a realistic style—the people have flat faces, and the backgrounds are flat, shadowless. But this symbolic, not realistic style appeals to kids; and my son liked looking at pictures of icons while I told him tales of the holy men and women they depicted.

Because the stilted hagiographies available to me had scant biographical detail, I confess I embellished the stories of the saints and took certain artistic liberties to be sure they captured my child's attention. Like many parents, I've found I can be more effective at enlightening kids if I'm at least a little entertaining. Ah, the challenge of imparting wisdom to children in the modern age.

He is nearly eighteen years old now and, like all of his generation, when he thinks of icons he first thinks of those little colored symbols on digital devices, including, but not limited to his laptop, tablet, smart phone, and smart TV. The most recognizable icon of our age? Maybe the iTunes icon, a music note in a circle. Or perhaps the Facebook icon, that plain white F on a blue background.

We are digitally besieged by hundreds, even thousands more icons, and emoticons, too, those smiling and frowning faces, those cats and dogs, attached by the millions to the end of text messages. Surely nearly everyone, even the most devout Christians among us, think of icons in terms of apps, not apostles.

And yet I know the lad feels connected to a few icons of the Orthodox Christian kind. This is a school day, and he ditched classes—third period Economics and fourth period Advanced Video Production—to attend this special service for St. Barbara. On the drive into the foothills above Santa Barbara to the church, he asks me to refresh his memory of the story of St. Barbara. "She was the one whose dad locked her in the tower, right?" he asks, stomping on the accelerator of my old BMW and speeding up Highway 154.

"Yes, that's our St. Barbara," I affirm.

Once upon a time in Heliopolis, there lived a bright and beautiful young woman named Barbara. Her father, Dioscorus, was a filthy-rich pagan, who locked Barbara in a tower in order to keep her under control and away from new ideas like those spread by the mostly secret, but nevertheless growing, movement of Christians.

Barbara's spirit was strong and she rejected an offer of marriage from a pagan suitor, one approved by Dioscorus; in fact, he himself presented the proposal on behalf of the young man he hoped would become his future son-in-law. Barbara turned him (them) down flat. Marrying an idolater would have released Barbara from the tower, but she chose to remain in confinement.

Why?

Because unbeknownst to her father, Barbara had become a Christian.

It must be said that Dioscorus attended to Barbara's material needs. Linens and food were raised and laundry and dirty dishes lowered by means of rope from tower to ground. Before departing on a business trip, Dioscorus ordered a private bathhouse built adjacent to the tower.

Construction plans called for two windows, but Barbara directed the workmen to put in three. The additional window shed more light on the indoor pool and seemed to make sense to the contractor, who complied with her request. Shortly thereafter, to the workers' amazement, Barbara used a powerful finger to inscribe the sign of the cross on a marble wall of the bathhouse.

When Dioscorus returned from his trip to find the extra window in the bathhouse, he got upset. His anger turned to fury when he spotted the cross on the wall. "Who made this mark?" he bellowed.

"Barbara," the workers answered, cowering at his rage. He became even more enraged when the workers told him that the cross was etched, as if by magic, by Barbara's finger.

Dioscorus stormed into the tower and demanded an explanation.

"The three windows are a symbol of the Holy Trinity," Barbara told her father. "Light from the Father, Son, and Holy Spirit. I am a Christian."

Hearing the "C" word put Dioscorus over the edge. He drew his sword and tried to kill her. Suddenly, however, a tower wall cracked and crumbled. Barbara escaped. She fled to the mountains, Dioscorus close on her heels.

Barbara shook her pursuers by hiking into a remote gorge. Here she was befriended by two good shepherds tending their flocks.

Make that one good shepherd. The first good shepherd refused to help Dioscorus find his daughter. But the bad shepherd betrayed Barbara and revealed to Dioscorus her whereabouts.

Divine retribution was swift: the duplicitous shepherd was turned to stone and his sheep changed to locusts. Unfortunately this bad end for the bad shepherd came too late for Barbara, in her father's clutches once more.

Rather than trying again to dispatch her on the spot, Dioscorus decided to drag Barbara before the regional despot, Martinianus, prefect of the province. Martinianus ordered Barbara to be disrobed and paraded naked through Heliopolis. However a thick fog came up all of a sudden, enshrouding the modest maiden and preventing anyone along the parade route from gawking at her.

After his attempt at publicly humiliating Barbara was thwarted by weather conditions never before seen in the "City of the Sun," Martinianus acted swiftly and without mercy. He threw her into prison—no residential tower this time, but a dark and dank lockdown—and ordered her tortured. But torches used by guards to burn her instead went out before the flames could reach her. Roman henchmen struck her with whips and clubs, and beat her head with a spiked club, but by morning Barbara's wounds had healed.

Word spread quickly throughout Heliopolis that Barbara, despite cruel torture, refused to renounce her faith. At night, for all to see, a light shone into the prison.

Faced with spooked jailors and a populace increasingly sympathetic to the Christian's plight, Martinianus condemned Barbara to death and gave Dioscorus the opportunity to carry out the sentence. On December 4, 280 AD, Dioscorus beheaded his daughter.

Traveling to his compound on the way back from the execution, Dioscorus was struck by lightning; his body ignited like a Roman candle and he was engulfed in flames.

"Christians are still getting their heads cut off," my son interjects at the conclusion of my tale of St. Barbara.

He must be referring to the recent horrific series of beheadings of captives by Islamic terrorists. "You talk about the killings in World History class?" I inquire.

Downshifting, he turns off the highway onto San Antonio Road and into the church parking lot. "No. Peter and I watched the video on my phone."

There you have it. Instant access online to videos about anything that intrigues him: daring mountain bike rides down impossible slopes, super-gross standup comedy acts, and fanatics, as crazed as any in the third century, decapitating people.

Has humankind evolved at all in the 1,734 years since Barbara lost her head? Is there any fundamental difference in beheaders between Discorus and pagans of Heliopolis and the guy nicknamed Jihadi John and the Islamic State of Iraq?

When I was a child, I could see through the icons, could imagine and recreate the lives and works of the saints. Like sunlight passing through stained glass, I entered, invisible and diffuse, radiated through the pictures, and emerged on the other side, transformed, given color and shape and form by the icon-maker and the Light of Lights. On the other side I marched into epic battles, witnessed conversions and cruci-fixions, the dawn of creation and the fall of Constantinople. I was there when Moses parted the Red Sea and St. George slew the dragon.

Like the children in the C.S. Lewis *Chronicles of Narnia* novels, who wriggled past old coats hanging inside a ward-robe and entered the kingdom of Narnia, I, too, left behind disbelieving adults and entered a landscape inhabited by the competing forces of good and evil, a kingdom where a child's imagination knew no bounds.

My journey began with the light of a single candle lit, in accordance with Eastern Orthodox tradition, at the church entrance. I made the sign of the cross and kissed the icon of St. Sophia, then entered the cathedral and looked to, and through, the particular icon that beckoned.

My Sunday school teachers explained that the icons por-trayed holy men and women of the early church, and told the story of the faith. Icons were integral to this storytelling because very few of the first Christians could read. The saints and their wisdom were still relevant to our faith, my teachers empha-sized. Orthodoxy was not a word-of-the-Bible-only religion, not *sola Scriptura* at all, but a living faith backed by two thou-sand years of tradition. Orthodox Christians do not worship icons, as some fundamentalist Protestants suspect, but merely venerate them for the holy men and women they depict.

The icons in St. Sophia Greek Orthodox Cathedral in Los Angeles were inspired by those that graced another St. Sophia, the great Church of Divine Wisdom, built in Constantinople in the sixth century. St. Sophia of Constantinople gave full expres-sion to the Byzantine notion of the Church as symbol of the universe, with the dome representing the vault of heaven. The architects and builders commissioned by Justinian, Emperor of Constantinople, carried out this idea so well that it became the model for Orthodox church building for the next millennium and a half. Many a chronicler of Byzantium reported that he found himself transported into a heaven on earth.

In fact, icons are intended to facilitate transport in a heavenly direction. Icons are known as windows into heaven in the Orthodox faith, and to pray with icons is to journey through these windows into heaven.

It was not exactly heaven I found when I attended St. Sophia of L.A., in the 1960s. True, there was Godly inspiration high above the pews: on the dome Christ, glowing, surrounded by the prophets who preceded him and the evangelists who followed him, looked down at me from the heavens. Also gazing downward at the congregation was the blessed Virgin Mother, arms outstretched, way up in the apse.

As the Divine Liturgy proceeded, my eyes were drawn, as a moth to light, to the icons at the base of the dome or to those stationed in the lower reaches of the cathedral, at eye level, in what Sunday school instructors called "the earthly church." These were the icons that inspired—St. Paraskevi, holding a palm branch, symbolic of victory for the early Christians (and often carried by the martyrs on their way to execution). And St. Constantine the Great, gripping a globe topped with a cross; this Roman Emperor's 313 AD Edict of Milan allowed freedom of worship. And St. Helen, who uncovered the cross of Jesus, and St. Theodora, who thwarted the iconoclasts and restored the holy icons. These early church fathers and mothers stood next to exquisite stained glass windows of similar height so that sun shone onto the icons and painted the saints with light.

Sunday school lessons provided only the most basic biographical information about the saints: when and where they lived, as well as how they suffered and died (often gruesomely) for their beliefs; thus certain artistic liberties were necessary to create a compelling story. Like a screenwriter whose producer offers only a two-paragraph biography and assigns him the task of scripting a two-hour bio-pic "inspired by the life story of—," I spun extraordinary stories from these brief synopses.

I took home coloring book pictures—black and white images of the saints that we kids filled in with crayons—and used them as inspiration for the stories I would compose. Among my earliest writings were fanciful accounts of the lives of the saints based partly on Encyclopedia Britannica entries and scant references I discovered in the Downey City Library.

If ever a church resembled a stage set, it's St. Sophia. The cathedral was built in the early 1950s, funded in large measure by the generosity of movie mogul Charles Skouras, a Greek immigrant who, beginning in nickelodeon days, had amassed a fortune in the film industry. Skouras employed set designers and other Hollywood artisans to work on the church.

The result of these artistic and architectural efforts was a magnificent homage to Byzantium. Inside the church, Skouras incorporated the very best state-of-the-art 1950 movie theater technology: a sophisticated lighting system, complete with spotlights and dimmers to highlight different icons or parts of the church; magnificent acoustics and sound system, all the better to amplify the liturgy, the priest's sermon, and the eighty-voice choir; an air conditioning system so powerful that parishioners shivered in their wool suits, even in summer, and declared that the cold would freeze the devil himself.

My favorite Skouras touch was "the electric saints," moveable icons on the altar screen, which disappeared to allow passage of the priest and altar boys, then closed again to secure the holy, behind-the-scenes mysteries.

The enormous brass baptismal font, the ornate Bishop's throne, two dozen enormous crystal chandeliers—everything about St. Sophia Cathedral is of epic proportion, reflecting the tastes of a man who loved, and believed the public loved, such spectacle. His brother, Spyros Skouras, Twentieth Century Fox studio chief, went on to green-light such cinematic spectacles as *Cleopatra*, starring Liz Taylor and Richard Burton. In a city

boasting such Hollywood picture palaces as the Egyptian Theater and Grauman's Chinese Theatre, with Middle Eastern
and Far Eastern inspirations respectively, Skouras, the proud
Hellene, may have thought it fitting to build a Byzantine Theater with Near Eastern decor. Skouras was entombed behind
the church in a magnificent mausoleum, a fitting final resting
place for a man who combined the spiritual with the theatrical.

With Sunday mornings spent in such surroundings, it
followed that the favorite films of my youth were Technicolor
spectacles: *Ben Hur, The Ten Commandments, Spartacus.* Like
the icons, those epic movies, as well as *The Robe* and *Deme-
trius and the Gladiators,* also told stories about events that
really happened and people who really lived.

Many were my own stories of adventures behind the
icons, but my strongest recall is of the final act of what might
be titled "The Fighting Christians." The story, set in about
140 AD, centers on the brave Captain Yannis, who saves his
fellow Christians by leading a group of guerrillas to victory
over a legion of Roman soldiers. The story had everything a
boy like me could imagine: an exotic locale, plenty of sword-
play and bloodshed, an epic battle between good and evil.

How easy it is in boyhood to dream of heroes, to imagine
that you, yourself could be a hero, too, if only you lived in
ancient times. And how easy it is in younger days to believe
that one day you would live the life you imagined.

*"O noble Champion, following God who is reverently praised in
Trinity, you abandoned the temple of idols."*

Near the icon of St. Barbara is a small table draped in a
white tablecloth, upon which rest two lighted candles and
a small ornate jewelry box containing a relic of St. Barbara
herself. The candles cast insufficient light to reveal St. Barbara's eyes, so it is impossible to tell where she is looking.
Near the icon stands a fifteen-foot tall Orthodox Cross with
Jesus upon it. The head of Christ is turned to the right, and

in the dim light it isn't possible to discern where our Savior is looking, either.

My son seems fully absorbed in the service. He watches the priests offer prayers in Greek and English, and listens to our family friend Randy chant in the ancient Byzantine way. He crosses himself at the appropriate time, looks to the icon of St. Barbara and then to the eastern windows of the church. Waiting for the light.

We worship and wait for the light in good company. Next to my son stands our longtime family friend Mike Pahos, eighty-five years old, chairman of the church's building committee back in the 1980s and the one in charge of selecting the icons and iconographers. Twenty years ago, he, too, journeyed to the Holy Mountain, a man on a mission: find a famed iconographer and commission a work for our church.

Across the aisle is another dear family friend, Nadya Penoff, a brilliant artist who works in stained glass, who has fashioned windows for Orthodox Churches across North America and was the one who created all the stained glass windows for St. Barbara.

"Struggling and suffering, O Barbara, you were not overwhelmed by the threats of tyrants."

In the pew in front of us is musician Chris Hillman, member of the 1960s rock group, the Byrds, famed for its pioneering efforts in folk rock, country rock, and psychedelic rock. And appreciated by Christians for the hit tune "Turn! Turn! Turn! (To Everything There Is a Season), with lyrics lifted from Ecclesiastes. "A time to be born, and a time to die…" Chris Hillman still rocks; my son and I are fans.

My son is a young man with an old soul, I muse. He likes classic cars with manual transmissions, repairing bicycles, and backpacking into the wilderness. As a baseball player he looks like a picture on a 1962 baseball card: 6 feet 1, 185 pounds, the brim of the cap over his close-cropped hair pointed straight, short baseball pants reaching to the bottom of the knee, high socks and stirrups. He is the only high school hitter for a hundred miles around who uses a wood bat, who prefers maple to metal.

He wears an Orthodox cross and chain. Sometimes the silver cross stands out boldly against his dark polo shirts, but more often it's tucked away under his clothing. The cross often pops out from under his jersey during baseball games; and, when he fails to cover it up, sometimes an umpire will notice and remind him of the "No Jewelry Rule." And as aggressively as he plays the game, it's remarkable he's lost only one cross—that while making a diving catch. Somewhere in right centerfield at Eddie Mathews Field at Santa Barbara High School lies buried a silver Orthodox cross. Other than the week he went cross-less while we ordered a replacement, he has worn a cross 24/7 since he was twelve years old.

He has all the latest electronics in his room, including a wake-the-dead sound system, but the speakers are small and hidden, and the digital devices discreetly tucked away. His room is spare, monk-like, with only two works of art: a large poster-size photograph of him high up, hurtling through the alpine air on his mountain bike, and an icon of one holy man hanging on the wall above his bed.

That icon, too, has a story.

"Dad, can you tell me again about the icon?" he asked recently. "The whole story this time."

By *whole* story, this man-child meant the full, grown-up version of how I became his father and how he became my son. I have told him age-appropriate versions from about the time he started Sunday school. But I have never told him the story in the way I would if I was a public speaker telling a long tale to an adult audience or in the way I would write the narrative for adult readers. We set a date for the storytelling—his name's day, a few weeks from then.

It's time. He's not a little boy anymore, that's for sure; he's a young man about to turn eighteen years old, to soon graduate from high school, and faced with huge decisions about potential colleges and careers.

I feel oddly nervous, though, about telling him the story. The end of innocence?

No, it's not that.

It's...the icons.

My faith in icons.

My lack of faith in icons.

Get over it, John. This is the one story only his father can tell him. This story is not online. Not on video. Had I access to today's digital technology twenty years ago, I most certainly would have used my camera phone to record high-def video of my journey to the Holy Mountain, edited it, added titles, graphics, and a Byzantine music soundtrack, and I would likely have shared it on social media and on my website.

But I have no video to share. All I have to help me remember the story are pages and pages of notes scribbled in my dreadful handwriting and a few dozen still photographs.

And icons.

Icons in our church.

Icons in our home.

Icons in monasteries at the end of the earth.

I've told this story in public only twice. I shared the story with friends and family right here in the church hall, just across the courtyard from the church on the day of my son's baptism. And I told the story to a huge audience at a mega-sized Christian church in Orange County. Both tellings were hugely successful, but...after hiking a lot and praying a lot... it came to me that this wasn't the right time to tell the story.

Ecclesiastes calls to me, rock 'n' roll style from the Byrds:

And a time to every purpose under heaven

Here comes the light. Out of nowhere. White light. It shines first on the top of St. Barbara's head. The light does not travel from east to west across the altar, illuminating each passing saint as it goes. It simply targets St. Barbara, fifth icon from the right, second saint from the left. One moment the icon of St. Barbara is lit by just two candles; the next moment her halo glows with the light of two hundred.

Amidst the congregants there are some intakes of breath and a few sighs. A little girl near the front of the church tells her mother, "Look!"

Out of the mouth of babes. We all want to shout, "Look!"

I know seeing is believing, but believing what I am seeing in this light is another matter. Only St. Barbara's face is spotlighted, not her red and blue garments, not the gold background surrounding her. I look closely to see if she is looking at us, but the light is so strong, so intense, that it is impossible to meet her gaze.

As strong as the light is on the eyes, it's even stronger on the heart. I feel unstuck in time, pulled toward the light on the icon of St. Barbara even as another light shines nearby. Another bolt out of the blue. A second light, brighter even than the one on St. Barbara, illuminates Jesus on the cross.

Behind the light I see a mountain, nearly obscured by clouds. And hikers, a half-dozen of them. The strongest hiker stands atop the summit; the weakest has fallen and lies on the shoulder of the rocky peak. The other hikers struggle up the mountain and into the thin air, into the white light.

They missed a switchback, I realize. They've lost the trail. And they are leaving the fallen hiker behind. I've got to help them. I've got to tell them where the trail goes.

The hiker at the top of the mountain raises his right hand and beckons to me.

I begin hiking.

Into another time.

Into another icon.

Into another story.

PART I

The Holy Mountain

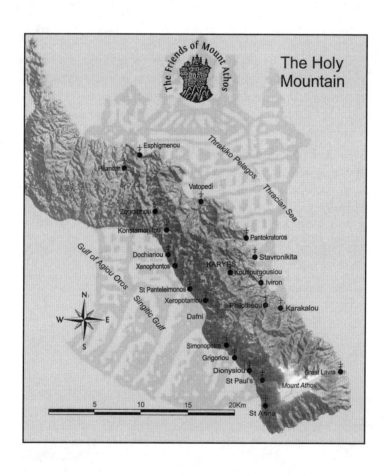

CHAPTER 2

THE NOVICE

"*O Lord I call to you; come quickly to me. Hear my voice when I call to you.*"

Late afternoon sunlight arcs through the west window of the church, spotlighting the bearded faces of the three chanters. It is visible light, given texture and three dimensions by candle smoke and heavy incense.

"*Set a guard over my mouth O Lord: Keep watch over the door of my lips.*"

The voices of the three monks blend as if they've chanted together in the Byzantine way for decades, though this is impossible, because the youngest of them has been at the Monastery of Xeropotamou for less than a year. A shaft of window light plays upon their three beards: a gray-going-white one on a monk in his late seventies; a black-going-gray one on a monk in his mid-fifties; a chestnut beard framing the face of a novice in his early thirties.

The novice is Dean Trigonis, brother of my fellow parishioner Alex Trigonis, of St. Barbara Greek Orthodox Church in Santa Barbara California. Dean is, or was, by all accounts a well adjusted young man raised in a tranquil suburb in the shadow of Pasadena's Rose Bowl. An excellent student, he earned scholarships and went to UCLA

He has come a long way, as they say.

Dean is a *rasophoros*, a cassock wearer. A year's worth of uncut hair is gathered by a rubber band and stuffed under his novice's cap. His beard is not one of those neatly trimmed businessman's beards, or one of those fashion growths so popular with movie industry execs, or even a sign of rebellion by a grad student seeking to emulate the philosopher of his thesis. Wild and woolly, his is the beard of a believer, of an ascetic-in-the-making, hirsute enlistment in the monks' battle against vanity, as well as testimony to the monastery's absence of mirrors.

"Let not my heart be drawn to what is evil, to take part in wicked deeds with men who are evildoers, let me eat not of their delicacies."

The two monks and the novice have strong voices; the psalms reach every corner of the church. Byzantine music, unlike Byzantine politics, is not complex. The chanting is homophonic—that is to say there is only one part—so that even when many chanters participate in the psalmody, they all chant together, as though their voices are coming out of one mouth. At the Monastery of Xeropotamou, the monks' three-part harmony is not with each other, but with God.

A psalm read is altogether different from a psalm chanted, I realize, as the monk's chanting vibrates the wooden prayer stall where I stand, sending a tingle up my arms, a shiver down my spine. Beauty, poetry, a Lord-is-my-shepherd kind of comfort—these are the ways psalms previously affected me.

Until vespers at Xeropotamou, that is.

The words are the same as those in the Bible, but the way the monks chant them, so fervently, so urgently, transforms the verses into battle hymns. Psalmodizing, as practiced at the monastery, is a weapon in the war against the devil.

Dean has that determined look of an earlier foot soldier for Christ, St. Demetrios, sculpted in marble and built, in all his full-length glory, into the western wall of the exo-narthex. But Demetrios is Byzantine bas relief; Dean is a nice boy from Southern California, offspring of parents I know,

18

a kid who grew up in a suburb near, and nearly like, the one where I was raised.

How—and why—does a man go from the most material of all worlds to a life without goods? How does a man travel in body and spirit from Los Angeles to *Agion Oros*, from the City of the Angels to the Holy Mountain?

Just transporting the body to Mt. Athos is an ordeal. A Byzantine journey it has been for the four of us: a hundred-mile drive from Santa Barbara to Los Angeles; a ten-hour flight from Los Angeles to Paris; then a flight to Athens; then a flight to Thessaloniki, where Mike, Ernest, Jack, and I spend a long day in Greece's second largest city confirming and securing our *diamonitiria*, our Athos visitor's permits; then a three-hour bus ride across the Halkidiki peninsula to Ouranoupolis, the Heavenly City, debarkation point and port for Mt. Athos. Then elaborate custom formalities, as if we are leaving Greece (which we are not) and entering another country. Here I, the blue-eyed, fair-haired Anglo-surnamed pilgrim am denied permission to board the Holy Mountain-bound boat by a trio of Athonite functionaries. I'm asked to prove that I'm truly an Orthodox Christian by producing a baptismal certificate. (No such proof is required for any olive-skinned, Greek-surnamed pilgrims in the disorderly queue around the harborside table that serves as the customs office. Outrage in the form of my shouting at them in my bad Greek does not sway the Holy Passport Control, but Ernest producing a letter from the Patriarch in Constantinople positively overwhelms them. In it, I am described as "a man of letters." One official nods, one makes the sign of the cross, and the third immediately wields his rubber stamps.

We board the small ferry for a three-hour ride along the peninsula named for its most prominent feature: Mt. Athos. As the boat chugs along the coast, we pilgrims peer through a light drizzle at the west-facing monasteries—Konstamonitou, Dochiariou, Xenophontos, Panteleimon—castles in the clouds. The Holy Mountain itself is enshrouded in mist. From the port town of Dafni, an hour's hike up a rough dirt road, past a two-tiered waterfall and a trickling stream, brings us to the Monastery of Xeropotamou. The Monastery of the Dry River, certainly a misnomer on a wet day like this one, looked four-square and bleak from the ferry, but is much more accommodating up close.

After the traditional welcome of *loukoumi* (a candy known everywhere but on Greek soil as Turkish delight), with a shot of ouzo and a glass of water, the guestmaster tells us the story of St. Paul of Xeropotamu and inspects our diamonitiria. Soon after we are shown to our quarters, the banging starts. A monk beats the *semandron*, a wooden gong, summoning the monks—and us pilgrims—to vespers.

The semandron, a great plank of wood, scarred and seasoned by long centuries of use, serves the monastery in place of a bell. Balancing the semandron on his shoulder, the *kampanaris* raps it in urgent rhythm with a little wooden hammer, as he carries it around the church, which stands in the middle of the courtyard. The church represents the ark of salvation; and the monk who walks around it three times while hammering on the semandron is in fact echoing the sound of Noah's tools summoning the chosen to join him aboard the ark while time yet remains. His first circuit is a call to reptiles and creeping things, his second for four-footed creatures; his last, for us sons of men.

"My prayer is ever against the deeds of evildoers; their rulers will be thrown down from the cliffs, and the wicked will learn that my words were well spoken."

The church is too full of light and music for me to pray. And packed with icons.

Xeropotamou's art is overwhelming in its quantity, visible at every turn. (What a contrast to our St. Barbara Greek Orthodox Church, unadorned by frescoes, and with a bare

minimum of icons!) The narthex is full of frescoes, domi-
nated by unsettling scenes from the Book of Revelation and
particularly ascetic-looking saints such as St. Onuphrios, a
fifth-century hermit, bare-chested with wild hair and waist-
length beard.

Inside, it is the icons that overwhelm: permanent icons
for centuries affixed in the same location and hundreds of
portable icons—displayed in the sanctuary, on the amazingly
carved wood iconostasis (altar screen) and all around the interior of the church.

Chief among the icons is that of St. Paul of Xeropotamou, introduced to us as we arrived.

Before he was Paul he was Procopios, son of the Byzantine
Emperor Michael Kuropalatos. Raised with extreme wealth
and privilege, he became a scholar of some renown, writing
treatises on the Holy Mother and martyred saints.

But tiring of the material world and the life of the mind,
Procopios abruptly left Constantinople and journeyed to the
Holy Mountain. After a stay in the wilderness and tonsure as
a monk, he adopted the name Paul. Settling near the ruins of
a first rendition of Xeropotamou, Paul soon attracted a dedicated group of ascetics.

Meanwhile back in Constantinople, a close relative,
Romanus, became emperor and summoned Procopios, now
Paul, to court. At the royal reception for him, Paul showed
up wearing a torn robe and holding a cross—which endeared
him to the most pious of the Byzantines. As it turns out,
Romanus was grievously ill, but thanks to Paul's healing
hands, Romanus rapidly rebounded to good health, and the
grateful emperor offered Paul his choice from all of the riches
and privileges of Byzantium. Paul declined, making only one
request: restore Xeropotamou.

Romanus granted Paul's wish and funded a big-time
reconstruction of the monastery, which returned to greatness;

and Paul, serving as Abbot of Xeropotamu, attracted a fervent community of monks. When Paul died, per his wishes he was to be buried on the other side of the Athos peninsula near the Holy Mountain; however, the ship carrying his body was blown way off course and Paul ended up in Constantinople, where he was entombed in the Great Church of St. Sophia.

St. Sophia. My mind drifts to St. Sophia, the cathedral in Los Angeles. Surely Dean worshipped there in his youth. Listened to the choir, looked up at the icons. What was it about Greek Orthodoxy, Southern California style, that put him on the path to monkhood?

I gaze through a cloud of candle smoke and incense at my fellow Santa Barbarans, each of them looking in a different direction at the hundreds of icons in the church.

The trio of church leaders is on a mission to learn more about icons, and by pursuing connections in Thessaloniki and elsewhere in Greece, they hope to locate just the right iconographer and commission one or more icons for display at St. Barbara. They even have high hopes for finding a top iconographer right here on the Holy Mountain and asking him to create icons for our church.

For Mike Pahos, this trip is a splendid passage into retirement from long service as the Santa Barbara County Parks director. Dr. Ernest Kolendrianos, pediatrician, avid student of Greek history, and the consummate organizer, was the driving force behind this trip. And Jack Guerrier, engineer and director of our annual Santa Barbara Greek Festival, is an easy-going traveling companion.

Our intention is to travel together to certain monasteries. The three other Santa Barbarans will concentrate on viewing the priceless art and architecture of ten monasteries on the jam-packed itinerary Ernest has prepared. I will focus on experiencing the natural attractions of the Holy Mountain, first on solo hikes, then hitting the trail with my friend Spiro Deligiannis, who will join me later in the week.

My mission to Mt. Athos is clear: Hike the Holy Mountain and write about its trails for my hiking column in the Sunday Travel section of the *Los Angeles Times*. I also expect to write other versions of the story for nature and travel magazines that have previously published my work.

"My eyes are fixed on you, O Sovereign Lord; in you I take refuge. Do not give me over to death. Keep me from the snares they have laid for me, from the traps set by evildoers. Let the wicked fall into their own nets, while I pass by in safety."

I can't wait to start hiking tomorrow morning. I have traveled by bus and boat and plane, and I am so ready to travel by my own two feet. I need to get into the fresh air and clear my head, all of a sudden uncomfortably busy with questions I've never before contemplated:

Do the monks see God?

No man can see God.

Do the monks know God?

Only fools say it is possible.

Do the monks love God?

Of course.

Do they praise God?

With song. With art. In prayer. In deed.

What does God want of those who say they want to be with Him alone?

I have no idea.

"When my spirit grows faint within me, it is you who know my way. In the path where I walk men have hidden a snare for me."

We adjourn, still in strict silence, to the *trapeza*, or refectory. The novice Dean Trigonis has apparently drawn mess hall duty, and he points us pilgrims to our places at the long wooden tables, where plates of food await. An older monk steps over to me and asks, "Are you Orthodox?"

"Yes," I answer. "I'm Orthodox."

"Yannis is Orthodox," Dean confirms.

I never thought of myself as particularly light complexioned, but I sure appear so in this crowd, I muse as I scan the refectory.

All of the monks and most of the pilgrims are of Mediterranean hue and height. Even the disciples depicted in the Last Supper fresco on the refectory wall are ultra-Levant-looking. No fair-haired angels and apostles around here.

Far away from the monks and pilgrims, at a table near the kitchen, are seated the only distinctly non-Greek-looking group. Germans, I guess. If I were not Orthodox the monks would no doubt seat me, too, in such social exile.

After a short prayer, we sit and eat in silence, while one of the monks reads what one of the early ascetics had to say on the subject of fasting. The reading is in Greek so archaic and difficult to follow that even the Greek pilgrims tune out and give full attention to their food.

To a man, every pilgrim who preceded us to Athos warned of the Spartan rations we would face, and our first dinner on the Holy Mountain is a light one: a Greek salad of tomato and cucumber, a slab of feta cheese, olives, *pastichio* (macaroni casserole), bread, and wine.

I try to eat rapidly (supper is over for everyone the instant the abbot finishes his meal), but the bread and cheese sticks in my dry throat. Where did those vexing questions at vespers come from?

Mike, who sits across the table from me, offers more pastichio. I accept. Carbohydrate loading, energy for my hike to Philotheou Monastery.

After supper, we are escorted back to the church where a young monk, custodian of the holy relics, brings out an assortment of cases and displays for us pilgrims to view.

"Xeropotamou has the largest piece of the Holy Cross," the monk explains, showing us a foot-long piece of wood encased in silver gilt. "Notice the hole made by one of the nails."

After the monastery was all but destroyed by fire in the mid–seventeen hundreds, Xeropotamou monks toured Europe, exhibiting this piece of the Holy Cross and raising funds to rebuild the monastery, the monk tells us.

We're shown bones of the Forty Martyrs in a special display, St. Auxentius the New Martyr (his skull in a special silver shrine), St. Tryphon's left foot in a jeweled slipper, fragments of Basil the Great and Gregory the Theologian, Timothy the Apostle and Jacob the Persian. As the pilgrims crowd closer—particularly the Greek ones, who do not know how to queue—it becomes clear that we are not merely to view the relics but to venerate them; that is, to make the sign of the cross, and kiss each and every one of them.

Ugh. I'm totally grossed out. I can't possibly kiss the bones. The pastichio sticks in my throat. My stomach somersaults.

How to explain my revulsion?

I have a strong stomach, as they say. Blood pouring from wounds, unusual ethnic foods, picking up insects or amphibians—these phase me not at all. But bones? I make my cross, kiss air over the bones, press tight lips to the side of display cases. I hurriedly exit the church, feeling as if I've flunked my first test of faith.

Xeropotamou's novice awaits me outside. Dean Trigonis appears nervous. His lips move almost imperceptibly, like a dance school student counting one-two-three during a practice waltz. He's repeating the Jesus prayer, I suppose.

He welcomes me warmly, if stiffly, politely inquiring about the parish, parishioners, priest. "I remember your face now," he relates. "Your daughter, your wife...." He stops, after listing everything he doesn't have, or ever will have.

But what are home and family when you have God? I wonder.

A few days before, at our church's Easter picnic in Santa Barbara, I said goodbye to Dean's mother. Catherine Trigonis asked me to take her son a huge, home-baked Easter bread with a red egg in the center and some *koulourakia*, Greek cookies. How will I be able to I tell her that this lovingly prepared loaf of bread and this tin of cookies, which I toted six thousand miles, ended up not in her son's private cell but in the monastery's communal kitchen? Unlike the soldier far from home or the student at college who may choose whether or not to share his mother's treats, a monk must share with all his brothers and it is the monastery, not the monk, who decides how such foodstuffs are to be divided. Apparently a monk—or at least a novice—may not own a loaf of bread, or even a single cookie.

Checking his watch, Dean says he has but forty minutes to spend with guests. The abbot is very strict about a novice's visitors. He suggests we walk out to the courtyard to watch the sunset.

Dean walks with a limp. No doubt the monastery's hard surfaces are unforgiving toward one who spends a lot of time on his knees or standing. We stroll into a spacious square that faces the Aegean and the setting sun. Alas, the Greek pilgrims who've staked out the square smoke like fiends. Repelled by cigarette fumes, we retreat to a bench that faces away from the sunset, but toward the Holy Mountain.

"It's understandable that visitors think monks have all the time in the world," Dean relates. "But actually we're very scheduled."

"Do you have a lot of studies, reading assignments and such?" I inquire.

He smiles indulgently. "This isn't like a college. I read the works of the early Mt. Athos monks, the lives of the saints, the Bible, but my main study is just being here, praying, working."

"They assign much work to do around the monastery?"

"Not really," Dean answers. When he becomes a monk, he'll receive a yearly assignment like the others, but for now, he has some simple duties—lighting candles at one of the outlying chapels, helping out once in a while in the refectory.

I compliment him on his singing. "The psalms—I've never heard them chanted like that," I tell him. "You have a wonderful voice."

"With God's help, my specialty—I guess that's what you'd call it in the world—will be chanting," Dean affirms.

Chanting, he explains, is recognized on Athos as one of the major kinds of "work" or activity that should be performed by a monk. It is a form of prayer in which both the soul and the body participate. Chanting is a social and physical activity, unlike purely mental prayer. The latter is the highest form of praying; such prayer is carried out solely by the mind and through the emotional center, or heart. Mental prayer is superior to psalmoziding but more difficult to practice because it requires great concentration and suppression of the senses.

"Mental prayer is reserved for one advanced in his spiritual life. And I'm not very spiritually advanced yet," Dean concludes modestly.

Holy Moly. If *he's* not spiritually advanced, I must not even be a blip on the spirit meter.

A visitor approaches. By appearance, he looks to be one of the Germans I spotted at the back of the refectory.

"Excuse me, maybe you can answer a question. I do not understand the Christianity practiced here."

"Maybe I can help," Dean replies, inviting the visitor to sit beside us.

Introductions are made. Hans Koppelburg is from Luxembourg. He's a tall, handsome, silver fox of a man of about fifty who speaks excellent, highly polished continental English.

"I traveled a very long way to Mt. Athos, and I find I am not permitted to join in," he complains to Dean. "I must observe the church service from the very back and may not worship with the others. I'm not permitted to view the icons or the relics. I must sit at a separate table while eating. All because I am not Orthodox. Are we inferior Christians? What kind of Christianity is this?"

Dean Trigonis is silent for a moment. His lips move slightly and I wonder if he is reciting the Jesus prayer again to give him strength. "We have traditions in the Orthodox faith, going back to the time of Christ. We preserve the doctrine of the Lord uncorrupted. We keep the holy traditions just as we received them."

Face-to-face with this challenge to his faith, Dean's jaw sets. His eyes flash, his countenance darkens—or perhaps only seems to darken in the lengthening shadows at day's end. The determined look he had while chanting pales beside his visage now. "Many Orthodox Christians have died to protect our beliefs. Many monks from this Holy Mountain have died for these beliefs. All of us, right now, would die for these beliefs."

Hans is plainly disconcerted by the ferocity of Dean's reaction. Perhaps he had been expecting a more academic, more collegial discussion. "I'm not asking you to die for your beliefs, or even change them. I am asking you to practice the Christian love that you preach and to stop judging others."

"I am not judging you or your Christianity," Dean replies. "You seem very sincere, perhaps a better Christian than I or anyone sitting here. But you are not an Orthodox Christian."

Has Dean become a zero-tolerance zealot? Persuaded that all those of other faiths, those who maintain that the Holy Spirit proceeds from the Father *and the Son*, or those who cross themselves from left to right, are irredeemably hell-bound?

"I'm sure you and other non-Orthodox, if you're sincere in your love of God, will feel God's love and mercy. But you cannot, in your present state, be members of the Orthodox Church, or fully participate in its practices."

Hans sighs. "I can understand there are historical reasons why we are not permitted in the church. But why not in the refectory? At supper, we had to sit apart from everyone, including the Greek guests and these Americans. I'm grateful for your hospitality. But you feed the body only, not the spirit. Why am I being discriminated against?"

"Orthodox are not allowed to pray with non-Orthodox. And the refectory is considered an extension of the church."

Hans points a finger at me. "I noticed *he* was permitted into the church and the trapeza."

"I'm Orthodox," I say.

"Yannis is Orthodox," Dean says again, the second time in two hours.

"Because I am not Orthodox, do you monks consider me a heretic? Because of some outdated and confusing theology about Apostolic succession? Other monasteries I've visited—the monks want to talk about their faith. Non-Catholics can pray with Catholic monks in Catholic churches. If Orthodoxy is the true faith, why don't you let fellow Christians get closer to the truth? How else can anyone be encouraged to join one true church if he's not allowed to pray?"

"You can pray—"

"Do the monks believe those in the right are called Orthodox and everyone else is wrong? If those are right thoughts, they're not for me."

"Try to—"

"While you're still a novice, perhaps you should reexamine the faith you've chosen if it excludes people."

Hans leaves us for the smoky courtyard and a look at the sun dropping into the Aegean. Behind us is the Holy Mountain, cloaked in a purple robe.

"Pilgrims need to understand that we're all novices," Dean tells me. "Elder Ephraim—he was the abbot over at Philotheou Monastery and is starting monasteries in the U.S.—says, 'There have always been laymen with the hearts of monks; and there have always been monks with hearts of laymen. It is not the place, but the means that makes the man.'"

Dean's commitment to monastic life was a matter of some discussion among our parishioners back in Santa Barbara. After seeing him chanting in church, and now defending the faith, no one could question his commitment. No matter what his father thinks, or his mother feels, Dean is here to stay. Dean is ready to do battle against the unseen forces of darkness.

In my mind, I write his brief biography in the stilted Athonite style: *Having reflected on the multitude of his troubles and feeling the whole Pacific Ocean could not wash him clean of them, and having seen and realized the vanity of the world and worldly things, he developed a love for solitude and fled from California, and from the world. At Xeropotamou Monastery in 1999, Dean Trigonis was tonsured a monk and renamed Efrem. A renowned chanter, he taught the art of psalmody and translated several works of Byzantine hymnology. Father Efrem stayed at Xeropotamou until 2055, when he died at the age of ninety-one.*

Dean lifts the sleeve of his cassock and checks his watch. "My visiting time is up," he announces.

I look at the clock on the monastery's great tower: 11:30. My watch reads 6:30. The clock isn't broken. It's on Byzantine time. The date is May 6, but according to the monks it's April 24; they follow a Byzantine calendar that is thirteen days behind.

Welcome to Mt. Athos. Set your watch back five hours, your calendar back thirteen days, your consciousness back one thousand years.

I have the sudden realization that, because of the strictness of the monastic regiment, I know where Dean will be and what he'll be doing, during every day, during every year to come. I hear him chanting far into the third millennium:

"My soul waits for the Lord, more than watchmen wait for morning."

"Years ago," Dean tells me, "I came to Mt. Athos, just like you, looking for something. Just what, I didn't know. Like you, I was searching for the right path on the mountain."

He gestures to the front gate of Xeropotamou. "And God brought me here. And he's brought you here, too. The Holy Spirit works in each and every one of us in mysterious and powerful ways."

"Out of the depths I cry to you, O Lord; O Lord, hear my voice. Let your ears be attentive to my cry for mercy."

"May God bless your trip to the Holy Mountain," he calls out, limping across the courtyard, "and show you the way."

CHAPTER 3

MARITAL ADVICE FROM A MONK

Karyes is a most inviting place to begin a hike. Nature is nearby.

At the edge of this town of 250 souls is a forest of walnut and hazel trees, as well as Koutlousiou Monastery, where the trail begins. Back in the States, Karyes could be a "gateway town," as visitor bureaus like to describe burgs located near national parks; that is to say, such a town is usually the last place along the highway to purchase supplies before reaching the park boundary and entering more commercial-free scenery.

The Holy Mountain is calling me, and I'm ready to answer with a walk in the woods along the ancient *monopati* (footpath) to Philotheou, a six-mile hike away.

But first things first. I'm here to experience Karyes, the capital of the monastic republic, and its can't-miss pilgrim attraction, the Protaton, church of the Protos, or president of the monastic community. A second mission is to buy supplies for hiking the Holy Mountain: Greek cookies, dried figs, and other snacks. And, most importantly, a good trail map.

Be prepared, I say.

Once an Eagle Scout, always an Eagle Scout.

Karyes boasts but one "Main Street," which extends east to west. Narrow side streets branch north and south, and lead to *kellia*, the cottages where one monk lives or a few brothers

31

reside together. Many of these small dwellings have their own tiny chapels with slate-covered domes rising above the roofs. Along the lanes and alleyways are workshops and shops full of crosses, rosaries, and icons.

Karyes could be a little town in Greece. Almost. However, there's something not-quite-Greek about it. It's ten A.M. and the shops aren't open. And there are no female shoppers, no women anywhere, of course.

In the hamlets on the Holy Mountain, no international symbols of a woman in a skirt are posted at the entrances to the *demotikes toualetes*, the public toilets. It's in the two (barely) commercial areas of Dafni and Karyes that the absence of the feminine is most noticeable.

That being said, Karyes is not all black robes and white beards. Pots of flowers brighten balconies and doorways. Curtains dress up some of the windows. Fresh paint and small gardens contribute to a feeling of tidiness.

Karyes, Byzantium has a nice ring to it. Karyes goes at its own pace, perhaps more like that of ancient Byzantium than of modern Greece. The men in black never hurry; in my professional evaluation of their gait, it's not really all that slow as much as it is deliberate. *They must walk and pray at the same time,* I muse, as a gray beard walking along the cobbled lane approaches me.

"*Kalimera* Good morning," I greet.

The monk breaks stride and, almost as soon as the words leave my mouth, I realize my mistake.

"*Evlogeite* (Bless me)," I hurriedly add.

"*O Kyrios* (the Lord)," he replies in a soft voice, almost a murmur, as he passes.

Evlogeite, evlogeite, evlogeite. In Thessaloniki, on the ferry and at the first monastery on our list, I was instructed repeatedly in the proper greeting for a pilgrim to a monk. Secular greetings are just not the way to go around here. And yet, at the first opportunity to observe proper Athos etiquette, I blow it.

Evlogeite, evlogeite, evlogeite.

In the window of a closed workshop, I spy the icon of Constantine—St. Constantine, as he's known around here. After lingering at the Byzantine Museum in Athens, getting a sneak preview of the just-opening Byzantine Museum in Thessaloniki, and reading short- and medium-length histories of the very, very, very, long Byzantine Empire, the icon of Constantine is familiar to me and one of the most recognizable portraits in my mental Gallery of Byzantium.

Nose against the glass, I admire the icon, a nice piece of work, hand-painted, not mass-manufactured. The iconographer has created a nuanced portrayal of the quintessential Byzantine, combining elements of church and state and giving us a Constantine who wears both a halo and a crown, and holds a scepter and a scroll. He is a leader triumphant in both the sacred and secular worlds, but at a cost. Circles under his eyes and worry lines show a man who has the weight of the world upon him.

As the story goes, Constantine the Great founded Karyes in the early years of the fourth century. "The Great" is no exaggeration moniker for an emperor who reigned for more than thirty years. Constantine was a successful military leader, prevailing in campaigns on the frontier and in the civil wars threatening to split the empire. While a soldier through and through, he nevertheless separated military and civil authority and stabilized the economy, introducing coinage that remained in circulation for a thousand years.

Inheriting the emperorship after the death of his father in 306, Constantine was forced to do battle with rival claimants to the empire's leadership intending to overthrow and kill him, including Maximian Golerius in the East and Maxentius in the West. The night before facing off with Maxentius at the Battle of Milvian Bridge, (a crucial route to Rome over the Tiber), Constantine prayed for help. The answer to his prayers came in the form of the sign of the cross in the heavens with the Greek words: "Through this sign, you shall conquer."

Constantine directed his men to mark the heavenly sign, a Chi-Rho monogram, ☧, combining the first two letters of "Christ," on their shields. Thanks to what would later be called the Vision of Constantine and superior generalship, his inspired soldiers crushed the army of Maxentius, who drowned in the Tiber when his troops were routed.

Constantine marched in triumph into Rome. But the now sole ruler of the empire doubted the good times would last in Rome, then brimming with politics, plots, and pagans. He moved the seat of government to Byzantium at the eastern fringe of the empire. Constantine built an imperial palace, government buildings, and walls around the city, which he soon renamed Constantinople.

It was an empire that lasted 1,123 years, an almost impossibly long time in the shaky history of human governance. In empire longevity, the Ming Dynasty at 276 years and the British Empire at 200 years or so are distant runners-up.

One wonders: What if *Konstantinoúpolis*, once the world's largest city with a population of 500,000, had endured? What if there were a modern state of Byzantium with Constantinople as its capital? What if it had not fallen to the Moslems in 1453 and did not become Istanbul, capital of Turkey? What if today it were mentioned in the same breath as Europe's other great capitals? *London-Paris-Rome-Berlin-Constantinople.*

While his secular successes at launching the Byzantine Empire are impressive, the accomplishments on behalf of Christendom on St. Constantine's CV are what are most admired here on Athos and in Orthodox circles:

Christian Leadership

- First emperor to convert to Christianity, and appointed Christians to high office.
- Promoted and implemented Edict of Milan that proclaimed tolerance for Christians.

- Called first Council of Nicea, and partnered with influencers to establish Nicene Creed for Christians.

Alas for Karyes, it was reportedly destroyed in the mid-fourth century by a later emperor, Julian, whose brief reign (361-363) garnered decidedly mixed reviews. "Julian the Philosopher" is remembered favorably for his military acumen, Hellenistic philosophy, and as an accomplished satirist. (Satire is a curious art for a high office holder; most politicians are objects of satire, not practitioners of it.) "Julian the Apostate" is remembered for his rejection of Christianity and for opposing its spread. "Julian the Transgressor" is remembered on the Holy Mountain as the Anti-Constantine, as a morally repugnant evil-doer. Supported by the Byzantine Empire and its capital, Constantinople, Karyes was revived some six centuries later and became the capital of the monastic republic.

I am curious about how Athos is governed and, if I have time before I hit the trail, I will visit the government building. I don't have high hopes for gaining entry and learning more about who runs the Holy Mountain. My experience of Greece is that government employees keep much shorter hours than the shopkeepers.

If it's a choice between church and state around here, the pilgrim just has to choose church. I am pleased to find the Protaton, the oldest church on the Holy Mountain, built in the first half of the tenth century, open for business.

To my untrained eye, the exterior of Protaton, with its too-perfect outer walls and Byzantine-styled roof tiles, appears to have been a bit *over*-restored. I am reminded of certain late eighteenth-century California missions, where restorers did their job just a little too well with the white stucco walls and red tile roofs, resulting in an unfortunate similarity to the late twentieth-century Spanish Revival–style office buildings and shopping centers located nearby.

Never mind the exterior, it's what's inside that counts, and the interior of the Protaton is oh-my-God dazzling, a mystical feast for the senses. At the end of the thirteenth century, the interior walls were frescoed—make that fantastically frescoed—by Manuel Panselinos.

Most compelling are the leading figures from the New Testament, presented with gestures, with movement, with expressions, with realism, with an imagination like nothing I've ever seen.

Not only is the quality of the images astonishing, so is the quantity! Like a muralist trying to utilize every bit of the space allotted, Panselinos filled the walls of the church to overflowing with color and light.

How in heaven's name did Manuel Panselinos get hired? I try to imagine how the Church elders agreed to contract with him.

Elder: Thanks for coming over from Thessaloniki. Father Cosmas briefed you?

Manuel: He did. I figure I need about a week here, making sketches and taking measurements. Another week back in Thessaloniki to get supplies and my team together.

Elder: Manny, I love your enthusiasm. And we want to move fast, we really do. What would you say about knocking out a few frescoes on the lower west wall? We can see where you're going with the project, put together a proposal, and take it from there.

Manuel: Just so we're on the same scroll, I thought you brought me here to talk about a commission. I'm way past the point in my career to work on spec.

Elder: Who said anything about spec? I mean no disrespect. We know what you've done in the Balkans.

Manuel: And last year with my work on the basilica of St Demetrios in Thessaloniki. You sent your man to check us out. You think we didn't know you were watching?

Elder: The reports we got did concern us. For weeks, nothing but blank walls.

Manuel: It's all in the prep. Those walls—it's no easy task to get them ready for the uncreated light of God.

Elder: We were told you and your crew do nothing more than stare at the walls, for hours, for days at a time. And then finally you put up what looks like small dots of paint.

Manuel: That's how we roll. One of the hardest parts of making frescoes is to locate and mark the center of the halos. We create off of those measurements. In my business, I start with the end in mind. Isn't that what we're supposed to do as Christians?

Elder: Can't argue with that. We know there's a lot of labor involved. Let's be clear, we're not just looking at frescoes from a cost standpoint.

Manuel: Good, it's all about value. Lasting value. We use the best materials—just the right mix of red clay. Only one supplier makes the kind of quality animal-skin glue I like. And the gold leaf, don't get me started.

Elder: Like I said, we're not looking for cheap. And of course we'll put you up. The best food and lodging in Karyes. You can't bring the wives, though.

Manuel: My guys know that.

Elder: We're your biggest admirers here on Athos. And if it were just up to me, I'd say "Paint, Manny. Paint for the glory of the God."

Manuel: But really this is about time and money.

Elder: Regrettably, yes. Heaven is a place without time and money. But here on earth—

Manuel: What kind of time are we talking about? Remind me, when was the Protaton built?

Elder: About 980.

Manuel: The first church. The most important church on the Holy Mountain. Built more than two hundred years ago. And you're just now getting around to ordering frescoes?

Elder: The Holy Mountain does move at its own special pace.

Manuel: I noticed the *outside* of the church has had a lot of recent work.

Elder: Praise God. As a matter of fact, the Emperor has been good to us.

Manuel: Andronikos II? With all the problems he has with the Latins and the Crusaders and the Moslems…he still supports the Protaton?

Elder: The signs from his people have been very positive, yes.

Manuel: Good, because I want to do the whole church.

Elder: The what?

Manuel: Top to bottom. All the way up to the arches.

Elder: The *whole* church?

Manuel: Elder, you want to sit down? You look a little shaky.

Elder: I'm fine, fine. I'm just saying: That's a lot of square cubits.

Manuel: I got a vision for the whole thing.

Elder: A vision. I'm not saying the Council of Elders won't approve. I think our chances are good. We're just going to need something more solid than a vision when we present to the Fresco Committee.

Manuel: Committee? Nothing gets done by committee.

Elder: Don't I know that.

Manuel: You want to wait another two hundred years for frescoes, or do you want to hear me out?

Elder: Please, have your say.

Manuel: I'm seeing this in four layers. At the lowest level, the saints, lots of them. We'll include all the traditionals, plus some surprises—the desert fathers and lesser-known ascetics. And unique to the Protaton, we'll do some Athos hermits.

Elder: I like that. We'd like to increase visibility for our
           saints here on Athos, the holy men the pilgrims
           don't know. Keep going with this.

Manuel: Way up top, on the arches, the prophets. Nothing
           surprising here. It is what it is. And in between the
           lowest level and the prophets way up on the arches…
           speaking of which, that's going to require a serious
           amount of ladder work. We're going to need to set
           up a lot of scaffolding to get up there. I can tell you
           now that's a big budget item.

Elder: One reason why I suggested we start with the bot-
           tom layer.

Manuel: That's a non-starter, your grace. I don't work that
           way. Let me tell you about the middle layers. This
           is what's going to set us apart. The Life of Mary and
           the Life of Our Savior. With the help of the Holy
           Spirit, I will tell the stories in pictures, all around
           the church, leading up to the Resurrection. Pilgrims
           from all across the empire will come to see the sto-
           ries of our faith, to pray in this church.

Elder: God willing. Very well, then. Give us an estimate,
           time and materials. Just remember we're not made
           of *stamenons*.

Manuel: All four layers?

Elder: The whole moussaka.

Manuel: Good, this is the right way to go. At the end of the
           day, you and your people are going to be very, very
           happy.

However the deal went down, the frescoes went up. And up
and up and up. Manuel Panselimos got in a zone—four zones
to be exact. At the lowest level are familiar figures, full-length
looks at the saints of the church, plus a lot of unfamiliar faces,
the ascetics from the Holy Mountain.

Fascinating to me are, for lack of a better word, the military saints. Men with swords. Warriors for Christ. What's the story with these guys? They look fierce, like they could kick some serious pagan butt. And who is St. Mercurius, anyway? But wait, there's Constantine, Warrior-in-Chief. No wonder that icon I espied earlier in the shop window was so darn good: it's a takeoff on the St. Constantine created by Manuel Panselinos.

Not far from Constantine is the flag of the Byzantine Empire. Imprinted on the yellow cloth is the two-headed golden eagle; one head to symbolize ancient Rome, the other head "new Rome" at Constantinople.

In contrast to the young saints-at-arms are the old saints. If with age comes wisdom, these are the wisest of men. The holy men in the frescoes are not just old, but very, very old. Ancient, in fact. At first glance, they appear seventy-five or eighty years old, with white hair and with a variety of beards from long and straight to 180-degree wraparounds from ear to ear. Deep thinkers all, with eyes that have seen much of the world, the saints come off as pious, not imperious. Such is the genius of Manuel Panselinos: that he's succeeded in making them appear twice their chronological age, not by making these saints more wizened, but more wise.

150 is the new 75.

The prophets gaze down from on high: Isaiah, Jeremiah, Ezekiel, and Daniel, who holds a scroll reading: "The God of Heaven will establish a kingdom which will never be destroyed." Far removed they seem, having spoken long ago, back in time before Christ. No one foretells anything anymore, so the prophets are placed on the arches, out of mind and nearly out of sight.

Perhaps this is part of the Panselinos layout and design intention—to focus most of the viewer's time and attention on the two middle zones of his frescoes—Biblical scenes, one following one another like a continuous painted frieze featuring the not-so-well-known life of Mary and well-known scenes from the New Testament: the Nativity, young Jesus in the temple, his baptism by John, the descent into Hades, Pentecost.

Particularly mind-blowing is the way he painted the Resurrection. Jesus stands atop the broken doors of hell, its capacity to imprison souls now demolished; the keys to hell are wrecked. Looking way more powerful than any commando who's kicked down a door to a terrorist stronghold and rescued hostages, Jesus leans forward to take Adam and Eve by the hand to lead them, to lead all of humanity, out of the abyss.

Panselinos pushed the limit—no, he went way past the limits—of Byzantine art. Perhaps this is how religious art would have evolved if the empire had continued past 1453. He reached with dramatic passion toward the Renaissance.

But it seems no one in Byzantium followed.

Doesn't anybody work around here?

In front of the Protaton stands the building of *Iera Koinotita* (Holy Community), where representatives of the twenty monasteries meet. It's closed. Also closed is an ancient tower, which houses a library that kept the first document of Mount Athos, written on goatskin and called *"Tragos."*

Prayer is the primary business on the Holy Mountain, and apparently the business hours of establishments engaged in the lesser businesses of governance and the sale of worldly goods reflect this. Here the few commercial businesses have short hours, but many of the churches are open long hours— before dawn, all day, and well into the night. This is the reverse of the way it is back in the Western world, where businesses are open long hours and the churches open rarely, sometimes just for an hour or two on Sunday mornings.

What looks to be the grocery store is closed. I look longingly inside at the rows of packaged goods. My stomach has been growling all morning. Bidding goodbye to my fellow Santa Barbarans, who have ambitious touring plans for this day that include a visit to Panteleimon, the Russian monastery,

I left Xeropotamou hours before the first meal would be served. All I've eaten is one of the last of my granola bars, devoured before I hopped onto one of the troop trucks that occasionally motor along the "main" road from Dafni to Karyes.

I'm also disappointed when I return to the little icon shop where I saw St. Constantine in the window and find it closed. An icon of Constantine will be a good souvenir of my visit, if the price is right and I can make a deal.

A *deal. Hmmm.* Does one deal around here? Anywhere else in Greece, no question I would bargain for arts and crafts. But here on the Holy Mountain? If a monk offers me Constantine at a too-high price, should I counter with a lower offer for the icon? Would this be normal business practice in Byzantium or a kind of blasphemy?

What looks like the largest gift shop in Karyes—and the one most likely to have that Mt. Athos trail map—is closed. I try to read the sign with the shop hours on the door, but a monk and a Greek pilgrim (well, he looks Greek and talks Greek) converse in the doorway and block my view.

"Evlogeite," I greet the monk. A little too loudly, I suppose. But at least I got it right this time.

"O Kyrios," he returns.

"Kalimera," says the pilgrim. "Father Theophanes," he gently nods to the monk. "My name is Alexandros."

"Yannis," I declare to both pilgrim and monk. "Kalimera," I say to Alexandros.

We are an interesting trio. The three of us are about the same age and of the same modest height. Alexandros is of beefier build than I, whereas Father Theophanes, with his dietary restrictions, is, of course, much thinner.

Here we are John, Alex and Theo shooting the breeze on a warm spring day in Byzantium.

"Where are you going?" Father Theophanes asks me.

Shopping for snacks and a map sounds a bit base. Perhaps I should tell the monk of my mission to the mountain. "I will walk from monastery to monastery. Perhaps eight or nine monasteries. From St. Anna Skete, my friend Spiro and I will walk to the top of the Holy Mountain."

Father Theophanes brightens. "Alexandros went to St. Anna."

Alexandros nods. "A beautiful place."

And one off the beaten track. A skete is a monastic community but not strictly a monastery, and I look forward to staying in a more relaxed, less regulated retreat.

"Why will you walk to St. Anna?"

Because it's the only way to get there is the obvious answer. "St. Anna, it is a good place to stay before we walk to Agion Oros."

Father Theophanes pauses. The Jesus Prayer. I just know he's repeating it over and over. Alexandros looks at me in a way that makes me think that I said something wrong in Greek.

"You have a woman?" Father Theophanes asks me.

The question startles me for a moment until I remember that the Greek word for woman (*gynaíka*) is the same word for wife. The monk wants to know if I'm married.

"Yes."

"Children?"

"Yes, a daughter. Sophia, two years old."

"And you want more children?"

Why is he asking me these questions? And why does Alexandros look so interested in my response?

"We want..." I begin. No, too secular; it's not supposed to be about what we want or I want, but what God wants. "*Theós*, God..." I begin again. I want to say *God willing*, but I don't know the correct tense... "*Theoú thélo-, Theoú thélon...*" Despairing of this conjugation, I look off to the Holy Mountain for help, but no help is forthcoming. I give up. "*Eh Theós...*" I say as humbly as possible, and palms up I look up to the sky. "If God..."

"Everything is by God's grace," affirms Father Theophanes after a long, even uncomfortable pause. Alexandros beams.

Both act as if I have said something profound. Perhaps they think I was struggling with my emotions, not grappling with Greek *grammatiki*.

Father Theophanes slows his Greek way, way down from the speed at which he was conversing with Alexandros when I first joined them. Monk talk as deliberate as monk walk.

"Sometimes it may be very difficult to talk to your wife," Father Theophanes relates.

Now there's an understatement. I think I see a grin on the face of Alexandros.

"Some women cook with a lot of salt. And not every man likes so much salt in his food."

Alexandros nods. Perhaps this a common problem between a husband and wife in Hellas.

"You must not shout at her. Or tell her she is a bad cook."

Not unless you want that hot-tempered Mediterranean you married to throw a plate at you. I married a Sicilian; I can only imagine Greek women run at a high temperature, too, particularly in the kitchen.

"If you want your wife to reduce the amount of salt in your meals, you must tell her in a loving way."

Wait a minute. A *monk* is telling us how to get along with our wives? Then again, who am I to boast of *my* understanding of women?

"Say something like, 'You prepared this meal with so much love and goodness. About the only way it could be better is if you would please use a little less salt next time.'"

After this example of conflict resolution, Father Theophanes and his Greek accelerate. A minute or two in, I guess he may be quoting scripture, a passage from Corinthians: "Love is patient and kind…" My thoughts turn to all those Protestant weddings I've attended where I've heard that verse. Cue up the music: Pachelbel Canon or the even more overused "Wind Beneath my Wings." Meanwhile the words hurtle past: …

God…Love…children…Wife…St…Anna…Wife….God…
God…Angels…American…Love…English…

"Would you like me to translate?" Alexandros asks in English.

"Please," I answer in Greek.

Father Theophanes is brief, his advice a fraction the length of what he just told us. Translation by Alexandros is rapid in mildly accented Greco-British English. "Remember, you are in partnership with the Lord. Pray together to get along. He hears the prayers of those he has joined together with the sacrament of marriage."

And just like that Father Theophanes halts and Alexandros stops his translation.

"Alexandros, may God bless you on your journey back home to your wife in Thessaloniki. And Yannis, may God bless you on your walk and visit to St. Anna."

Thank you Father Theophanes," says Alexandros.

"Thank you, Father," I add as the monk glides away.

"Did you understand what Father Theophanes was telling us?" asks Alexandros.

"Yes. Thank you for the translation."

"Where are you walking?" asks Alexandros.

I shrug. "Everything is closed."

Alexandros smiles. "I know one business that is open. Please join me for lunch."

God provides. Food for my afternoon march to Philotheou.

"*Thavma*," I answer enthusiastically. "A miracle."

Alexandros laughs as he leads me down the street to a small café.

CHAPTER 4

"I *LOVE* GIGANTES!"

Queue is not a Greek word.
Queue is not a Greek practice.
Queue is not something Greeks do.

I am reminded that Greeks cannot and will not queue when I find myself in the midst of a cluster of two dozen hungry customers pressing toward the counter of the café. When we entered the modest eatery, I got in line behind one party of four and one party of two, establishing (I thought) me and my new acquaintance Alexandros as numbers seven and eight to be…served? Seated?

Alas, as a result of my long cultural conditioning to queue and failure to recall just how queue-challenged Greek nationals can be, we have slipped closer to the back of the non-line than the front of the non-line. I am clueless as to where our non-queue is headed. Does the café offer table service? Are we pressing forward in order to be seated by the maître d'? Do we place our orders at the counter and seat ourselves?

A quick survey of the café reveals ample tables for all, so no diner need worry about getting seated for lunch. What kind of lunch we might be served is a complete mystery to me because no menu is in sight: no printed menus, no list of entrées with prices posted on the walls, no chalkboard with the daily specials. *Tipota*. Nothing.

Lunch patrons are construction workers and road repair-men—at least that's my guess after spotting the trucks parked outside—along with a few cleaner and better-dressed gents who might be civil servants. A jovial lot, the men carry on a lively discussion about a soccer match, while one of them asks who wants a bottle of beer.

Beer. We can have a beer?

I figure we are surging toward the counter wherein lie trays of food, but instead our small wave of humanity breaks toward a white-apron clad, mustachioed fellow, who is taking lunch orders. Too many torsos prevent a clear view of the counter and the day's offerings, but I manage to glimpse a macaroni dish with a lot of oil floating on top and a second casserole that I cannot identify. The scant offerings behind glass are at odds with the heady aromas of Greek cooking that fill the café—olive oil, feta cheese, oregano....

Oh my, am I hungry! The Mt. Athos Meal Plan for monks and pilgrims alike is two meals, the first at about ten or ten-thirty in the morning and the second about seven in the evening. As I missed the first meal of the day, fully fifty percent of my day's rations, I am eagerly looking forward to lunch. And lunch in a secular setting at that, with beer served, and conversation permitted.

Alexandros cuts in front of me and I follow his lead as we wedge past our friendly rivals and regain much of our lost ground. Nearing the man I adjudge to be the order taker, Alexandros glances over his shoulder at me and inquires loudly above the din in Greek: "Do you like *gigantes*?"

"I *love gigantes*," I respond in Greek at even greater volume. Alexandros grins and the workers behind me laugh. Perhaps at my accent. Maybe I sounded a bit too enthusiastic about beans.

Ah, but these are not just any beans, these are giant baked beans, white beans to be exact. Gigantes (pronounced *yee-gan-dess*), true giants, one of my favorite Greek dishes and one I rarely get the opportunity to enjoy.

"And two beers," I call out to the man in the white apron. "Amstel." Amstel and Heineken share a near monopoly on the Greek beer market, so it's a safe bet they serve that beer here.

"Amstel," he confirms with a smile.

"I *love* gigantes!" a customer calls out from the back of the pack. Good-natured laughter follows.

Somehow I amuse them. Fair enough. Here I am the only blue-eyed, fair-haired pilgrim in town, clad in full hiker garb, boots and a Patagonia fleecy pull-over (packing the burgundy one rather than my gray one was a poor choice if I hoped to travel unnoticed), and speaking their language badly....

We find a table in the back near the kitchen, and Alexandros and I rapidly introduce ourselves. I tell him about my traveling companions from Santa Barbara, my hiking writer profession, and about my plan to meet Spiro and climb the Holy Mountain.

A high school history teacher by trade, Alexandros is slowly finishing his doctoral studies and hopes to teach at a university one day. His specialty is modern Greek history, which dates from Greek Independence in 1836 to modern day.

I wonder if Alexandros came to Athos out of academic interest. "Are you here to learn more history of the Holy Mountain?"

Alexandros shakes his head. "Too much history here, even for a history teacher."

I smile. "I was hoping someone like you could help me understand who's in charge of the government of Mt. Athos."

Who's in charge here? Wherever I travel, my natural curiosity (and trained journalistic instincts) drive me to ask that question. Even here on the Holy Mountain, where all I really want to do is take a few good hikes, I feel compelled to learn who's in charge. I can't help myself and ask that question in tourist bureaus, in businesses, and at all levels of governance.

Who's in charge here?

The answer in Greece is usually "Everyone and no one."

Alexandros returns my smile. "Later, I will try to explain."

I hope not, I think, regretting that I asked Alexandros for his expertise. For heaven's sake, I can't comprehend how this café in Karyes operates, much less Mt. Athos. Really, I want to know more about Alexandros, not Athos. "How many times have you traveled to the Holy Mountain?" I ask.

"Four times," he answers. "This time I went with a friend to Simonopetra."

And to Skete St. Anna, I remember from our conversation with Father Theophanes. St. Anna, my trailhead for the hike up the Holy Mountain. "And how did you find St. Anna?"

"By boat," Alexandros replies.

Oops. Alexandros took me a little too literally. I was inquiring about his impressions of Skete Anna, not his transport to it.

"You don't have to walk to St. Anna," he continues. "You can take a boat."

Not a hiker, Alexandros.

Like many things around here, the boat schedule is difficult to understand, Alexandros explains, but he and his friend Nicholaos were able to secure passage from Dafni to the little harbor located far below.

"Nicholaos, a fine name, I interject. "My godson, a year old, is named Nicholas." I tell Alexandros of my hope to purchase an icon of St. Nicholas for the little guy—if the stores ever open in Karyes. Otherwise, I'll buy one when we get back to Thessaloniki.

"And what's it like at St. Anna?" I ask.

"Nicholaos was the one who really wanted to go there," Alexandros replies, oddly apologetic. "He wanted to—"

His answer is cut short when the waiter brings us two bottles of Amstel and glasses.

"So you *love* gigantes," says Alexandros with a smile, suddenly changing the subject. "Does your wife like gigantes?"

"Cheri *hates* gigantes."

The first time she cooked them the flavor was fine, but she substituted lima beans, which are not genuine gigantes, for the big white beans. Reluctantly, my wife made gigantes for me once more, this time with the regulation beans; however she added lots of spicy sausage, which overwhelmed the baked beans—a success for a chef who dislikes gigantes, but a defeat for a gigantes purist hoping for the real thing.

Helen, my Greek-American mother, dislikes the dish, as does my Irish-American father, so I grew up largely deprived of the pleasures of gigantes. A dislike for gigantes might be the only thing my mother and my wife have in common.

I've managed to order the beans occasionally at Greek restaurants and from a Greek deli in Southern California, but only during my travels in Greece have I been able to find them served in a variety of eateries. Ah, the glory that is Greece and its gigantes!

Cheri cooks difficult-to-make Greek dishes, including a delicious moussaka and pastichio, and she can do wonders with lamb—not an easy meat to master. Bless her hands, she even makes a good loaf of altar bread, *prosforo*. But gigantes, in her view, are just gross in look, texture, and taste, and she is averse to cooking them.

"Does your wife like gigantes?" I inquire.

Alexandros grins. "Christina *hates* gigantes."

We agree that we are lucky men indeed, each with a wonderful gynaíka. But our wives hate something we love. Cheri and Christina refuse to cook gigantes for us. What would Father Theophanes say about this serious issue in our marriages? The monk scripted how a husband could gently tell his wife to use less salt in her cooking. Might the good monk also know a way a husband could coax his gynaíka into cooking gigantes?

Together we raise our glasses of beer.

"To gigantes," Alexandros toasts.

"To gigantes," I echo.

Just as we clink glasses, the waiter arrives with two big bowls of beans, a side of warm bread, and a look that says *You two must be out of your minds.*

The café serves basic gigantes, just as I hoped: white beans, tomatoes, onions, olive oil, and sugar. Yes, a little sugar. And they look to have been cooked perfectly: baked in the oven until they are of perfect texture and, importantly, the top layer of the beans is charred from the sugar.

We take our first spoonfuls and sigh with satisfaction. But while I grow silent, Alexandros, to my surprise, begins talking about *who's in charge here.*

Mt. Athos, as a monastic republic, got started in the tenth century by Byzantine Emperor Nicephorus Phocas, explains Alexandros. He was the first of the Byzantine Emperors to really support the monks. The monasteries, particularly Great Lavra, were supported by all the later Byzantine emperors, too. After the fall of the empire, the Ottomans were surprisingly tolerant of this outpost of infidels—at least in comparison to how Christians fared elsewhere under the sultan's rule—and after the collapse of the Ottoman Empire, the Athos monasteries got support from Orthodox Christian countries and the faithful from around the world.

Ah, the gigantes are served exactly how I like them. Warm, not steaming hot. Sprinkled with feta and parsley. Served with bread.

It follows that any form of governance set up during the Byzantine rule would be, well, Byzantine in nature–that is to say excessively complex, Alexandros continues. And so it is with Mt Athos, subjected to the law of Greece, international law, and European law.

Alexandros has an easy manner of delivering complex history in a simple way, and I imagine he is a favorite of the teen-aged students at the *lykeio* where he teaches. I'm simply astonished that he can deliver the most informal of lectures while eating gigantes. And he is eating like a gentleman, not talking with his mouth full. I marvel at how he has managed to eat as many gigantes as I have while he does all the talking and I do all the listening.

I survey the café and see many more happy diners. The vast majority of lunch patrons chose the gigantes, with only a few opting for the Greek macaroni and cheese casserole. Maybe gigantes are a strictly a guy thing. Perhaps a preponderance of Greek wives refuse to cook gigantes for their husbands, with a resultant frustration and pent-up demand for the beans. One thing for certain, in this world without women, gigantes sure are popular.

"All monks and novices, from whatever country, when they are admitted to a monastery, become Greek citizens."

"I thought of becoming a Greek citizen myself," I say.

"Seriously?" Alexandros asks, as if I am joking.

I decide to give Alexandros a break from his Mt. Athos mini-lecture and tell a story: Because my grandfather, Charles Gekas, was born in Greece, I am eligible to apply for Greek citizenship, and gave the matter some thought a few years back. Certainly there are pluses for an American to hold dual citizenship with both American and European passports. However, it was pointed out to me that, were I to have a son, he would automatically become a Greek citizen, and not just an honorary one: service in the Greek military would be compulsory.

That was the deal-breaker right there.

"I had a year of service. Believe me, you don't want to be in the Greek Army."

Alexandros has used the interlude to equal—no, surpass—my gigantes consumption.

"If you became a citizen, you would need to learn to speak Greek," he teases.

True. If I acquired Greek citizenship, I would feel under cultural pressure and moral obligation to learn to speak Greek fluently. And also learn how *not* to wait in line.

Mount Athos has twenty monasteries, and they are ranked in influence, not by age or size. Alexandros continues after the break. After the monasteries in preeminence come the sketes, cells, and hermitages. A Holy Community of twenty monks representing the monasteries make policy, with an executive committee overseeing the villages of Dafni and Karyes first, as well as the police force and forestry department.

"That government is best which governs least." I stand with Henry David Thoreau, who supports that notion in his essay "Civil Disobedience." Likely the free-thinking Transcendentalist would find few who would agree with him on the Holy Mountain, where both Church *and* State are under Byzantine-style governance.

I look around the dining room at the men finishing their meals and realize that for all my failures in Greek language and culture, I have at least mastered one Greek skill: I know how to use bread as a utensil, dipping into the gigantes and getting mostly sauce, then wiping the bowl clean of all its drippings.

Alas, Alexandros and I are getting to the bottoms of our bowls of beans.

The most important law of the land, continues Alexandros, is found in the Charter of Mt. Athos, created long, long ago by Athonite monks representing the monasteries and ratified by the ecumenical patriarch of Constantinople and the Greek Parliament. This charter essentially grants Mount Athos status as a self-governed and nearly sovereign part of the Greek nation.

More important around the Holy Mountain is its religious governance. Spiritually, Mount Athos is under the direct jurisdiction of the Ecumenical Patriarch in Constantinople—*er,* Instanbul.

"More?" Alexandros asks suddenly.

"Yes," I nod politely. I'm overloaded from talk of the history and government of Mount Athos, and don't want to hear another word; however, I don't want to tell Alexandros that and risk insulting him. His presentation, in a second language, while eating gigantes, was brilliant.

"Good," he says. "I want more, too."

To my surprise, Alexandros gets up from the table, pokes his head into the kitchen of the restaurant and comes back with...

More gigantes.

Two plates-full of gigantes. This second batch is a little warmer, a little more savory, the feta sprinkled on top just a little fresher than the first batch.

"More?" I ask.

Now it's Alexandros's turn to be confused, as I rise from the table, walk into the kitchen and return with…

Two more bottles of beer.

I notice other customers returning from the kitchen with more gigantes and more beer. We men are such simple creatures. All we need to be happy is beans, bread, and beer.

Our conversation turns from the monastic kingdom to friends and family. Alexandros has quite the extended family.

"Do you have children?" I ask.

"Not yet," he replies. Alexandros repeats the words and gestures I made when Father Theopanes asked me that question. "If God…." he says, raising his palms upward and looking off to the heavens.

As the café empties, I realize it's getting late and I'd better hit the trail for Philotheou.

"How far to walk to Philotheou?" asks Alexandros.

"About ten kilometers."

Alexandros shakes his head. "Ask in the square. Maybe you could ride the bus to Philotheou."

Not a hiker, Alexandros.

In my sodden state, I'm not much of a hiker myself. As I walk through Karyes I feel so full of beans I could burst. Perhaps when beer is added to gigantes they swell to twice their size.

St. Constantine looks at me from the window of the iconographer's workshop (still closed) as I walk past. I cross the square where the buses and transport trucks arrive and depart, and follow the main street past the (closed) *Epistasia*, the government building out of town. A ten-minute walk brings me to the outer gates of Koutloumousiou Monastery.

Founded in the fourteenth century, the central church is said to be one of the most magnificent on the Holy Mountain.

Chapels are dedicated to the archangels, my St. John the Baptist, and my friend's saint, St. Spyridon. Spiro would love this monastery, and would want to look at one of its greatest treasures—what is supposedly the largest relic of the True Cross. (Wait a minute. Don't the monks at Xeropotamou claim to have the largest part of the Cross?)

Maybe later in the week, all the Santa Barbarans can do a proper visit to Koutloumousiou (with a stop at the Karyes Café, because all the guys, and especially Mike, appreciate gigantes). But time is short this afternoon and I have to hit the trail. It's about a six-mile hike to Philotheou.

I locate the start of the footpath to Philotheou near the monastery's gate. I wish I had a good map, but the Tourist Map of Mt. Athos will have to do. At the trailhead, I stretch, pushing against a wall and feeling my calves tighten.

"Are you walking to Panagouda?" a voice from behind me calls out.

I turn to see two of the better-dressed patrons from the café; I guessed they might be civil servants on a lunch break, but their presence at the monastery gates suggests they are pilgrims. The shorter one does the talking while the other stands near, holding a well-thumbed guidebook to Mt. Athos.

"Philotheou," I answer, pointing to the trail sign.

"Not Panagouda?"

Just ten minutes ago I traced my route on the map and can recall no *Panagouda* on my route. I shake my head.

"Elder Paisios," he prompts.

"Father Paisios of Mt. Athos," adds the other pilgrim. He withdraws a baseball card–sized color photo from a shirt pocket and hands it to me. "Please take this with you on your walk."

"Thank you." I expect to see the picture of a St. Paisios on a Byzantine icon, a holy man with a halo from distant history, but, no, this is a contemporary portraiture of an elderly monk who is…there are no dates of birth or death on the back of the card.

"Father Paisios was first a monk at Philotheou," the shorter pilgrim begins.

I don't mean to be rude, but I need to leave. I have ten kilometers to hike—twenty kilometers round trip. And already I have to pee.

"He went and prayed in the wilderness," he continues, gesturing toward Mt. Athos, "and then went to live in Panagouda, a hermitage between Koutloumousiou and Philotheou."

I fidget with the shoulder strap on my daypack. Perhaps realizing I'm in hurry to get hiking, he launches into a high speed telling of the life and times of Elder Paisios. Of course I understand almost nothing of what he says. A minute later, just as I decide to take my leave, the other pilgrim presses a small pamphlet into my hands. It's a brief account, in Greek and English, of the Elder's life. I nod, as the pilgrim speaks, all the while consulting the pamphlet.

Elder Paisios became known on and off the mountain for his piety and wise counsel. He became a beacon of light for those in spiritual darkness, and legions of men walked down the trail to his hermitage to see him. By day he received the suffering men, counseled them on their mental, physical and spiritual illnesses, their broken marriages, their addictions to drugs and alcohol. He gave advice, emptied them of their pain and sorrows, filled them with hope and love for God.

By night he prayed, long spiritual vigils that left him only two or three hours of sleep.

Along with his full-time counseling practice, Elder Paisios made metal icons of the Theotokos. He gave these icons of the Holy Mother to visitors as a blessing and wrote books of wisdom, compiled into thick treasuries of his work. Elder Paisios, beloved by the Greek people and Orthodox in the know, died in 1994.

"He will be a saint one day," concludes the pilgrim. "Blessings on your walk."

As I thank them for the photo and story and hike down the trail, the pilgrim with the guidebook calls out: "Did you *love* the gigantes?"

I'm never going to live this one down.

Following the monastery wall, the trail descends to a creek, crosses it, and meets a dirt road signed for Philotheou. After a half mile, I reach a junction: left for Philotheou, straight ahead to Xeropotamu and Simonopetra. Later in the week we will stay at Simonopetra, where I hope to connect with Father Makarios, whom I have dubbed the "Eco Monk" because he has written about monastic life, nature, and the ecological crisis.

About a mile out, I join a length of *kalderimi*, an ancient stone pathway, suitable for mules and donkeys and, of course, hikers. Wonderful. I'm hiking back into the Byzantine times, with the birds singing on a perfect spring day.

I look southwest to the Mt. Athos, named in pre-Christian times for the Giant Athos who, during the "Battle of Gods and Giants," flung an enormous rock at Poseidon, which landed where the peninsula is now. An alternate story is that Poseidon hurled a large rock at Athos, which squashed him at the place where the Holy Mountain stands today.

As for the gigantes in my stomach, they shrink as the miles pass. The route is an engaging combination of dirt roads, footpaths, and more lengths of kalderimi, uphill, downhill, and even a stream-crossing.

I step off the trail to pee. *Yannis*, I write in big Greek letters in the dirt with a strong stream flowing from the beer in my belly and the sheer joy of being on the trail. The Trailmaster, back in his element, wild and free.

In the months before our pilgrimage, I read all the books I could find about Mt. Athos in libraries all over Los Angeles, and I pestered Eric, my next-door neighbor and an antiquarian bookseller, to order me a few long-out-of-print titles. Nearly all books about the Holy Mountain detailed the monasteries and their treasures. The books were organized by monastery alphabetically, geographically, or haphazardly. All emphasized the monasteries first, monastic life a distant second. Maddeningly to this mountaineer, mentions of the Holy

Mountain itself, that is to say its, geology, flora, and fauna, were few and far between.

But never mind. I'm in nature now, with the red squirrels, pink cyclamen, and lots of lizards.

As a writer about hiking, I love a hike that saves the best for last, and the last mile to Philotheou is the best. Awesome. I leave the road for a narrower track on a mellow descent, then onto a stretch of kalderimi, dropping into a valley. I cross a shaky bridge over a stream, and on my right is a lovely little waterfall. A steep gain makes up for lost elevation, followed by a lovely bit of stone path leading between buildings to the entrance of the Philotheou monastery.

Philotheou is most welcoming to the pilgrim afoot, offering a gentle transition from nature wild to nature tamed in the form of lawns, trimmed trees, and plants in pots. It displays nothing of the Medieval fortress–like appearance of other monasteries, perhaps because in 1871 it all burned down except the main church. Philotheou's late nineteenth-century rebuild with elaborate brickwork and bold use of red paint makes the monastery easy on the eye.

I join a tour of the church already in progress. A young monk speaks to five Greek gentlemen in their fifties and sixties, who have that look of scholars or university professors.

"Please join us," the monk greets me.

"Please," adds one of the men, who beckons me to stand near.

"*Efharisto*," I reply, thanking him.

"We will now see the icon of Panaghia Glykophilousa," the monk says.

As we migrate over to a pillar on the left side of the church, a kindly gentleman with a goatee and wire-frame glasses falls into step with me and asks me in English: "Would you like me to translate?"

"Yes, please," I answer gratefully. Wait a minute. I only spoke one word of Greek. How did he know I would welcome translation services? But before I can figure that out, we are before an icon of the Holy Mother, Theotokos Sweet Kiss, and he is quietly giving me the gist of the monk's narration.

The icon depicts the Holy Mother leaning toward Christ, who embraces her. It belonged to the devout Victoria, who lived in Constantinople in the ninth century, at a time when the Iconoclasts held power. She was the wife of Symeon, a senator who was, like Emperor Theophilos, an iconoclast.

Symeon demanded that his wife give him the icon so that he could burn it. She refused and threw the icon into the sea. It floated away, traveling upright over the waves. A few years later, the icon arrived on the shores of the Athos peninsula below the Monastery of Philotheou, where it was greeted with great rejoicing by the monks, who had been tipped off of its passage and arrival via a revelation of the Theotokos.

It really is a sweet icon. The Holy Mother seems to be embracing the Christ child more closely than in other icons, and the expression is a bit more humanly affectionate.

At the conclusion of our tour, I'm surprised to find a fresco of St. Christopher, portraying him with a face of a dog. This is certainly not the St. Christopher, the popular protector of motorists that I recall from my youth. One of my Scout leaders, a devout Catholic with three sons in my troop, kept a small portrait of Christopher on the dashboard of his old truck. Christopher rode alongside a plastic Jesus, and I dimly remember a prayer that went along with the saint, something like:

Lord, give me a steady hand and watchful eye
So I don't hurt or kill anyone as I drive by...
That *can't* be right.

Anyway, forget the patron saint of travelers; this is an altogether different St. Christopher. This Christopher was a thief, a murderer, cursed with a face so ugly it looked like that of a dog—and no Best of Show winner either—a homely cur indeed. Later Christopher repented and became a saint. I suppose the point is that outward appearances don't matter and can conceal true beauty—found in the human heart.

Another version of the story begins with Christopher born with the head of a dog. When Christopher converted to Christianity, his face changed into human form—and not just your everyday average male either, but a man of such compelling handsomeness that he was able, working by himself, to convert no fewer than forty-eight thousand people to Christianity–including even the courtesans sent to seduce him.

A third version of the story presents a St. Christopher so drop-dead good looking, so irresistible to the ladies, that in order to avoid temptation, he prayed to be made ugly! However the story goes, fresco artists and iconographers must find it far easier to depict St. Christopher as a dog; he is instantly recognizable in canine form.

As I take leave of the friendly Greeks and thank my translator, our guide steps toward me. "Did you know our Elder Ephraim is in America?" he asks in fluent English.

"Elder Ephraim," I say slowly, in a way that I hope reflects reverence and hides my ignorance. Wait, I remember now. Novice Dean mentioned Ephraim.

Elder Ephraim is a master of the art of spiritual warfare, the young monk tells me. Such is the power of his prayers that they carry far and wide and into some unexpected places. A quite upset Satan himself appeared in Father Ephraim's dreams and demanded: "Why did you come here, in my kingdom and pray?"

For twenty years Elder Ephraim served as abbot at Philotheou, but he recently decided to leave Philotheou in order to construct a monastery—a real Athonite monastery—in Arizona.

Do monks equate the United States with the Devil's Kingdom? I wonder. *Is Arizona hell on earth?*

"Elder Ephraim will open fifteen to twenty monasteries over the next ten years," the monk tells me.

"We will be blessed to have the spirit of the Holy Mountain in America," I say.

"Where do you walk now?" he asks, suddenly changing the subject.

"Back to Karyes," I answer.

He nods. "On your next visit to Philotheou, you could take a bus."

Back in Karyes, I am pleased to find a gift shop open and even more pleased to find that the Austrian-made topographic map I'm seeking is for sale.

Cartographer Reinhold Zwerger's "Paths and Tracks on Athos" looks like a fine map to me, but the ancient shopkeeper who sells it to me seems reluctant to vouch for its accuracy.

"Is it a good map?" I inquire.

He shrugs, blows the dust off the remaining half-dozen or so maps in his inventory.

"Depends on where you're going."

"I'm climbing the Holy Mountain."

"I don't know anyone who's climbed the Holy Mountain with this map."

I must be losing something in translation, I think, as I place the map and two packages of Greek cookies on the counter.

Seems like anybody who walks around here should have a map and the shopkeeper should sell a lot of them. Any hiker who heads out on the trail without a map, without knowing where he's going, is a fool. Me, I want to study the terrain and know exactly where I'm going. That's why I like maps. With a good map and my good sense of direction, I can find my way most anywhere.

"The roads…footpaths," I persist. "It's a good map?"

"Most men who come here, they go to one monastery. They know where they're going. They don't need a map. Why do you need a map?"

The customer is always right. Have you ever heard the expression? "I need to find the way to the Holy Mountain."

He points out the south window of his shop. "The Holy Mountain is right there."

CHAPTER 5

FATHER NIKON'S ICONS

Mike Pahos and Ernest Kolendrianos plotted our journey to New Skete on the south side of the Athos peninsula to meet a monk named Father Nikon, and to see his icons. Mike is the parishioner most responsible for the iconography at our church in Santa Barbara. He and his wife, Vivian, toured Greece and Italy looking at icons and artisans for the new church, built in the late 1980s, and a work in progress during the '90s.

"This Father Nikon is considered one of the best iconographers in Greece," Mike proclaimed. "Wouldn't it be something if we could commission him to paint an icon for us?"

It was surprisingly easy to arrange transport to New Skete. Ernest cornered the driver of a big Mercedes work truck and negotiated passage in American dollars. In minutes we climbed aboard one of the high-wheeled vehicles that in recent years have all but replaced the donkey as the beast of burden on Athos. Passengers are accommodated by two long benches extending the length of the truck bed, which is covered troop-truck style in canvas. Riding down the spine-jarring dirt roads, pitched side to side, fore and aft, makes any journey longer than ten minutes a kind of penance for pilgrims and monks alike.

A monk from Xeropotamou Monastery telephoned ahead for permission to visit; nevertheless, Father Nikon looked just a little bit startled to find four Americans at his door. Several cups of strong coffee in Karyes plus the jarring, stomach-turning drive has left us a little on edge.

"Welcome," he greets us. "How was your journey?"

We whine in discordant Greek chorus: "Long. Bumpy. I would rather walk." Then simultaneous embarrassment at our weakness and a quickly modifed narration: "It was fine. We're fortunate to have trucks to help us get around the Holy Mountain."

He must know we need to chill out because rather than beckoning us inside his quarters, he leads us into the adjacent chapel of St. Spyridon. We make the sign of the cross and admire the tiny house of worship that Father Nikon shares with a handful of artisan and scholarly monks who live alone in the hillside cottages scattered nearby.

For a few moments, it feels like I'm still jouncing around in the back of the truck, but under the watchful eye of St. Spyridon, I soon calm down. I stare back at the icon of Spyridon and try to remember why he's a saint. On the island of Corfu, most of the male population are named Spiro. My friend Spiro, who will meet me in a day or two at Simonopetra and will hike with me around the Holy Mountain, will no doubt know. I wonder if Father Nikon painted this icon.

Father Nikon takes us back to his cottage, where Mike makes introductions. Jack is introduced as an engineer and the director of our church's Greek Festival. Ernest is presented as a leading pediatrician, fellow elder in the church, one keenly interested in icons and the man co-responsible (with himself) for contracting the art installed in our church.

"In Thessaloniki, so many admire your work," Mike praises. "We have even heard of the beauty of your icons in Santa Barbara, California."

Father Nikon's eyes look away. A monk must always be humble.

Father Nikon is modest about his English, too, and we continue in Greek with a little English mixed in.

Mike finishes introductions with Yannis, a writer who's going to hike over to Skete St. Anna and then up the Holy Mountain.

Father Nikon's intense gaze turns to me. "Yannis, it's a very long walk to St. Anna. But you will find some special icons there."

Father Nikon leads us into his studio. "I am blessed to have such light."

Indeed he is. His studio is a spare, well-lighted place. Those artistic people needing serenity and retreat would be happy to work here, unlike those requiring big-city social and cultural stimulation.

Inside the studio, we are struck by a few remarkable photo prints. Father Nikon's photographs of his brother monks and life on the Holy Mountain are positively radiant, but he dismisses his craft as "mere picture-taking."

He is reluctant, shy about showing his photos. "Just some pictures I took while visiting other monks on the Holy Mountain." Why are the most accomplished the most humble?

Father Nikon (pronounced not like the famed camera, but *Nee-cone*) is no mere shutterbug of the sacred. His black-and-white and color images glow like icons, but are a whole lot better composed. I spotted a few of his framed photos when he led us into his studio, admired them, and asked to see more.

He seemed a bit taken aback by the request, but nevertheless he now brings out a wide-leaved portfolio and shows us his work. Meanwhile, my fellow Santa Barbarans regard me as if I'm getting off track from our goal to commission Father Nikon to paint an icon for our church.

Ever since I studied filmmaking at the University of Southern California and California Institute of the Arts, I've seen the world in pictures. And Father Nikon's pictures are most compelling to me, more so than much of the art and architecture I've viewed thus far on my travels.

The monk's photos offer an engaging view of the Athonite world. As a photographer he's far from technically perfect, but the obvious affinity he has for his subjects comes right through. His use of light and shadow and depth of field, particularly in his black-and-white work are excellent. Certainly he has had access to his brother monks—an insider's point of view that any pro photographer would envy.

When we praise his work, he's supremely modest.

Away from the Holy Mountain, away from this world of men without mirrors, Father Nikon might be described as handsome. A mostly black beard surrounds a small mouth and underlines a long thin nose. Beard and black cassock accentuate his luminous eyes, which in their intensity more than make up for the other facial features that are hidden or subdued by hair and cloth. He looks like an artist, so much so that I find it difficult to imagine him in his previous line of work: the *archontaris*, or guest-master, at a big monastery. Living alone in a whitewashed cottage perched on a hillside, looking out toward Mt. Athos, seems far better suited to the life of an artist than the regimented life of a monk in a large monastery.

Obviously Father Nikon's subjects trust him. Some of his best portraits are of elder monks; they remind me of Edward Curtis's photographs of the vanishing Native Americans, whose elders of the tribe, in portraiture, retained their dignity and courage.

Cheri would love these photos. For a moment I review them from her critical eye. From her days at *Runner's World* and a half-dozen other magazines, she's picked the best from among tens of thousands of technically professional, properly illustrative images, looking for photos that conveyed an emotion. Of Father Nikon's work, I know what she would say: "That monk's really got an eye."

Maybe so, but Father Nikon dismisses his photographs as a mere hobby. When we praise his work, he averts his eyes.

"*Thavmassia* (Splendid)" I proclaim. "You know and love your subjects. They trust you and it shows."

Photography is not his real work, he reminds us again.

That would be his icons, which he seems even less inclined to show us than his photographs. Perhaps iconography is no longer his real work, either.

While reviewing Father Nikon's photography, Mike and Ernest glance nervously around the studio. It's apparent what's bothering them: there are almost no icons around. Two icons, backs toward us, lean against a wall. One work in progress looks back at us from an easel near the window.

After our photo review, Mike asks Father Nikon to show us his icons. The monk responds by closing up his photo portfolio and walking over to the easel. "This St. Nicholas is for a church in Thessaloniki. It's my last commission for at least a year."

Mike tries not to show his disappointment.

"Maybe two."

Father Nikon's St. Nicholas lacks facial features and is not very far along. Another reminder to me that I need to find at least a small icon of Nicholas for my godson.

Once Father Nikon completes a commissioned work, the icon is shipped immediately to the parish that has paid for it, he explains. Therefore he has very few actual icons to show us.

When he sees the disappointment on Mike's face, he brings out a three-ring binder. Here he has arranged more than a decade's worth of his work.

We gather around the book for a look.

Maybe Father Nikon is one of the best iconographers in Greece, but who can tell? The icons appear textbook Byzantine, and so much smaller than life in photographs.

Mike and Ernest are intrigued though, and appear quite genuine in their praise of his work.

"Ah, I'm being such a poor host," Father Nikon interjects after the first compliment. He disappears behind a curtain.

"Maybe in a year or two, after his sabbatical or time off or whatever he's doing, we can still get him to make us one," Mike muses.

"An icon from Athos, from such a superb iconographer— it would be very valuable," Ernest affirms.

Mike looks up from the Disciple Peter to me. "John, didn't you talk to a policeman in Karyes who told you how valuable icons are?"

This morning I learned the old icons might be worth something on the black market in Karyes when I chatted with a policeman. (I had met him during our brief stop in town when I was walking toward the café. I was hoping for more gigantes, or at least another fine meal, but alas the eatery was not yet open.) He told me what ends up on the Holy Mountain police blotter.

Law enforcement on Mt. Athos is in the hands of a dozen ecclesiastical gendarmes, bearded in the approved monkish fashion and wearing battle dress of celestial blue, with caps bearing silver badges of the double-headed eagle—the symbol of the Byzantine empire. The policeman told me that the most common problems are men who overstay their permits and women who drift too close to shore on passing boats. Then there's the occasional ruckus created by the drunken workers who miss their wives, and forget they are living in a holy place.

But the worst crimes on the Holy Mountain have been the theft of religious art. He and his fellow policemen must be ever on the watch for international criminals who might attempt to smuggle icons or other holy treasures off the peninsula.

"I think the holy cops were referring to *ancient* icons. I can't imagine there's any market, legal or illegal for modern icons."

Ernest, Mike and Jack ignore me, turning through the pages of Father Nikon's icons and marveling at what they see.

Honestly, I don't understand what they see. Sure, the monk's icons are well drawn, the color and composition fine. I'm sure his work is as good as—and likely better—than anything else out there, but they're still, well, Byzantine.

As a child I liked icons, but after I completed Art History 101 in college, I developed scorn for the icon-maker's art—for the pie-pan faces and steam-rolled, cartoon-figured bodies. Why, I wondered, did the icon "artists" continue painting the same subjects in the same way, century after century?

Hey guys, ever hear of realism, perspective, shadows, three-dimensionality? Any of the many evolutionary art movements of the second millennium? Ever think the fall of Constantinople and the fall of the Byzantine Empire might have been a good time to stop painting in the Byzantine tradition?

No wonder school children liked icons. The holy men and women were depicted as a child would draw them—eyes starting straight ahead, curious flat noses, tight lips around too-small mouths. They looked like they walked out of a coloring book.

Father Nikon returns with a tray bearing the traditional lokoumi, with glasses of ouzo and water. He offers me the tray first. I take the little ouzo glass and the glass of water and, as always, pass on the Turkish delight.

After making the rounds with the tray, Father Nikon opens the door to a patio and directs his visitors outside. "The mountain is out," he declares.

What an odd way to put it. *The mountain is out.* Where have I heard that expression?

I'm about to join my fellows outside on the patio, out with the view of Mt. Athos, but Father Nikon blocks my way. "Let us talk, Yannis."

Uh-oh. Culled from the herd. What could he possibly want with me? I take a quick look up at Mt. Athos before he steers me back inside.

Now I remember: Mt. Rainier. On those rare clear days when Seattle residents can see snowcapped Rainier, they say, "The Mountain is out."

Father Nikon closes the door behind him. "Now, tell me more of your walk to St. Anna."

"Spiro and I are walking the coastal trail to St. Anna's and spending the night. The following morning we'll get an early start and take the trail to the top of the Holy Mountain. Have you climbed it?"

"Once."

"How is the path?"

"Very long. And hard to follow in bad weather."

"Did you take pictures?"

"No. A cloud covered the top of the mountain."

"The view is supposed to be wonderful. Some times the best photos arc with dark clouds. Very dramatic."

Father Nikon should have been able to shoot some pictures in low light, I muse. That's why God made f-stops. "It's hard to imagine it was too dark on top of the Holy Mountain for photos."

He shakes his head. "Too light."

Before I can object, he locks in on me with those intense eyes. "You appear more interested in photographs than icons."

"They're both excellent," I rush to say. "Mike says you're one of the best iconographers in Greece."

He takes the last glass of ouzo from the tray and joins me for a midmorning aperitif. He smiles gently. "But you are moved more by photographs than icons?"

Thank goodness Father Nikon didn't bring Byzantine perspective to his photographs. Thankfully the church patriarchs didn't hand down orders dictating the proper way to photograph. If Father Nikon had brought a Byzantine eye behind the lens, his photos would probably have been slightly over-exposed, with no shadows or depth of field. He would have posed his subjects so that they stared straight into the camera and used a face-flattening wide-angle lens.

"Yes. I don't really get why our church has such basic, such simple art. The perspective is all off."

Eyes, nose, mouth, and hands. He admits the faces are artistically exaggerated. That's because the church fathers in their wisdom understood that seeing, hearing, smelling, tasting, and touching are the doors to a person's soul. All the senses on these great men and women, these saints, have been made holy by God; they're no longer mere sensory organs. "So you understand why an icon-maker makes faces like he does?"

"I think I remember what my Sunday school teacher said about the eyes—they're larger because they've seen such amazing things. But the noses and mouths?"

"The noses are long and thin because the saints have smelled the fragrance of the Holy Spirit. The small mouth indicates that the saints fasted often and had little use for food."

What with the quiet and the few opportunities to talk and with the short rations, perhaps every pilgrim returns from Athos with a smaller mouth than when he arrived.

"But this perspective," I begin to object, then catch myself. I can't believe I'm having this conversation with a monk with my poor Greek and his few words of English and that I'm actually understanding him. I also can't believe I'm expressing my doubts about icons. To a monk, no less.

"I understand why the icons were powerful to the early Christians, but this perspective…. I take a deep breath. "People today are more sophisticated."

"We're more sophisticated? We're better people? There's less greed? Less war? More love?"

Orthodoxy and ouzo. A delicious, licorice-flavored warmth flows down by throat, spreads from my heart to my stomach, and I relax to Father Nikon's message. He is speaking mostly in Greek, I mostly in English, and yet we are communicating almost perfectly.

"Most of the monks on the Holy Mountain are well educated," he tells me. "Many monks study, study for long hours, but the wisest of the fathers on the Holy Mountain know we learn best by our daily schedule of prayers—our job as we see it. We hear and repeat and chant the words of Christ and of the early fathers of the church. As we pray, the icons remind us of the lives of the saints, of the holy saints, particularly the martyrs, who knew better than we how to live a life in the light, closer to God. Yannis, what is it that you think the monks are trying to accomplish by contemplating the icons?"

"Honoring the important men and women from the early days of the church."

"More than that. Yannis, have you ever looked at an icon and seen more?"

"More?"

His eyes twinkle. "More than an old man with big eyes, a big cross, and a long gray beard?"

"A very long time ago. When I was a child."

"And when you were a child—you saw more?"

I hesitate. "It was silly, really...."

Father Nikon smiles encouragingly.

"On Sunday mornings I sat in church—St. Sophia in Los Angeles. At ten years old, I was kind of (*I can't say bored*) restless during the service. I didn't really understand much of the liturgy, because more than half of it was in Greek in those days. I looked up at the icons and my imagination kind of took off—I made up stories about the people in the icons."

Once a guest-master, always a guest-master. As if by magic, there's suddenly a small carafe in Father Nikon's hand and my glass of ouzo is refilled.

"Stories about what kind of saints?'

"I looked in the back of the church at St. George and the dragon and imagined fighting monsters with him."

"That would seem an image that a ten-year-old boy would like. What other Bible stories?"

"No, the stories I made up weren't true stories, about what really happened to the saints and the holy people in the icons. They were stories about me mostly, doing things, battling evil, and the saints were just part of the story—nearby, giving advice."

He is intrigued. "So did you pretend to be superman or a TV policeman in your stories? And the saints came with you around Los Angeles on your adventures?"

"No. I traveled back in time. To be with the people in the icons."

Now he's even more intrigued.

"There was one story, one fantasy adventure that I most remember."

He nods encouragingly. "Please tell me."

His burning eyes. The ouzo. I can't refuse him.

"It's so silly." Nearly thirty years have passed since I thought of my childhood alter-ego, Captain Yannis, his band of Christian guerillas, and his battles against the Roman legions. Post-puberty I've never repeated this to anyone, and yet I recall it in remarkable, indeed embarrassing, detail, as if I were a child again, back in St. Sophia Cathedral looking up at the icons.

Father Nikon listens intently, but I tell my story in rather rapid English and I wonder how much the monk really understands.

"Have you ever thought about painting what you told me?" Father Nikon asks.

"I can't draw at all. I have absolutely no talent with a brush."

"There are many ways to be an iconographer. You know the meaning in Greek?"

"*Ikonographos*—Icon writer," I translate.

"Perhaps you'll write a story about the icons some day."

CHAPTER 6

MONASTERIES OF THE ROCKS TRAIL

Monasteries of the Rocks Trail.
That's how The Trailmaster would name this pathway.

If I were writing about this trail for my *Los Angeles Times* hiking column, I would summarize it thus:

> Monasteries of the Rocks Trail links Simonopetra, Gregoriou, and Dionysiou, three abbeys perched spectacularly on the cliffs above the west coast of the Athos Peninsula. It's a moderately strenuous hike of 7.2 miles round trip from Simonopetra to Dionsyiou, with lots of ups and downs along the way.
>
> The route offers splendid views of the western coast of the peninsula and the bold summit of Mount Athos. Hiking time is about three and a half hours, but you'll want to linger to see the art and architecture of these seaside monasteries.

Departing from Simonopetra's main gate, Spiro and I soon join a handsome length of kalderimi. We descend the stone pathway past the monastery's outlying buildings, then meander through a vineyard and garden.

A lovely garden it is. The monks told me they practice organic farming—another reason why Simonopetra is becoming known as the "eco-monastery." Nearby woodlands and hillsides, burned in a recent wildfire, are being carefully restored.

Ernest, a marvel of good planning and executive function, and so encouraging of my nature interests, has arranged a late-afternoon meet for me with Simonopetra's Father Makarios, a monk-scholar who has written papers about the relationship between Orthodoxy and the environment. I look forward to meeting the monk, though I fear I will not understand his message, because as a low-level nature writer and chronicler of trails, I will be way out of my academic—not to mention spiritual—depth with Monk Makarios.

Today's jaunt along the coast is a fine practice hike for our upcoming trek from Great Lavra to Skete St. Anna to the top of the Holy Mountain. I want to get an idea of Spiro's pace and hiking style, get to know him better, and find out what brought him to the Holy Mountain and where he's going after his visit.

From bits and pieces of our conversations, I surmise there is *a lot* going on with Spiro. He hasn't come right out and said it, but I have the feeling things aren't working out with his One True Love. The Right One. The One You Marry. And at the same time he's dealing with that personally, he's at a crossroads professionally. BS and MS engineering degrees aside, as well as having worked as an engineer for a few years, he's realized it's not the career path for him going forward. Right education. Wrong profession.

Spiro appears untroubled, though, by disappointment, claims to be unworried about what the future may bring, and repeats that old joke: "Want to make God laugh? Tell Him your plans."

We are rapidly getting to know one another, and quickly cover all the usual guy topics about school and our city sports teams, the Los Angeles Dodgers and Los Angeles Lakers, the Chicago Bulls, Chicago Bears, and the hopeless Chicago Cubs. More unusual for us guys, we dive right into weighty topics about faith and fate, eternity and evil. Perhaps there is an Athos Effect: conversation and camaraderie is deepened by time on the trail, in the monastery guest quarters and at prayer in candlelit sixteenth-century churches.

We look back to a wondrous view of Simonopetra, mounted upon a rock like a monastery in Tibet. The mighty façade of the monastery is as impressive from our cliff-side trail as it is from up close. Maybe even more so.

The monastery's name "Rock of Simon" originated with its founder, the thirteenth-century hermit Simon, who is said to have decided to build a monastery after witnessing a mysterious light lingering over this rock tower. Simonopetra's original walls were destroyed by a severe 1891 fire, and the monastery rebuilt with *lots* of plaster and cement.

Ten stories high, Simonopetra is visible from more than five miles away. And the views *from* Simonopetra are terrific, too, if you have the courage to step out onto one of the worn wooden balconies outside the top floors of the monastery. Truly it was an act of faith for Spiro and me late yesterday afternoon to stand on the creaky boards, perched 800 feet above the rocky shoreline below; however, our faith was rewarded with fine views of the sun setting over the Aegean.

Most trails north, south, east, and west of the Holy Mountain offer vistas of the sea, so The Trailmaster would categorize them as coastal trails. The Athonite Peninsula measures twenty-eight miles long and three to six miles in width; therefore every trail on the peninsula lies three miles or less, as the Eastern Imperial Eagle flies, from the sea.

Coastal trails are near and dear to my heart. I pioneered the California Coastal Trail, a 1,600-mile pathway along the beaches and across the bluffs of the state. I walked from the Mexican border to the Oregon border, from the white sand beaches of SoCal to the redwood forests north of San Francisco, met an array of colorful characters en route, and wrote *A Walk Along Land's End*, a narrative account of my journey.

When I return from the Holy Mountain, my publisher will be sending me around California on a book tour.

That will be some transition. From the monasteries of Mount Athos to the TV studios of San Francisco and Los Angeles.

Back home I am The Trailmaster, an authority on hiking. Here I am…what's The Trailmaster in Greek? *Kýrios Monopati*? Mr. Trail? No, I'm just Yannis around here.

We spot a tour boat chugging along, perhaps a quarter-mile or so offshore.

"That's about the closest women can get to Mount Athos," Spiro comments. "I think the rule is boats with women aboard have to stay 500 meters away."

By all accounts the boat tour that begins in Ouranoupolis and travels along the west coast of the Athos peninsula is extremely popular with women; certainly it offers the closest look at the monasteries available to them.

The boat slows, nearly to a stop.

"And this is the closest we're going to get to women in the next week," I add.

We laugh and wave at the boat.

I imagine a trilingual tour guide explaining the prohibition against women to the passengers in Greek, German, and English: "*Avaton* (pronounced Áh-vah-ton) is Greek for 'what may not be set foot upon.' A thousand years ago, when first pronounced, the Mt. Athos Avaton barred women—plus boys, beardless men, and eunuchs. Avaton remains one of the most strictly enforced rules in all of Christianity. It includes domestic animals as well—though there are many housecats around the monasteries so we suppose female cats are the only exception to the rule.

"European feminists say this ban on women is discrimination and talk about fighting it in the courts. But the Mt. Athos Avaton is guaranteed by Greek and international law. The rule is that a female is not to enter a male monastery, nor is a male to enter a female monastery; and this rule is an accepted part of Christianity, as well as other religions.

"Mt. Athos has so many monasteries concentrated in a small and very beautiful area, and would indeed be very attractive to tourists. As you might know from your visits to Greece, even very distant Greek islands get tourism, so why not the Mt. Athos peninsula? But the fact is, ever since...."

We march toward the sea, cross a streambed, and begin a steep ascent. Our efforts are rewarded with an eye-popping view of Gregoriou Monastery, truly a monastery of the rocks. A footpath leads through an olive grove, then across a small bridge close to shore at the monastery's little harbor.

We ascend a kalderimi past a shrine with a fountain dedicated to St. Nicholas and along the ancient brick pathway up to Gregoriou. If the bricks were painted yellow we could be off to see the Wizard, the wonderful wizard of Oz....No wizard around here, though there resides here the powerful spirit of St. Nicholas.

The Monastery of Gregoriou is dedicated to St. Nicholas, and I'm reminded of my godson Nicholas. I *must* return with an icon for him. I failed to purchase a St. Nicholas in Karyes, and none of the monasteries have a Gift Shoppe, so I'll need to go shopping in Thessaloniki before I head back home.

Many are the miracles of St. Nicholas, who has protected Gregoriou from wildfire, saved monks who have fallen from steep cliffs, and rescued boats from perilous seas and certain shipwreck on the rocky Athos shores.

Hanging from a strong ring above one of the chandeliers in Gregoriou's main church is a silver scale model of a ship saved by St. Nicholas. A lumber schooner, nearing the monastery's tiny port in the midst of a terrible storm, was about to capsize when the sailors called out to St. Nicholas. Their entreaties to the saint were heard and Nicholas interceded by quieting the tempest and saving ship and crew from a watery grave.

Frescoes in the narthex of a small chapel illustrate more miracles: drowning victims resurfacing alive from treacherous waters; dead and buried people rising from their graves; people eaten by animals regurgitated intact from the mouths of these beasts.

Leaving Gregoriou, we hike about a half-mile to a bridge, which carries us over a rushing stream. A frisky flow it is, cascading down from Gravanistis Fall, mightiest on the Holy Mountain. If we were hiking in Mount Athos National Park, doubtless we'd find a trail junction here, with a signed pathway leading to the waterfall. No trail to the cascade, though, so we'll have to be content with admiring it from afar.

I suppose the monks are not completely insensitive to the beauty around them and with good reason call their environs "The Garden of the Virgin Mary." Still, when I tell them about my plans to hike through the Garden to the top of the Holy Mountain, the monks repeatedly change the topic from where I will be hiking in nature to which monasteries I will visit, and soon start asking questions about my family and life back home.

John the trail writer is becoming more than a little frustrated. If I had planned this journey as a hiking trip, no way would I be spending so much time here, there, and everywhere. I would march from the port of Dafni to Skete St. Anna and then hike to the top of Mt. Athos. Point A to Point B to Point C. Maybe take an alternate route back, maybe not.

I understand that our *dormitrion*, our Athos passport, has us scheduled for certain nights in certain places, and that this restricts our itinerary and my ability to go hiking. And truly I appreciate Ernest's successful efforts at getting us around; most pilgrims are content to visit two or three monasteries over a three-day period, but thanks to him, we have ten days of touring.

Nevertheless, by the time I get to Skete St. Anna trailhead for the climb to the Holy Mountain, I will literally and figuratively have circled it. I will have visited nine monasteries and I don't know how many churches, chapels, and shrines. I wonder, at week's end, if my time spent in churches will exceed my time on the trail.

After our visit with Father Nikon, I could easily have hiked from his community at Nea Skete to Skete St. Anna. Today Spiro and I could continue hiking along the coastal trail past Dionysiou to Agiou Pavlou Monastery and on to St. Anna.

We hike steeply again uphill, and are soon rewarded with vistas to the top of Mt. Athos, which is particularly alluring to a hiker from this angle. The promontory of the Holy Mountain is faced with marble, gray mostly with a hint of green fallen pillars of rock lying in diagonals

Then it's downhill again. The trail peters out near the water at a little port, where we join a wider track to the gates of Dionysiou Monastery.

The main church is dedicated to St. John the Baptist. Completed in 1547, the church is cross-shaped, with a substantial dome and elaborate frescoes.

"Here's your saint, Yannis," Spiro says quietly, nodding his head toward the icon of St. John the Forerunner.

Wow, this is some Yannis! A sixteenth-century icon showing St. John in action. Scroll and scepter in left hand, he beckons us to follow him. John has a very faint halo, a shadow really, a crown of light in its early stages of formation.

I immediately like this John. John of the *Mountains*. He's not depicted in his usual environs—the desert or on the banks of the Jordan River—but more like the great naturalist John Muir in the High Sierra. John steps through a mountain pass, a gap between impressive high peaks, rock towers with scattered conifers clinging to life below the summits.

Rather than wearing attire colored in usual Byzantine blues and reds, John is dressed for the great outdoors in what resembles a military-issue olive-colored robe. His light brown wings look like shouldered weapons. This is a saint in camouflage, ready to do battle.

At the bottom right of the picture I spy what looks to be a mountaineer's axe. But at the bottom left corner I see John's head, in repose, a distinct halo behind it. Obviously John lost his head to this axe, that of a henchman, not a hiker.

"No doubt, you're a John the Baptist kind of guy," Spiro says as we exit the church and take a seat on a stone wall. "I mean, he is your saint, right?"

"Absolutely," I confirm. "But when I was a kid I didn't know for sure. For reasons I still don't understand, my mother would not declare whether I was named after John the Evangelist or John the Baptist."

"Really?" Spiro questions, taken aback at my mother's ambiguity. "What was your Name Day? What icon did you have?"

"My family didn't have icons around the house," I explain.

Spiro is incredulous. *"Seriously?"*

"It was left up to me to figure out which John was my saint."

John the Gospel writer appealed to me, for I was that odd kid who loved to write stories and imagined becoming a writer one day. At St. Sophia Cathedral, John was stationed at the base of the dome with the other three evangelists, and while I cannot remember their faces, I recall who else, and what else, was painted into the pictures with them: St. Mathew with a man looking back at us over his shoulder; St. Mark with a lion; St. Luke with a calf, and St. John with a mighty eagle, with a large hooked beak, muscular legs, and powerful talons.

I really connected with John the Baptist, though, "the voice crying out in the wilderness," the man with clothes of camel hair and a diet of locusts and wild honey. When I went hiking with the Scouts in the Mojave Desert I could picture John out there with all those twisted Joshua trees.

A man of action, John baptized Jesus and multitudes of the faithful. His one mistake was mixing it up with Herod over points of Jewish law, with the bad result of getting his head served up on a platter. And you've got to admire a saint who keeps working after his death, who goes down into Hades to preach to all those tortured souls that the Messiah is coming.

And then there was the matter of visibility. John the Evangelist has a very low profile compared to John the Baptist, who is given a place of honor on the iconostasis. John's Baptism of Christ and the beheading of John the Baptist are staples of Christian art.

Unlike my mother, Greek friends and relatives had no doubt John the Forerunner was my saint and wished me a Happy Names Day on January 7. By the time I was twelve or so I had chosen the wild man of the desert over the author-theologian.

"Of course by the time I was a college student, I was sure Baptist John was the one for me," I conclude. "I learned more about Gospel John and really got turned off by him and the whole prophecy thing."

"The what?"

"Prophecy, predicting the future."

"I know what it is. What's your problem with it?"

"Okay, writer John, the Evangelist, leaves us 'The Gospel According to' and three short epistles. He was an eyewitness to so many events in the life of Christ, he's a good reporter, he had access to first-hand accounts of things, he writes well. He should have stopped right there. But at the end of his life, he's all by himself on the island of Patmos where the Romans exiled him, and he gets all these visions. Hallucinations. He writes the Book of Revelation totally out of his head."

"Well he did get the visions from God," Spiro points out.

"That's the story. It's soooo Old Testament. We're left with this crazy end-of-the-world stuff; it brings out all the crazies and conspiracy nuts to interpret it."

"You mean like product codes supposedly with the devil's sign, 666?"

"Yeah, like that's a clue to the end of the world. And then there's Gorbachev's scar—the Mark of the Beast. Seriously? I mean, I'm no Mikhail fan, but he's not the Anti-Christ."

Two monks walk by.

"*Evlogeite*," Spiro and I say together.

"*O Kyrios,*" the monks say, one after another.

Thank goodness for Spiro. I forgot the pilgrim's greeting again, and without him would have greeted the monks with a "Good afternoon."

Evlogeite, evlogeite, evlogeite.

"What's your new Orthodox Study Bible say about the Book of Revelation?" I ask, after the monks bless us and move on.

"Got to say Orthodox scholars have some issues with it."

"No doubt. And whether you believe in these 'revelations' or not, I don't think Christians should be waiting around to be raptured out of a horrible earthly life; rather, we should get to work and do our best here and now, on this planet."

"What about *your* John?" Spiro asks.

"My John?"

"Seems like *he* was a prophet—getting into everyone's face and declaring 'Repent for the Kingdom of Heaven is at hand!'"

"Jesus was right there with John," I counter. "Contemporaries. They were cousins. That's not prophecy, that's just looking around and paying attention. He doesn't claim to be more than the 'voice of one crying in the wilderness.'"

"Yannis, you just can't explain away the prophets. The Bible is filled with recorded events the prophets foretold, years, centuries even, before they happened."

"So if there's no rational way to explain how these predictions turned out to be true, you—"

"You just have to accept that it was the Holy Spirit working inside them that helped the prophets see into the future."

CHAPTER 7

MAKE NATURE THE STUFF OF
YOUR PRAYERS

"Are you eating a lot of Greek food?" Cheri teases. Considering the notorious Greek phone service, my wife's voice is remarkably clear coming through the pay phone located close to the waterfront in the nearly deserted port of Dafni.

"I'm not eating a lot of anything here on the Holy Mountain," I answer. "Two meals a day: lentils, feta, and bread. I did have one amazing lunch. My favorite: gigantes."

"Gigantes! The monks made you gigantes!" She laughs.

I love her laugh. In this tiny town without women, on this peninsula without women, how strange—and delightful—it is to hear a female voice, even if it's merely over the phone. My heart feels light and even my legs feel light—despite hiking the Monasteries of the Rocks Trail with Spiro and walking the winding road from Simonopetra to Dafni.

"I had two enormous bowls of gigantes. Absolutely delicious. In a café in the little town of Karyes. And beer."

"So this is paradise for you, right? Gigantes and beer and hiking around. Maybe you want to stay a few more weeks."

"Well, I am spending a lot of time in churches. And there aren't any women. Speaking of which, tell me about my girls."

"Sophia misses you. Mornings in day care at Miss Eva's are working out great with playtime and storytime and all, but not the afternoons. She won't nap there. I have to pick her up after lunch."

"You're such a great mom."

There's a pause before she answers and, for a moment, I imagine I've said something wrong.

"I went into the Adoption Center today," she says hesitantly, her voice tight.

Another pause. "You've been wanting to go in for a while now," I prompt.

"It was very discouraging, meeting with Dani, even though she gave me her usual 'Have Faith it's Going to Happen' pep talk. I can't see how we're ever going to find another baby."

"Sure we are," I assure her.

"It's been more than a year. No action on our file. Zero response to our mailings. We got Sophia in a month."

"Everybody tells us we were very, very lucky." Given the truly Byzantine world of adoption, with layer upon layer of government and social service agencies mixed in with slow-moving secular and religious charities, not to mention expensive lawyers, it's a wonder there are any adoptions at all.

"Maybe the problem is we specified a boy," she says. "Makes it twice as hard. I so want Sophia to have a little brother." Her throat catches; I can hear it from six thousand miles away. "And for you to have a son."

"Oh honey, it's just a matter of being persistent. We'll figure out how to make you a mother of two."

"We've tried just about everything."

"No way," I object. "We haven't been aggressive enough on the marketing side. When I get back we'll do another letter and picture package, send out mailings to the adoption lawyers and Christian counseling centers."

There's another pause and I hear white noise over the line. Like wind in the trees.

"How's Spiro?" Cheri asks, suddenly bright and bubbly again.

"We hiked together today. A great guy. And a true believer. We really get into some talks."

"About what? Women?"

"Well of course, women. And deep stuff, too. Faith, the monks, the saints, icons."

"Icons?" She giggles and for a moment all is right again with our world. "Have you told Spiro about our funny experience with icons in Florence?"

"I will, though I'm not so sure he'll see the humor in it."

We continue, light and easy for a time. So much to say, and the cost per minute so high.

"Love you."

"Love you, bye."

As I sling my daypack over my shoulders and start walking out of town, my eye is captured by the reflection of the late-afternoon sun on glass. I veer over toward the glitter on the waterfront and, to my surprise, discover crate upon crate of beverages stacked near the dock. Beer, lots of Amstel. And soda, Sprite and Coca-Cola.

I look around. Not a monk or sailor or pilgrim in sight. A beer would be nice, but not a warm one, and not before I have to hike back to Simonopetra. Suddenly I am overwhelmed by the desire for a Coke. I pull a bottle from a crate. Then another.

Wait a minute, Yannis, my conscience speaks. You can't *take* the Cokes. That's stealing. On the Holy Mountain, no less.

But I can *buy* the Cokes, I scheme. But from whom? No one is around the waterfront. I open my wallet and withdraw a ten-dollar American bill and place it in the cavity once occupied by a soda bottle. Now that I'm paying for the Cokes, I rationalize, I should be getting more for my money, so I take two more for a total of four. I open one Coke with the bottle opener on my Swiss Army knife and slip three Cokes into my daypack. I write a single word thank-you note (*Efharisto*) on a slip of paper, leave it next to my ten-dollar bill, and begin the hike back to Simonopetra.

Oh, that sweet liquid, so American. And Coke has caffeine, so welcome because coffee is absent from the monastic diet, and I really miss my morning cup. Maybe I can sub Coke for coffee at breakfast time. Somewhere I heard that a remarkable number of Americans drink caffeinated soft drinks for breakfast.

Call me John, or call me Yannis, but never call me late for dinner. The Coke jolts me *and* my appetite, and suddenly I'm very hungry. The monastic meal schedule—we are fed two meals a day, with a ten-thirty A.M. "brunch" after matins and a seven P.M. supper after vespers—is wearing on me, as is the menu of lentils, cooked vegetables, brown bread, and olives, washed down with wine.

Spiro must be more deprived than I by one fewer than the usual number of meals per day and by the conservative portions; he has thirty or forty more pounds than I to fuel. Of course I guess the point is *we're supposed to be hungry.* Keeps us sharp and on edge, makes us appreciate the monks and their regimen, helps us stay alert to thwart the devil's advances.

Eating—what we eat, how we eat, and where we eat—I've learned, is very much part of the monastic experience. The refectories have impressive décor, and we eat surrounded by frescoes of the saints. From a pulpit, a monk reads from the New Testament or other holy writings throughout the entire meal, as we eat in silence. At the head table sits the *Igoumenos* (Abbot), who starts and finishes the meal by ringing a bell and saying a prayer. The wise pilgrim checks on the pace of the Abbot's eating and matches his to the elder; once he's done, you're done, and with only two meals you don't want to leave food on the plate. You can only eat in the trapeza. No snacks. No trips to the kitchen to find leftovers.

I pick up my pace. I don't want to be late for our meeting with Eco-Monk Makarios. Or for dinner.

Before I've hiked a quarter-mile, I swig the last of my Coke. As I slip the empty into my daypack, a truck rolls up alongside me.

"Would you like a ride?" the driver calls out from the cab of a small diesel-powered truck.

"Yes, please!" I answer enthusiastically. As I climb into the passenger seat, it occurs to me that nearly all vehicle traffic travels along the main road between Dafni and Karyes; not along this little spur road to Simonopetra. Better confirm my destination with the driver. "I'm going to Simonopetra," I say.

He nods. "So am I."

And that is the end of our conversation, for the driver listens intently to a sports talk show that plays at very high volume on the radio. The truck looks familiar, as does the driver, a man of about forty, with thickly calloused hands and a neat mustache.

As the Holy Mother watches over us from an icon affixed to the dashboard, we motor rapidly along the little road, and what was a tedious hike north is a comparatively short drive south. Nearing the main gate of Simonopetra, the driver makes a U-turn and stops, the motor running.

As I disembark, it occurs to me that this kind soul went out of his way for me. He had no reason to go to Simonopetra—except to give me a ride. For which I am so grateful.

"Thank you so much! You—"

"Gigantes," he says with a smile, as he waves goodbye. "I *love* gigantes, too."

"Lions lived with the holy hermits, St. Kyriakos the Anchorite and St. Savas the Sanctified," begins Monk Makarios.

The monk-scholar recounts how the holy men of old communed so well with wildlife. Surprisingly, they got along with lions—the most fierce of animals.

I remember reading, in an old *National Geographic* maybe, about Asiatic lions roaming Palestine and all over the

Holy Land at the time of Christ. Ruthless Roman authorities ordered the earliest followers of Jesus thrown into the arena with hungry lions; to say the least, lions do not have positive associations for Christians.

The only Biblical character I can recall who escaped becoming lion food is the Prophet Daniel, who, when left overnight in the lions' den at the command of King Darius of Persia, was not harmed by the hungry beasts but saved by his great faith in the Lord. (The evil men who had cajoled the King into this action were themselves thrown into the lions' den and suffered the fate they intended for Daniel.)

If this was Simonopetra University, we might be in a graduate student seminar. We sit at the end of a long table, with Professor Makarios (if the monk exchanged his cassock for slacks and a blazer, he'd easily pass for a college teacher) and his teaching assistant at the head of the table, his four pupils close by, and a dozen empty chairs.

Translators d Ernest, as well as Mike and I, have an awkward start when Father Makarios mixes in some French (apparently his language of choice and scholarship). Ernest only dimly remembers some French from college days and French is a language I speak and understand *worse* than Greek.

Mon Dieu!

O Theós mou!

My God!

From a stack of photocopied documents resting on the table, Father Makarios selects a rather svelte one and hands it to me. It's a ten-page summary of his work in English, and I am most grateful for it.

By way of introduction Father Makarios told us that the monks approach the world's environmental problems from an altogether different perspective than scientists and politicians. Whatever he has to contribute on the subject of Nature is not original thinking; rather, he shares the wisdom of the saints, as well as the wisdom of the elders on Mt. Athos.

I am intrigued and Ernest appears to be enjoying the talk. The good doctor has the kind of brilliant mind and wide-ranging interests that would make him an A student in almost any field of endeavor. Likely Ernest exaggerated my credentials to get an audience with Father Makarios: *Yannis studied at the University of Southern California and is a well-known writer about nature and the environment...."*

Yeah, right. Mostly what Yannis does is tell people to "Take a hike!"

Mike, recently retired as Santa Barbara County Parks director, has long been personally and professionally interested in the environment. And Spiro? Count on him to be fascinated by stories of the saints.

Kyriakos, born in Corinth in the fifth century, lived in the desert outside of Jerusalem and was said to always have a lion with him for company and protection, tells Father Makarios. "This may seem surprising, but we must remember that before the Fall, wild beasts lived with Adam and Eve in paradise."

The lions who lived with the saints are not the lions of the storybooks, I realize. Not Simba, Nala, and all the colorful characters in the wildly popular *Lion King* movie beloved by my Sophia and children around the world. For a moment, I drift off, back to our living room, watching the video with my little girl. Sweet. *Hakuna Matata.*

St. Savvas lived in the remote wilderness and preferred lions' dens as his retreats, continues Father Makarios. When Savvas moved in, the lion moved out and gave it to the Holy man. Once Savvas noticed his disciple, Agapios, asleep, as a lion was sniffing about him. Savvas prayed, and the lion, rather than attacking Agapios, brushed his face with its tail, waking him up. Savvas used the opportunity to tell the young ascetic: "You must not sleep so soundly or you'll be vanquished by both visible and invisible creatures."

"Bears, also very fierce animals, kept quiet company with the saints," Father Makarios continues. "Seraphim of Sarov and other hermits lived in harmony with bears in the forests of Russia in the eighteenth century."

And the saints' peaceful co-existence with creatures was by no means limited to large mammals, Father Makarios relates. Holy men lived in harmony with birds, too. Crows carried half a loaf of bread to St. Paul every day for seventy years.

My own relationships with animals known to kill humans have not been so harmonious. On several occasions while hiking alone, I have been stalked by mountain lions. While on a trail in Big Sur in the Ventana Wilderness, a mountain lion walked silently along one side of the creek while I walked along on the other. The big cat followed me for several miles. Near dusk, I could see the lion's amber eyes looking at me from across the creek as I made camp. I kept my campfire going a very long time. I slept fitfully, knowing a silent, stealthy, lightning-fast predator could be just one pounce away from my tent.

Never will I forget or forgive that Yosemite bear for eating my food supply. The big black bear batted down my food cache strung (sufficiently high and out of reach, I thought) from a tree limb.

The incident occurred in a High Sierra trail camp located just off the John Muir Trail. The bear made off with about three quarters of our foodstuffs before ambling off to the sound of our shouts, our beating of pots and pans, and our blowing a whistle. My trail companion and I were forced to make do with mighty lean rations for several more days of hiking before reaching our next food cache.

As for birds, the winged things steal food from me; never do they bring it. Scrub jays and sea gulls have snatched snacks and sandwiches from me at trailside meal stops.

"A monk shows respect for *all* creatures," Monk Makarios emphasizes.

Before I can say "Amen," he tells the tale of *another* Makarios, one of the great desert ascetics, circa 300 AD. Such was the extreme discipline of St. Makarios of Alexandria that it was said that no one ever saw him eat, drink, or even sit down.

One day Makarios squashed a mosquito, a reflexive action no doubt, an instinctual human response to a pest. Even if noticed, easily forgotten. Not by Makarios, however. For penance, he immersed himself for six months in a mosquito-infested marsh, daily wading into the buggy waters and getting all but devoured by insects.

When I think of the number of mosquitoes I've slapped, clapped, and trapped, the number of skeeters I've squished, squashed and pinched to death before they bit me, or in revenge for biting me and sucking my blood....

If there's hell to pay for killing mosquitoes, I'm going straight to the devil.

I picture Makarios covered toes to scalp with a thousand bites, every bit of skin swollen and infected. Apparently the mosquitoes left Makarios so deformed he was recognizable by his brother monks only by his voice.

So Kyriakos and Savas became saints, in part, because they weren't bitten by lions, and Makarios because he was bitten ad nauseam by mosquitoes? Wouldn't St. Markarios be better remembered if he *hadn't been* bitten by mosquitoes?

I say "Praise the Lord" for mosquito repellant made with the strong chemical agent DEET, one of the great benefits for hikers, and for all of humankind. I only wish DEET's purpose were to kill the damn things, not merely repel them.

Given that mosquitoes spread malaria and other diseases, you wonder: why would God create a mosquito, anyway? Don't some of the funds raised by our Orthodox diocese for missions in Africa go to the eradication of mosquitoes?

Quite suddenly, Monk Makarios literally and figuratively turns the page, and abruptly transitions from simple tales of saints and animals to a complex thesis of how the monks view nature and the ecology crisis. It all began with Adam, whose fall and getting locked out from Paradise caused our estrangement from nature. The wealth God has given us, we have wasted in wantonness. The only way for us to again become good stewards of nature is for each of us to repent for our own sins and, like the monks, take individual responsibility for our actions.

Father Makarios describes a very deep spiritual ecology, way beyond the oft-cited Biblical directive for believers to be good stewards of creation. He presents an altogether different relationship between humankind and the natural world than any I have ever heard before. What the monks teach us, he expounds, is that with enormous spiritual struggle, we can move from a sinful and egocentric relationship with creation to a spiritual one, through the purification of our souls.

In less than five minutes, I am lost. Lost in translation. Lost in understanding. Likely I would be lost even if the monk's presentation were made in plain English.

Fortunately, before my translators despair and the monk-scholar notices the blank looks on our faces, we hear the call to vespers, and our lesson abruptly concludes.

"Bless the Lord, O my soul!"

Vespers at Simonopetra. Spiro at my side, Ernest, Mike and Jack nearby. From the first words the chanting at this monastery is…

Out of this world.

"You who laid the foundations of the earth, so that it should not be moved forever."

The single voice. The responses. The many monks together in unison.

"The sun knows it's going down. You made darkness, and it is night."

The first part of Vespers are psalms that remind us Who's In Charge.

The young lions roar after their prey, and seek their food from God. When the sun rises, they gather together and lie down in their dens.

The Lord even rules over lions. Over saints and sinners, believers and seekers, bears and mosquitoes.

"Yannis," Spiro says quietly, directing my attention to an icon of St. John.

Simonopetra's John the Baptist is pictured in the most traditional way: with halo and angel wings, with scepter and scroll. The wild man of the desert looks nicely put together in this depiction with a neat blue shirt and dark gold robe.

One needs to look closely at this John to distinguish him from other holy men because the differences are subtle: eyes more intense, locks of hair out of place, a beard a bit more scraggly than that of the other saints.

This is a much different John from the one located just a few miles down the Monasteries of the Rocks Trail at Dionysiou. That icon was of a wilder saint, rough around the edges, a bigger-than-life hiker in a mountain wilderness.

While contrasting the two icons of John, my tired mind adds a third, the icon of the saint on the altar screen at St. Barbara. That portrayal of the saint shows an in-between John—more wild than the one at Simonopetra, less wild than the one at Dionysiou. For a moment in the candlelit darkness of the church, the icons of the three Johns appear to me one after another in the same place. Wild-wilder-wildest. The images repeat, flashing before me in time to the chanting.

Oh Lord, how many are your works! In wisdom You have made them all. The earth is full of your creatures.

I blink and the icons disappear; I turn to Spiro but he is out and about in the dusky interior of the church. He and a half-dozen or so pilgrims, mostly Greek I guess, are venerating icons, crossing themselves before them, one of the pilgrims doing prostrations before a saint I cannot identify, others moving in time with the chanting, from icon to icon as the spirit moves them.

Beautiful chanting. The chanters are holy instruments, haunting beyond words.

The chanting adds to senses already overloaded by the day—by the smell of salt air, ripening olives, and heavy incense; by the touch of my boots on a thousand-year-old trail; by the sights of monks and monasteries and icons....

So many icons. From the Early, Middle, Late, and Post Byzantine periods. From the Comnerian Age and Palaeologan Age. Small and large, permanent and portable, poorly rendered and magnificently expressed.

As if the scores of permanent icons in the churches and chapels weren't enough, dozens of portable icons are displayed high on the iconostasis, on the wall with doors that separate the nave from the sanctuary. Tier upon tier, each tier with niches, each niche with an icon, with the largest icons displayed in the most prominent places: Christ, Mary, John the Baptist, and the saint for whom the church is named. The icons are arranged in some kind of hierarchy that I do not understand—likely in an order, and in a ranking, as Byzantine as the icons themselves.

Of course icons aren't the only Byzantine art on the Holy Mountain. The monasteries also have ivory diptychs and illuminated manuscripts, crosses with ornate metal work and tapestries with gold embroidery, bishop thrones, lamp stands, and even caskets. But it is with the icons that the monks communicate; it is the icons that the monks venerate.

The monks who founded Athos are known as *iconophiles,* those who love icons and, to this day, *iconophilism* is not too strong a word for their love of icons. To a man, each monk is an *iconodules,* one who serves icons, one who strongly supports their veneration.

Lord, I call upon Thee, hear me. Hear me, O Lord. Let my prayer arise in Thy sight as incense.

I wonder: does the quality of an icon matters to a monk? The "best" icons, and surely the most numerous, are of the Theotokos, and a fair number of these are "miracle icons," the Holy Mother working wonders for those who prayed to her.

But monks and the most pious of pilgrims also give their full devotions to obscure saints, badly worn icons, and to a scattering of "happy icons," those overly-restored, way-too-bright.

As I consider the varying quality of icons, the voice of Mr. Ledford comes to me from the home dugout at Rockview Dairy Little League Field: *"It's not the arrow, it's the Indian."* My baseball coach told me this when I arrived before the game with an expensive new bat. His point to me, the ten-year-old lead-off hitter for the Bears, was that good tools are fine, but, more important to success is the skill of the hunter shooting the arrow or the skill of the batter hitting the ball.

So maybe I'm missing the point to look at the quality of the icons; it's not the icons so much as the skill of the one venerating them and praying. When I approach icons, poor Christian that I am, I can't get a hit. I strike out looking. The monks, in contrast, so skilled at venerating icons, are clutch power hitters. And it doesn't matter who's the pitcher. Or in the picture, in the case of icons.

And let the lifting up of my hands be an evening sacrifice. Hear me, O Lord.

With regard to icons I am one of those who practice Yi-ya Orthodoxy: we light candles, make our crosses and approach icons the way our grandmothers taught us.

Spiro's approach to icons is one of a true believer, more like that of the most devout pilgrims and the monks. When we return to our room, I must ask Spiro about icons.

After a modest (what else?) dinner highlighted by what I think was chickpea soup, Spiro and I retire to our quarters. Our accommodation at Simonopetra is smaller and more private than we've had so far, and a nice change from the larger dorm rooms of other monasteries. Our two beds are near a window with a view of the Holy Mountain.

As we enter the room, we fumble without success for the light switch. Simonopetra must be taking its charge to become the "eco-monastery" seriously, for its energy use is low indeed.

There is the most minimal light in the hallways and bathroom, a feeble glow coming from the lowest possible watt bulbs. Candles might provide more light than these dim bulbs.

My small flashlight helps guide us across our room but nevertheless Spiro stumbles over my daypack, which rests on the floor near my bed. There is a clanking sound as the pack falls open and two bottles of Coca-Cola roll across the floor.

Spiro laughs. "Yannis, I must have missed it. There's a Coke machine down the hall?"

"Right next to the vending machine with the chips and the candy bars."

I pick up the Cokes. "Breakfast," I promise, as I stow them away.

Spiro laughs some more when I tell him of my purchase (he calls it "theft") of soda on the Dafni waterfront and the ride back with the truck driver who, like me, *loves* gigantes.

"And were you able to call Cheri?" he asks.

I recap for Spiro our conversation—Sophia's nap resistance and Cheri's visit to the Adoption Center.

"I had no idea adoption was so difficult," Spiro responds. By the light of a very dim desk lamp—the only light that works—I see him, in silhouette, shake his head in sympathy. "It must be really hard for women, for Cheri."

"It is. I kind of thought the pressure would be off after we adopted Sophia. But she really wants another baby."

"So what are you going to do?"

"More marketing. There are ways to get our family profile out there. We haven't tried everything yet."

Spiro slips under the covers. "So we're doing the three-thirty service, right?"

"Right," I say with as much enthusiasm as I can muster. Without Spiro as my spirit guide I'm sure I would ignore the three-fifteen A.M. knock on the door, the tapping of the semandron, and decline the opportunity to attend another two-and-a-half-hour service.

"Spiro?"

"Yeah?"

I can tell he's about to fall asleep. "Spiro, I see you with the icons. And you and some of the other pilgrims and the monks, you seem so connected to them."

"Yeah?"

"I started thinking a lot of icons after visiting Father Nikon, the icon painter."

"Yeah, you were so lucky to talk to him one on one. He's a disciple of Elder Ephraim, the one bringing monasteries to America."

"He is?"

"He's special. Next thing you know he'll be Elder Nikon and people will be coming from all over just to get five minutes of his advice."

"Spiro, it was kind of a strange conversation. Father Nikon didn't seem to know much English. And you know my Greek. But we had this deep conversation. And I was understanding him, and I'm sure he was understanding me."

"No kidding. That's how things work around here."

"I told him my issues with icons."

"You told a monk about your issues with icons?"

I can't tell from Spiro's voice if he is amused or horrified. Or both.

"About the faces, the way they're drawn. I told him about how I liked them when I was a child, and didn't as an adult. "

"What advice did he give you?"

"Nothing very specific. He reminded me that *iconographos* in Greek means 'icon writer.' And he wished you and me a safe journey to St. Anna and the Holy Mountain."

"So you have issues with the icons as…bad art?

"I guess you could say that." Cheri's voice comes back to me: *Have you told Spiro about our funny experience with icons in Florence?* "Cheri asked if I told you about our experience with icons…are you still awake?"

"I am."

But not for long, I guess.

"A year before we got married, Cheri and I rendezvoused in Florence. Romantic Florence. We had so much fun taking in the city's art and architecture, street life, the trattorias. Magic. We even had a room with a view on the top floor of Mario's Bed & Breakfast Inn."

The darkness. Spiro's calm voice. The cross on the wall. This feels like Confession.

"We wanted to absorb as much Renaissance art as possible, so we hung out in the Uffizi Gallery. But we made a few wrong turns in the museum and walked out of the Renaissance into, like, miles of corridors. We couldn't figure out where we were going with the awful museum map, and Cheri's poor Italian couldn't get us back on track, so we ended up in this seemingly endless special exhibit of icons.

"So after all this amazing Renaissance art, we're looking at the icons and it isn't long before our icon-viewing gets pretty irreverent. First smiles, then chuckles. And then we start laughing, because we play a game, 'Guess the Age of the Icons.' One of us covers up the date at the bottom of the icon while the other guesses when it was painted. (Loser buys the gelato.) From the fourteenth century to the eighteenth century, all of them looked the same. Who could tell if an icon was painted in 1384 or 1843? Our guesses were centuries off the mark. We really thought it was the funniest thing at the time—though the other visitors in the gallery did not share our amusement.

"Then I guess you could say we got even more wicked. We started wisecracking: maybe the Florentines and all the Renaissance art lovers were simply too polite to hang Byzantine icons where they belonged—in what used to be called the Primitive Art Gallery and is now 'Indigenous Cultural Expressions' or 'Early People Folkways' or whatever the politically correct term is these days.

"So there you have it: 600 years after the last Byzantine walked this earth, iconographers are still painting like the Renaissance never happened. It's an art movement that never moved. The saints are painted in the same two-dimensional way century after century.

"So in the midst of our guess-the-age-of-the-icons game, I get red-faced trying to keep from laughing and Cheri gets a severe case of the giggles. First the museum attendant shushes us, and when we don't take the hint (we don't follow his Italian but his talking hands make it obvious) he suggests that we should exit the museum."

There is a long silence, and I fear Spiro has fallen asleep.

"That's it?" Spiro says, stifling a yawn.

"What do you mean 'that's it?'"

Spiro fluffs his pillow. "Lots of people have doubts. Like half the kids I went to college with. You just get over them."

"I saw all that crossing and kissing of the icons in church tonight. I didn't see much doubt on display." My words come out in a torrent. "I mean, how's it supposed to work between the believer and the icon? Does the believer make the greater effort? Or is the icon supposed to do the majority of the work? What are the monks trying to connect to? What—"

"Good night, Yannis. We'll talk about it in the morning."

"Good night, Spiro," I reply, but by the time the words leave my lips, my companion is sound asleep.

I am wide awake, with a stomach that needs filling and a mind that needs emptying. I open my notebook and begin to write:

Letter from John to the Hikers

Brothers and Sisters in Christ. From the time Adam and Eve were exiled from Paradise, humankind has mourned its lost relationship with the natural world.

Adam took a fall for us all. Never again would he or Eve or any of the billions of humans who followed them walk the Earth without sin against God, against one another, and against nature.

Adam's fall corrupted nature. Adam's fall corrupted human nature. Adam's fall was the hiker's fall.

Hikers fall. Rarely. Frequently. Softly. Seriously. All hikers eventually fall. And just as we fall when we are hiking in nature, we fall and we fall short in our care of nature.

Listen now to the cry of Creation.

Today we are more disconnected from nature than ever before. We chop down the great trees of the world—in the cold forests of the north, in the tropical rainforests, and in the woods near our homes. We foul streams and rivers, lakes and oceans. Every day another species of plant or animal is lost from earth for all time.

We want more than we need, and take more than we need from nature. We fail to moderate our desire for material things, which causes us to view nature as a commodity and merely as a collection of resources to be used as food and fuel. We refuse to acknowledge nature is more than the sum of its resources.

To reconnect with nature, reconnect with God, and remember that it's you, not another, that is the cause of the despoiling of nature. The hiker's contribution to halting the abuse of nature is for each of us individually to correct ourselves.

Do not seek more control over the holy forests, the holy mountains, or the holy waters. Do not seek more control over other people.

Instead, control yourself. Learn from the monks: Take personal responsibility for your own thoughts and actions toward nature. Avoid blaming others for the abuse of nature, and do not hide behind broad excuses about corrupt politics, a perverted economy, and immoral humanity.

Begin the restoration of nature by restoring yourself. One fitting time for self-reflection is during Great Lent, which should be a period of repentance and reduced commercial activity. But no need to wait for Lent; bring a little bit of Lent on each hike. Give up blame. Set aside anger. Give thanks for God's many blessings, for friends and family, and for the natural world around you.

Make nature the stuff of your prayers. Bring the tall mountain, roaring river, and singing bird into the sanctuary of your heart. An appreciation of the beauty and power of nature adds to appreciation of our Lord. When we are right with God, we will do right for nature.

Hike as children of light. Leave ego and arrogance at the trailhead and you shall see and hear nature in all its glory. In nature, find refuge from cities full of idols. In nature, find yourself. In nature, find the Holy Spirit or allow the Holy Spirit to find a way into your heart.

Blessed be the one who loves to hike and blessed be the one who hikes to love.

Remember the words from the Holy Mountain of St. Silvan the Athonite: "The heart that has learned to love, has pity for all creation."

Love the red dawns, golden sunsets, and sky of many colors.

Love the still waters, burbling streams, and thundering waterfalls.

Love the ancient oaks, the cedars, and the palms.

Love the sandy beach, rocky shore, and tide pools.

Love the desert dunes, slot canyons, and badlands.

Love the lupine, the lilies, and the daffodils.

Love every day of God's light. Love everything in nature, and you shall discover the heavenly mystery in all living things. And once you have discovered it, you will come to feel it more and more, as you hike mile after mile, and with each passing day and week and year of your life.

CHAPTER 8

BREAKFAST IN BYZANTIUM

After a week of lean rations, I am thrilled beyond all bounds by our breakfast in Byzantium. Never have string beans looked so good.

"Thank you very much for this wonderful meal," I tell a young monk as he places a platter of *fasolakia* in front of me.

"The two weeks after Easter is the best time on the mountain for eating—we really celebrate," the monk replies, without a trace of irony.

Geronimos, who sits across the table from me, nods in satisfaction. With his gray beard and gray garb he at first glance resembles a monk-in-training; actually, he's a tour guide/entrepreneur and the proud owner of a green, heavy-duty, high-wheeled Mercedes truck. Ernest hired him, and he drove us pilgrims—Spiro and the Santa Barbarans—to the Holy Mountain's largest and wealthiest monastery, Great Lavra, every bit as huge as its name suggests.

Geronimos told the friendly monks that we were visitors of great importance; this resulted in a first-class tour and in a regal breakfast: red-dyed hardboiled eggs, feta cheese, beans, bread, and red wine.

On approach, Great Lavra is quite impressive. It occupies a commanding rock outcropping at the end of the peninsula where the Holy Mountain itself slopes down to the sea.

Meghisti Lavra, Greatest Abbey, the first monastery founded on the Holy Mountain, holds 300 monks and by far the greatest number of sacred relics, our tour guide monk tells us on a pre-breakfast walking tour. Father Guide (he's apparently too modest to give us his name) speaks excellent, if heavily accented, English, and he guides us in a manner that we pilgrims agree is superior to most secular European tour leaders.

Father Guide tells us the intriguing story of the monastery, which dates from its founding in 963 AD by St. Athanasius, as we approach the saint's tomb in the Chapel of Forty Martyrs, one of the fifteen chapels within the huge abbey.

We admire the thousand-year-old cypress trees in the courtyard and visit a shrine containing a piece of the Holy Cross, the left hand of St. John Chrysotomos, the skulls of Basil the Great and St. Michael of Synadon….

Inside the church, Father Guide tells us about the murals created by the famous Cretan painter Theophanes in 1535, when the master was at the height of his powers. When he leads us into the trapeza and shows us more amazing frescoes adorning the dining hall walls, we figure we're about to get a second discourse on the religious art of Theophanes, but no, we are blessed instead by a bountiful breakfast.

Geronimos beckons us to join him at a long table, where he drinks wine with three old monks who could stand in for the three Wise Men in a nativity scene. While wine at ten in the morning is a first for me, our driver, obviously undiscouraged by the early hour, imbibes liberally.

We pilgrims, along with Father Guide, join Geronimos and the monks at the table. The briefest of blessings emanates from the cassocked side, ten men make the sign of the cross, and suddenly we're all drinking wine and doing brunch.

And talking. Obviously talking in the trapeza is permitted, perhaps even encouraged, during such informal gatherings with visitors. The conversation—about our parish in Santa Barbara, about the Orthodox Church in America, about the revival of monasticism, and more—swirls around me. Intent as I am on devouring this breakfast, I am content to let my fellow pilgrims carry the conversational ball.

Greek is becoming easier on my ear, and I'm starting to think, just a little bit anyway, in Greek. A trio of translators has really helped me get around. Ernest is simply a brilliant man, with a photographic memory, a very quick mind, and a tongue to match. A few more weeks in Greece and he'll be ready for translation duty at the UN. Mike probably understands nearly as much as Ernest, and the two sometimes consult and arrive at a consensus translation. Spiro, too, is a good translator in his own way. His Greek isn't as practiced as that of the older men, but he has a great instinct for translating only what's most critical. He'll let me swim along with my tourist Greek until I start to drown, then rescue me.

Since Greece is such an impossible language to learn as an adult, perhaps it could be combined with a more sensible tongue like English, I muse. Yes, Greeklish ought to be the official language of the Holy Mountain. Combine Greek, the historic, liturgical language, the link with Byzantium, the language in which the writers penned the gospels, with English, the modern international language of trade and ideas. Greeklish would enable pilgrims to understand Greek words and ideas that have no direct English translation and form the perfect language for spreading the good Word from the Holy Mountain.

"Yannis."

Greeklish. Learning it would help the outside world understand the monks on Mt. Athos. And the monks on Athos could learn more about the outside world. On the other hand, what more do the monks need to know about the outside world?

"Yannis."

I look up from my food to find everyone at the table staring at me.

"They want to know about your walk to Skete St. Anna," Ernest says.

I manage to swallow a too-large bite of feta cheese with the help of the last of my wine.

"I'm going to climb the Holy Mountain. To the top. Skete St. Anna is at the start of the trail up the mountain."

This answer seems to satisfy my fellow pilgrims, but not the monks, who wait expectantly for me to continue.

"Spiro is coming with me," I add.

They continue to regard me with great expectation, as though I have something more profound to tell them.

"Back in America, I like to climb mountains," I ad lib. "The Holy Mountain will be a very special climb, I'm sure."

Father Guide confers with his brother monks, then turns to me. "The monks of Great Lavra take care of the brothers at the far end of the Holy Mountain. We watch over the monks who live as hermits in the hills and caves. We are responsible for the skete, and some of us know St. Anna's quite well."

"What will I find there?" I inquire.

"What are you looking for?" he returns.

"A place to stay for two nights."

Father Guide translates for his brothers. The oldest monk shakes his head, and another brief conference takes place.

"Do you want a family?" Father Guide asks.

"Already have one," I reply.

"Children?"

"A daughter, two years old. Sophia."

"Beautiful name, Sophia."

"Yannis and his wife Cheri adopted her at birth," Mike tells them.

Father Guide translates and the three monks, like a Greek chorus, nod in satisfaction, then speak rapidly in low tones to him. "They would like to hear about adoption, how a child is adopted in America these days," he tells me.

I look down to find that, as if by magic, my wine glass has been refilled. A monk's day begins at midnight; therefore ten in the morning is really like six P.M. for someone who begins work in the outside world at eight A.M., I rationalize. And therefore Happy Hour at ten in the morning makes perfect sense.

Between sips of wine, I give them the executive summary of adoption, American style. First, how rare adoption really is. About a country of around 280 million that manages but 60 thousand adoptions per year. About the two million American families that say they would like to adopt, but lack the willpower, resources, or know-how to battle such long odds to adopt a baby. Even if a couple has the commitment and determination to adopt, it's faced with the difficult, nearly impossible task of finding a baby, especially a healthy baby, to adopt, because the number of babies available for adoption are very few indeed. About ninety-nine percent of young, unwed mothers choose to keep their babies and raise their children themselves; few of these women are prepared for motherhood and able to support themselves and a child.

Mike listens intently. He brought up adoption because there's a part of him that wants to talk about the subject, get affirmation that he did the right thing by adopting two. But he is from a generation that didn't talk about things. And I am from a generation that does. Adoption, it's all so open these days. For Mike, adoption today must seem like a foreign landscape, a trek into the territory of rarely explored feelings, as strange in its own way as the monastic kingdom of Athos.

First you need a matchmaker, I go on. A few government agencies still help with adoption as well as a few religious organizations (Jews and Catholics mostly—no Orthodox, I add). And there are a small, and dwindling, number of private agencies, like the Adoption Center in Santa Barbara, which we used. But mostly it's lawyers these days. The trend is for lawyers to handle everything, including the matchmaking. Even if the match is made by an agency or person-to-person, the lawyers get involved to close the deal.

When my words in translation reach the monks and they hear about lawyers, it appears as if they might spit.

"Lawyers," the old monk mutters. It appears as if he's silently praying, repeating the Jesus Prayer to ward off the devil.

Apparently, even here at the end of the earth where the rule of God prevails over the rule of men, lawyers have a bad rap.

How can you get a lawyer to sell his soul to the devil?

Hire him.

How hard it must be for them to get past the pearly gates!

God decided to take the devil to court and settle their differences once and for all.

When Satan heard this, he laughed and said, "And where do you think you're going to find a lawyer?"

I'm tempted to tell all the lawyer jokes my friend Tim McFadden, a lawyer-turned-theologian told me. But something about the seriousness of the monks, even while drinking wine in the off-hours, tells me such jokes would not go over well.

Q: What do you get when you cross a lawyer with a demon from hell?

A: Another lawyer.

No, definitely not.

"Yannis, your adoption of Sophia," Father Guide presses. "Was it difficult?"

"No. After all I've told you about how difficult it is to adopt, it was really quite easy to adopt Sophia."

"You had lawyers involved?"

"Only at the end of the process, to make the adoption official."

"Did you name your daughter Sophia or was she already named Sophia?"

"Cheri and I named her."

"Did you pray for her arrival?"

"Well, not exactly pray."

"Tell them about the angel who came to you," Mike interjects.

When Mike's words are translated, a complete silence falls over the table.

"An angel!" declares the old monk with a smile. The reverential way he says *angel* makes the word seem like the antonym for lawyer.

"Well, it wasn't exactly an angel," I correct. "But it seemed like one at the time."

"Yannis, the whole story, please," Mike requests. "We only heard the story once, at Sophia's christening. And I'm positive the monks will be interested."

Mike's right about the monks. They give me their full attention. I know they're going to be disappointed, though. The story about the angel isn't that spiritual.

Dani, one of the counselors at the Adoption Center was a great believer in the power of positive thinking and the technique of creative visualization, I begin.

I've barely embarked on my story when it comes to a near halt: *creative visualization* does not translate well. Ernest, Mike, and Spiro all try their explanations and the monks return with explanations of their own and gospel passages.

Father Guide sums up the monk's take on this technique. "Tell us, this 'creative visualization' is really just another name for prayer, isn't it?"

"No, no, it's psychology," I tell them.

The monks look altogether disbelieving.

"An actor imagines himself in the role he will play," I elaborate. "A businessman imagines the sale he will make. People who want to adopt try to picture a baby, concentrate on that image of a baby, believe that the image, that baby, will become part of their lives."

"Why not just ask God for a baby?"

"This is a psychological technique. You don't have to believe in God to use it."

An imaging technique that leaves God out of the picture does not go down well with the monks, all three of whom simultaneously dissent. Father Guide moves to quell the protest in Greek that I understand. "Brothers, let him get to the angel."

The old monk beckons me to continue.

Dani asked me if I could visualize a baby. I could, clearly, in fact: I'm walking the beach with a baby in a backpack. The baby's head is next to mine. The sound of the surf is calm and restful, and the soft south light wraps it all in a peaceful glow.

Great visualization, Dani tells me. And Cheri?

Cheri freezes. She has no visualization. For fifteen years, ever since she learned she would never bear children, she hasn't allowed herself to dream, to imagine a baby in her arms. Dani asks her what she sees when she thinks of a baby and all she can do is cry.

Cheri can't imagine what her baby will look like, what color eyes. She can't visualize feeding an infant, playing with a toddler. Nothing. And so Dani works with her for hours, coaxes Cheri into a visualization: a baby, in a sleeper.

Sleeper is another of those English words that doesn't translate very well, but Ernest, the pediatrician, who's seen so many kids in sleepers, quickly explains.

Cheri goes to the department store. It takes her an hour to get up her courage to walk in. She buys a sleeper. Not an infant-sized one, because she can't imagine anything so small, but an eighteen-month-size sleeper. She doesn't buy a pink one because she can't visualize a girl, and she doesn't buy a blue one because she can't visualize a boy.

She hooks the yellow sleeper, still on its plastic hanger, over the curtain rod in our bedroom window. Visualization: the sleeper will be the last thing she sees before sleeping, the first thing she'll see upon waking.

One warm night in July, about a week after Cheri bought the sleeper, I woke—or, at least I think I woke—to light filling our bedroom. Outside was a big full moon, low in the sky, beaming into our room. A wind rustled the trees and whisked into the bedroom. It wasn't the usual wet ocean breeze from the west that cools our house located close to the beach. No, this was a dry wind, from the east, a Santa Ana. People in Southern California say very strange things happen when these desert winds blow over us.

I woke in a sweat with a dry mouth and throat and watched an angel fly about the room. It was the sleeper on its hanger in the window, backlit by the moon. As the breeze swayed the sleeper, its shadow flew around the room, projecting what looked like an angel on the walls.

Just a sleeper, I told myself. Just my imagination. But I closed my eyes and the angel continued to fly around the room. Only now it wasn't a little sleeper-sized angel but one of the fierce-looking seraphim that I'd seen on an icon. I couldn't see the angel's face, just its powerful wings, beating like the wings of some great bird. And it seemed three-dimensional, not like a shadow at all. But that image vanished. And I was certain I was having a dream because when I sat up in bed, the sleeper was motionless, the air still.

The next morning I said nothing of what I had imagined. Buying the sleeper had seemed to make Cheri more sad than hopeful. As we had our coffee, she asked me again: Do you think we'll ever be able to adopt a baby?

It's only been three weeks since we signed up with the Adoption Center, I reminded her. I'm very hopeful, I said. Now more than ever.

How can you be so sure? she wondered.

I just am, I told her.

A week later we got a call from the Adoption Center. It was the news we'd hoped to hear. A Women's Clinic in Iowa, two thousand miles away, had contacted the center. A young woman, five months pregnant, saw our letters and pictures and picked us to adopt her child. We called her, wrote to her, brought her to Santa Barbara to give birth. Cheri and I became the parents of Sophia.

When the translation finishes, there is silence at the table, and everyone waits for me to continue. Perhaps they missed something, I think.

"End of story," I say in Greek.

They still wait for more.

"So that's creative visualization for you," I add.

Nobody translates this for the monks, who sit impassively. After what seems a very long time, while I twice scout the table for more wine and discover there's not a drop left in anyone's glass or in the two decanters, the old monk speaks.

"Have you and your wife tried more visualizations for more children?"

"No, Cheri and I registered with the Adoption Center."

"Did you 'visualize' your trip to the Holy Mountain?"

"No. At home, just before I climb a mountain, I usually visualize it. I'll do that before we climb Athos, too."

"Thank you for telling us about your adoption. You and your wife are very special for adopting a child."

"We're very fortunate, anyway."

Father Guide moves closer to me, so that his translation is going into my left ear, almost as fast as the old monk is speaking; it's almost as if I'm understanding the elder's Greek.

"We Christians are children of God by adoption. As adopted children we are in God's family and have the opportunity to become more like the Creator—not because this is solely in our nature or because we are smart enough to figure out the right way to be, but because of God's grace."

My fellow pilgrims finally come to life and there is affirmation and wonder at the notion that in the cosmic sense of the word, we're all adopted.

"You know, Mike knows a lot about adoption," I volunteer. "He's the father of—"

"Adoption takes place when the Holy Spirit, stirring in our hearts moves us to pray to the Father, the Father in Heaven, the Father of us all," the old monk continues. "There is a passage in Romans: *For you did not receive a spirit that makes you a slave again to fear, but you received the Spirit of Adoption.*"

The Spirit of Adoption. Cheri will be happy to hear about this. We're going to need a strong spirit in our attempt to beat very long odds and adopt another child.

"May God bless your travels on this Holy Mountain."

CHAPTER 9

THE HOLY MOUNTAIN
IS IN THE LEGS

Where God left his shoes. This was a favorite phrase of
the late Gaetano Bisso, my wife's Sicilian grandfather,
who used it to describe a remote place and/or one difficult to
reach. The backside of Mt. Athos, along the trail crossing the
forested lower slopes of the Holy Mountain from Great Lavra
to Skete St. Anna, is definitely where God left his shoes.

What a glorious day. Spiro and I are bound for the most
striking and wild country on the Holy Mountain. It promises
to be a long day on the trail, and perhaps the second best day
of my time on the Holy Mountain; only tomorrow's climb
to the top of Mt. Athos is likely to be a better hiking experience. Should our summit plans be hindered or canceled due
to foul weather, today's tramp through the wilderness might
very well prove to be the highlight of my trip.

We leave Great Lavra behind (such is the enormity of
the greatest of monasteries that we hike quite some distance
before it is lost from view), and hike south. Our packs are of
low to moderate weight, thanks to Ernest and Mike, who let
us offload nonessentials and agreed to transport our surplus
clothing and recently acquired souvenirs until we meet again.

No wonder this side of the mountain was an early and
favorite pick of the ascetics; if you want to get away from it all,

115

this is getting away from it all. The far end of the Mount Athos Peninsula remains the domain of hermits, and Spiro and I will be on the lookout for them, though the monks at Great Lavra warned us that even getting a glimpse of them is rare.

We ascend an hour or so on the path, up and over a ridge, and reach a cross and wooden bench. From this vista point, we enjoy grand vistas of the Holy Mountain and the heavenly sea.

The region of Greece known as Halkidiki has three peninsulas. Kassandra and Sithonia have gentle coastlines, calm seas and natural harbors; only the one named for the Holy Mountain is wild. Athos, the easternmost peninsula, rears right out of the sea, and the very height of the Holy Mountain creates its own ecosystem and microclimate.

I recall the four layers of frescoes of Manuel Panselinos on the walls of the Protaton and try to imagine how he might have painted the mountain's four layers of flora: the rugged coastal bluffs with Mediterranean shrubs; woodlands of oak and chestnut; Aleppo pine and fir; the hardy, low-growing alpine vegetation on the rocky summit.

And my, what a grand fresco of the natural world it would be if Panselinos had added the creatures of Athos: the gray wolf, red fox, and hedgehog. And then added the gulls over the coastal cliffs, the grouse in the woods, and golden eagles circling high over the shoulders of the Holy Mountain.

Glory to God and Creation.

But this day is more than a walk in the woods. At Great Lavra, Spiro learned of a wondrous icon of Mary and baby Jesus and we agreed to put a visit to venerate it at the top of the day's itinerary. At our viewpoint, I scan the map in my hands and the terrain at my feet and choose an unmarked trail that leads in the general direction of Skete Prodromos.

I pick the correct trail and a half-hour's hike brings us to the skete, one of two Romanian outposts on Athos. This is a really large skete, quite a complex, and I wonder why it never became a monastery. Late to the party I suppose; by 1855 the Mt. Athos Top Twenty had already been well established.

With its brick buildings, wrought iron balconies, and many windows overlooking both mountains and sea, Prodromos offers the appearance of a rather odd East European hotel. Our intention is to take a quick look at the miracle icon and get back on the trail, but somehow Spiro and I wind up in front of frescoes that are almost unimaginably horrible in their depiction of Holy ones suffering for their faith at the hands of Romans and devils.

One fresco shows a martyr, his ankles pierced by meat hooks, hung upside down from a cross-arm as Romans soldiers torment him further, one slicing the holy man with a knife, two others sticking him with their spears. A second holy man is tied (not nailed) to a cross while a half-dozen black devils armed with bows and arrows, and even chains and muskets, step menacingly toward him. A third holy man (all of the afflicted men have halos) is pinned from behind by a Roman soldier, while another attacks him with an axe. His legs have been severed, the left at the ankle, the right at the knee, and blood gushes from the stumps of his legs. Both hands have been chopped off and lie on the ground. The holy man looks skyward past his attacker, raising his handless arms to heaven.

"Wrong turn," Spiro says, heading off in another direction. He consults his guidebook as we walk. "Prodromos has relics of your saints."

By *my* saints, Spiro means my saint, John the Baptist, and my parish and hometown saint, St. Barbara. The skete's reliquary is said to include the right hand of John the Forerunner, the one with which he baptized Jesus, as well as relics of St. Barbara.

At the mention of St. Barbara, I remember that I am a long, long way from home: from dear Cheri and little Sophia, from family and friends, and from St. Barbara Greek Orthodox Church, where there is another relic of St. Barbara, located in a bejeweled box in a glass case before her icon.

Like us, most pilgrims who detour to Prodromos via trail or dirt road come not to admire the skete's architecture or to view the contents of the reliquary (and certainly not to see those frescoes!), but to venerate the Icon of the Theotokos. This particular icon of the Holy Mother and Child is one of the most mysterious icons on the Holy Mountain, the monks of Great Lavra told Spiro.

As the story goes, in 1863, Skete Prodromos founder Father Nifon commissioned veteran iconographer Iordache Nicolau to paint an icon of the Theotokos. Even before his first brush stroke, Nicolau felt on a mission from God and adopted a stricter-than-usual regimen for his workday. His highly disciplined approach included a daily reading of the *Akathist* to the Theotokos, a long and beautiful hymn usually presented only during Lent. And Nicolau fasted—he didn't eat a thing until he finished work for the day.

After laboring long and hard, he finally (and lastly, in the Orthodox tradition of iconography) painted the faces of Jesus and Mary. The master iconographer was disappointed in his work. It was more than a case of an artist being his own worst critic. Nicolau knew that as hard as he had tried to write this icon, it was not his best writing. This was not the window into heaven he had tried so hard to create. At day's end, he covered the icon with a cloth and prayed well into the night for guidance.

Next morning, Nicolau and his brothers, to their astonishment, found the icon complete, a now radiant Christ and Holy Mother. The icon became known as Theotokos *Acheiropoieta* ("made without hands" from the ancient Greek).

Like so many other stories about icons, you just have to take things on belief, I ponder as we get a quick look at the Theotokos Made Without Hands from a non-English-speaking and barely Greek-speaking old monk. No before-and-after photos of the icon exist: we have no clue as to the appearance of the icon made by the hands of Nicolau or of the divine upgrade "made without hands."

Spiro appears moved by the icon, and certainly untroubled by any doubts. Before the icon, Spiro makes his *stavro,* as do I. But his sign of the cross is the one of a man connecting with Christ and the Holy Mother and mine…well, I'm not feeling it this morning.

It is impossible for a pilgrim to view much of the Theotokos Made Without Hands, as it is now almost completely shielded by hammered silver, with cutouts for the faces of Jesus and Mary. Such encasement is necessary to protect it from the pilgrims who come to venerate it, but severely limits the amount of the surface area of the icon offered to public view.

From the courtyard of Skete Prodromos, I look up at the cross topping the Dormition of the Theotokos Chapel, and out to the peak of Mount Athos. Now there's beauty you can see.

As we walk up a dirt road to rejoin the Lavra-Anna Trail, I wonder: if I were to paint word pictures of the Holy Mountain, how well could I? What if, as is often the case, precisely the right words didn't come to me? What if I threw a shroud over my final draft, prayed through the night and came back to find my narrative perfected, my work edited to perfection, and passages "made without hands"?

In a strange twist, Athos is described better by early pagans than by later Christians. Thucydides mentions the mighty mountain in his accounts of the Persian Wars, as does Herodotus, who called it "a great and renowned mountain."

According to the most ancient of Greeks, Athos was occupied by a race of Giants who waged war against the gods—most particularly Zeus. The task of ridding the mountain of the giants was assigned to Hercules, who destroyed the "impious and lawless nation."

Legend has it that a great ivory statue of Zeus stood at the top of Athos. For eyes, the statue boasted two huge diamonds; these gems reflected starlight and flashed at night, so that they functioned as navigational beacons for the mariners sailing around the Athos coast.

Strabo, the Greek geographer, describes Athos as mamma-ry-shaped; for obvious reasons, ever since the mountain became a male-only monastic province, the grand teton profile of the Holy Mountain is rarely mentioned. Likely Strabo's observation has not been ignored because of any fear of the female form by the monks, but rather because the mountain bears no resemblance whatsoever to a breast. I've viewed it from the west, east, north, and now south, and can find nothing teat-like about the crest and summit of the Holy Mountain.

Given the time in which he wrote, Strabo might have gotten away with calling Athos pyramid-shaped—less of a stretch in imagination than characterizing it as breast-like—but even that comparison is weak. The mountain is what you make of it.

Or would like to make of it.

Strabo also records that the bold architect Denocrates pitched his most grandiose proposal to Alexander the Great: If Alexander would grant him the necessary expenses, he would transform the summit of Athos into the king's statue holding a falling river in his right hand and a town full of people in his left. Denocrates never got this megalomaniacal project off the ground, perhaps because Alexander was a bit distracted at the time—speeding eastward with his armies to conquer the world.

As outlandish as the idea of shaping an enormous face of a mountain to honor a great leader might have sounded to Greeks in 320 BC or to Americans in 1920 AD, it did not dissuade fervent patriots from blasting the faces of Presidents Washington, Jefferson, Roosevelt, and Lincoln into the Black Hills of South Dakota. The iconic symbols of presidential greatness at Mount Rushmore National Memorial attract millions of tourists a year.

At 6,670 feet in elevation, Mount Athos stands about 500 feet higher than Mount Rushmore, so Alexander, or whoever was sculpted into or out of the limestone summit,

would be a commanding figure indeed. Had this Grecian
Mount Rushmore been created, it would have been quite an
attraction, though no doubt would have forever secularized
the Holy Mountain.

We tramp a length of an ancient cobbled path that Spiro
says reminds him of Camino de Santiago, Europe's premier
path for pilgrims. From medieval times, pilgrims have walked
across Spain to the legendary shrine of St. James the Apostle.
And dating from late Byzantine times, pilgrims have journeyed around the Mt. Athos peninsula. We wonder: what if
there were a way-marked trail that circled the Holy Mountain
and connected the monasteries and sacred sites?

The trail writer in me imagines the cover copy of a guidebook: *The Mount Athos Trail— Experience 20 Monasteries, 60
Miles of Trail, and 1 Very Holy Mountain.*

We hike into a mixed forest of oak and chestnut, with some
scattered fir as well. It's a moist world of mosses, lichen, and
more than a few varieties of mushrooms. We pass numerous
spur trails, mostly unsigned, that we guess lead to hermitages,
but there is only so much we can explore in one day, so we stick
with the main trail. An hour past the cross, the trail meanders
through a thickly forested canyon and we reach a signed path
leading to Kafsokalivia. The trail crosses a cold brook, and we
linger a moment in the shade.

We hike through a handsome woodland and emerge
above Kerasia. A path leads downhill into a little valley and to
a modest gray stone church and a few small buildings. Above
Kerasia looms *Profiti Illiou* (Prophet Elija Rock)

Strictly from a hiker's point of view, Kerasia is a better
starting point for a hike to the top of the Holy Mountain,
because the elevation here is 2,000 feet, whereas Skete St.
Anna is scarcely 500 feet above sea level. But pilgrims can't
spend the night at Kerasia. No guest facilities are available—
and there are few monks around to provide for visitors.

We hike on into "The Desert." Oddly, that's how the
monks characterize the anything-but-arid topography around

Mount Athos. The Desert—the desert wilderness—is where the earliest prophets dwelled, where Jesus himself retreated to prayer, where the earliest monks found seclusion. And "The Desert" is the name the monks give this most secluded and rugged part of the peninsula.

"Wilderness" is what the monks really mean by a wild landscape, but for once the Greeks don't have a word for it. The Greek word for desert is *eremia*. And the Greek word for wilderness is one and the same: *eremia*.

The wilderness of Mt. Athos is like no other I have experienced. It is not at all the kind of American Wilderness with a capital W that has challenged my fortitude and stirred my soul—nothing like those vast tracts with snowcapped peaks and alpine lakes that characterize the wilderness areas in the Rocky Mountains, Cascades, or High Sierra.

Were it on American soil, the Mt. Athos Wilderness would not meet the criteria for official wilderness designation in the U.S., as defined in the federal Wilderness Act of 1964: "An area where the earth and its community of life are untrammeled by man, where man himself is a visitor who does not remain." By that definition of wilderness, Athos falls far short, having been trammeled—and inhabited—continuously since the tenth century.

Another one of my country's best ideas, the National Park, wouldn't work here either. Mount Athos National Park, a *Greek* National Park would be a terrible idea, adding another bureaucracy to the already massive flotilla of bureaucracies around the Mt. Athos Peninsula. And as for providing visitor services, Karyes and Dafni would never make it as gateway towns to a national park.

However it compares to wildlands elsewhere, this wilderness sufficed for the great ascetics in times past, and today it serves the needs of the sparse population of brothers in the *kellia* (cells), *kalyva* (huts), and *kathismata* (settlements). Perhaps it doesn't matter if you live a two-hour, four-hour, or eight-hour hike from the nearest monastery; it's wilderness enough if you can live the life of prayer you imagine.

From Kerasia, we ascend for a half-hour or so on the steep trail, which crests at a four way-junction at about 2,500 feet in elevation. Tomorrow we will ascend the right (north) trail to Mt. Athos peak; another straight ahead leads to St. Anna, as does a path leading to St. Anna in a more indirect way, which beckons us today.

Seconds after arriving at the trail junction, we are joined by an unshaven pilgrim with a large backpack, the first hiker we have met all day. The young man is as out of breath as Spiro, which is surprising, because he is coming down and Spiro and I are going up. In rapid Greek between deep breaths, Spiro and he introduce themselves and me. From what I understand, we are: Spiro from a big Greek family in Chicago; Costas, a *botanismós*, a botanist from Greece; John, a writer about nature and trails from Santa Barbara, near Los Angeles.

Thankfully, in a half-minute's time, Spiro and Costas switch to English and, as one, we remove our backpacks and sit. The trail sign posted on a tree reads *Panaghios* with a red arrow pointing the way.

I suspected that his breathlessness was nervousness—perhaps he had overstayed his Mt. Athos permit—but no, indeed Costas is a botanist who is collecting plants from all around the Athos peninsula, and his labored breathing is caused by carrying a heavy backpack stuffed with specimens.

His research efforts, he says, are contributing to the compilation of a comprehensive flora (Greece's first in a hundred years). I tell him I'm a nature writer back home in California and Costas tells me he's always wanted to go there, particularly to Southern California, which has a Mediterranean flora with similarities to that of Greece.

"The collecting is going very well," he reports. He's gathered and photographed rare plants, including a species of iris botanists previously believed to be extinct.

"Are there plants that grow here and nowhere else in Greece?" I ask.

Costas beams. "Yes, maybe twenty, thirty different species are...*endimikós.*"

With his translation services not required, Spiro looks like he's tuning out. Likely this is too much nature talk for a city boy. I can appreciate that. Yesterday, drowsy from drinking wine at our midmorning meal, I drifted off and shut down during what seemed like an endless guided and self-guided exploration of Great Lavra. For me it was way too much art, and far too many chapels; my fellow pilgrims Ernest and Mike, and particularly Spiro, were fascinated.

"Endemic," I confirm. Same as in English. "Are the monks interested in your work?" I ask.

Costas shrugs. "Maybe a little. And yours?"

"Just a little," I return. "When I tell the monks about the Holy Mountain's beauty, they point up to the sky—to God and Heaven, I guess—and say: 'That's where it's truly beautiful.'"

From the field work of Costas, I see emerging a beautiful coffee table book, *Flowering Plants of Mount Athos*, with gorgeous photos, or perhaps watercolors, of the native plants—the shrubs, wildflowers, trees, the many plants of the forest understory, and the hardy specimens that manage to survive under the mantle of snow that blankets the summit of Athos every winter.

"The flora has survived here because of *Avaton*. You know about Avaton?"

"No women permitted for a thousand years," Spiro pipes up, re-entering the conversation.

"Just men, now and forever," I add.

Costas nods. "It's more than that. With the Avaton, nothing female higher evolved than a bird is permitted on Mt. Athos. No domestic animals have grazed the Holy Mountain for a very long time. Especially goats. And Yannis, if you've hiked around Greece—"

"I have."

He smiles. "Where?"

"Sparta, Crete, and some islands. And Cyprus."

"Then you know that the goats, they eat everything, all the native plants. But here, no sheep or goats, so the flora has survived."

I never thought of it that way. Certainly Avaton has kept the human population low and thus lessened the impact on the environment. (If the population in a remote place can be sustained only by highly restricted immigration rather than by the more typical unrestricted onsite reproduction, it is bound to be low.) And carrying the edict to the extreme, as the monks have, with a ban on all higher-order mammals has unintentionally resulted in the preservation of nature primeval. Avaton, in this regard, is proof positive of the Law of Unintended Consequences.

"Because of Avaton," continues Costas, "this is one of the most natural, un-touched places in Greece, maybe in all of Europe."

Paradise, I think, at the same time wondering about the trail leading to it. "How's the trail to the summit?" I ask. "Spiro and I are up there tomorrow."

"Good to the Chapel of the Panaghia. A little confusing past that, but all right."

"You've gone to the summit?"

"Yes, once. It's mostly rocks up top. I mostly work the middle slopes, where there is more plant life. I must warn you: the weather isn't good up on Athos."

"Is a storm coming in?"

"I don't know about the weather tomorrow, but conditions change very fast on the Holy Mountain. Strange winds and clouds." Costas rises and hefts his backpack.

"You might get wonderful views. You might not see anything at all."

Still very hungry after lunch from our scant foodstuffs (Greek biscuits, figs, and the last of my trail mix), we leave the four-way junction and hike southwest. Taking the "scenic route" to St. Anna gives us the opportunity to traverse the Hermit District, where dwell the most solitary of solitaries, said to live in caves on the cliffs, eating only crusts of bread and drinking rainwater.

We descend perhaps a thousand feet in elevation and in an hour dip in and out of a canyon to the outpost of Katounakia, a collection of little chapels and cottages scattered about the hillside. We see no sign of any Katounakians; the monks are at work, at prayer, or God knows where.

Perhaps we have not reached the end of the earth, but we are close, less than a mile away from the edge of the peninsula. I lead Spiro just a little bit south, though the main trail here turns north to Skete St. Anna.

A flash of black across the trail interrupts my thoughts. "Spiro, did you see that?"

"What?"

"I saw a hermit." I know I spotted the monk—a small bandy-legged fellow, gray beard like a billy goat's, arms flapping, descending rapidly.

"On the trail?"

"Off the trail. Going down the slope through the brush. Toward the sea."

"You sure it wasn't a donkey?"

All day I have been on Hermit High Alert, and I know I saw one. "After a week on the mountain, I know the difference between a monk and a donkey. I think he saw us coming. And he didn't want to be seen."

Spiro shrugs. "We've gone a week without showering. He probably smelled us coming."

"Seriously."

"So now, it's *you* being serious."

"I saw a hermit, I'm sure of it."

Spiro looks as if he suddenly remembered something. "The monks told us about this side of the mountain."

Here, where the south slope of Mt. Athos plunges near-perpendicular into the sea, live the most isolated hermits, the most ascetic of the ascetics. Some hermits retreat here in their twenties, live sixty years, and rarely see another human being. Some live in caves in complete isolation, others in tiny sheds perched precariously on the cliff face a thousand feet above the Aegean.

On our hike we witnessed the mountain's lush green beauty, but in gazing down at the coastal bluffs far below, we see an altogether different Athos. A landscape of barren rock, one that would expose the hermits to hot sun, frequent storms, and an unrelenting salt-laden wind. I suppose if you're a hermit, you scorn living on the beautiful, sheltered side of the coast, or in the peaceful forest, and pick the least accommodating part of the peninsula with the worst weather in order to suffer all the more.

Truly we have reached the place where God left his shoes. We stand nearly at the extreme southwest end of the Mount Athos Peninsula that bears the decidedly pre-Christian name, Cape Nympheon.

"*Karoulia*," Spiro says quietly, reverently, as if he is in church.

Karoulia. The most severe of the hermitages are known as *Karoulia*. The most severe monks are *Karoulia*. The Greek word *Karoulia* means "Pulleys," after the preferred method of hoisting supplies before any precipitous narrow footpaths were built. The cave dwellers accessible only by rope and pulley depend for their subsistence entirely on the nearest monasteries.

At regular intervals a monk lowers a basket of provisions down to the cave mouth. If the basket is not emptied, the visiting monk lowers himself to the cave. If the hermit is found dead, the body is removed, a new occupant takes his place, and the deceased's skull is returned to the monastery to take its place among his numberless predecessors on the special shelf reserved for them.

I'm letting the Karoulia get away, I realize. I drop my pack and take a few steps after the fleeing hermit, when Spiro calls out.

"Yannis! You're not thinking of chasing after him?"

Guilty as charged. "I just want a better look and—"

"And what? *Talk* to him? He's out here because he doesn't want to talk to anyone. And if he did talk, you wouldn't understand him anyway."

True enough. And if I did chase him, I'd never catch him. He was moving at ten times the usual monk speed, and even if I could drop down that steep slope as fast as a hermit, it would be impossible for someone unfamiliar with the terrain to find him.

I sigh mightily and suppress the colorful words of disappointment that I would express at most other times and in most other places. The Karoulia, the monks and their caves and any pulleys that may still be in use, lie to the south of us down faint paths on precipitous slopes. And the way to St. Anna is north.

This is their Desert.

This is their Wilderness.

And like in the wilderness of my own country, I am the visitor who should not remain.

Nevertheless, poor Christian and sore loser that I am, it is with grudging reluctance that I lead us away from Karoulia to rejoin the main trail to St. Anna. I shall have to speculate—not determine for myself—the state of mind of the Karoulia monks.

"He was waving his arms, like a crazy person," I tell Spiro.

"I bet he saw you and *pretended* to be crazy to scare you off."

Pretending to be crazy. Doubtless an old trick, but probably an effective one, passed along from one hermit to another for a thousand years.

"Spiro, you think these guys that end up as hermits are crazy when they come here, or do they just get crazy in their isolation?"

Spiro does not answer right away, and I notice he seems to be moving along at a monk's pace, quietly and deliberately, just taking in the scene; for the last mile or two, I've suspected he might be at prayer.

"Maybe some of them are a bit off," he allows. "Way off. But it's also possible, from what we've learned about this Holy Mountain, that living somewhere on those cliffs is a really holy man. A totally unknown hermit, praying day and night without stopping. Maybe nobody knows him now, but he might just turn out to be a saint."

"But if these guys stay hermits and never come back into the world, how will we ever know what they learned by giving up the world? I mean, if a saint falls in the forest and there's no sound…?"

"Yannis, I don't think they're in it for recognition from the outside world."

"But humans are social animals. It's not natural for us to live alone for so long. I mean, yeah, wandering into the wilderness for forty days to get your head together is a cool thing to do, but forty years?"

"I can think of a lot of crazier things to do with your life than praying all day."

"I bet psychiatrists would say these guys are crazy or on the way to being crazy."

"And what do you think the monks would say about psychiatrists?"

That gets a laugh out of us.

And then Spiro is quiet again and, for what seems a very long time. The only sound is the scrape of our boots over the trail.

"Crazy is relative," Spiro offers. "We came all this way to Mt. Athos on this pilgrimage, talked to all these monks, visited all these churches, got up in the middle of the night for services, all presumably for the purpose of getting closer to God, and you know what? After getting more calm and centered and hopefully more spiritual, I'm returning to Chicago and you're flying into LA. How crazy is that?"

I imagine myself looking out the window of the plane as it descends toward Los Angeles International Airport into a photochemical sunset. "Now that you put it that way...."

I shake off thoughts of the murky metropolis and hike on. Our trail offers a glimpse of Skete St. Anna, located off to the northwest and a thousand feet below us. The buildings sparkling in the afternoon sun are our departure point for tomorrow's climb of the Holy Mountain. And also, I realize, Anna is our last stop before hitting the trail for home—the coastal trail from Pavlou to Dionysiou to Grigoriou to the port of Dafni and the ferry back to Ouranoupolis.

My thoughts return from the hike tomorrow and the hike the day after tomorrow to the hike today. What a marvelous time we had on the trails.

The *trails*. Suddenly I have an awful thought and exhale mightily, as though trying to rid myself of a breath of polluted air.

What if the trails vanish from the Holy Mountain?

I've seen trails disappear all over the U.S. and elsewhere around the world: trails replaced by roads; old trails paralleled by new roads; trails on one side of a mountain abandoned when roads are built on the other side the mountain.

It could happen on the Holy Mountain.

My Austrian map, "Paths and Tracks on Athos," shows the obvious roads and trails, as well as old tracks that have been covered over by new forest or transport roads, and whose original condition is no longer recognizable, which are shown by a long broken line; also shown are paths that either end abruptly, or ones that the authors found impossible to complete, which are shown by the use of a crossed line.

Warns cartographer Reinhold Zwerger: "Should the tendency of building new roads continue, it would not be necessary to bring out a map in ten years' time because then there would hardly be any more paths or tracks worth mentioning."

Clearly there is good reason to fear for—and every reason to pray for—the future of the ancient footpaths leading to the most remote places on Athos. The network of dirt trails and cobblestone-paved paths date from late Byzantine times and are as old or older than much of the art and architecture on the Holy Mountain.

If trails on the Holy Mountain are replaced by roads, if the mountain becomes a drive-up instead of a walk-up, something will be lost from a pilgrimage to Agion Oros. If the occasional "troop truck" with hard bench seats is replaced by air-conditioned buses that make strictly scheduled stops at the monasteries, and if the small boats that ply the Athos coast are replaced by bigger, better, all-weather ferries, will a destination easily gained be as meaningful as one well-earned with a hard hike?

Extraordinary efforts are under way to restore the rich architecture of the monasteries and to preserve its treasures in environments worthy of the world's top museums. Could there not also be at least a modest effort made to preserve footpaths? Surely with all its Byzantine governance, one Trailmaster Monk, one *Monopataris*, could be assigned the responsibility of overseeing the construction and maintenance of trails on the Holy Mountain.

Doubtless I have a minority viewpoint. Hikers like me, or like Spiro, are but a fraction of the pilgrims who visit the Holy Mountain. "Life is a journey, not a destination," said Ralph Waldo Emerson. But who around here would listen to a Transcendentalist?

We hike in companionable silence. Spiro is just glowing—from whatever combination of God the Father and Mother Nature the day has blessed us. In contrast to dour Skete Prodromos, Skete St. Anna beckons as warm and welcoming as a Greek island village.

Truly, I must come to terms with my own peculiar spirituality: the farther I hike from the city, the closer I get to God.

That's not to say I *can't* pray in a church; it's simply much more difficult for me to shut out the busyness of the world, turn down the volume on the voices of negativity, and get out of the way of my selfish self when kneeling in a pew than when hiking on a path.

Unfortunately for *my* spiritual convenience, all houses of worship are found in cities, towns, and suburbs, and nearly all services, sermons, and communal prayers take place indoors. This Christian is the odd man out. Or at least left outdoors.

For the smartest and most well-read pilgrims, the Holy Mountain is in the head.

For the most spiritually advanced of pilgrims, the Holy Mountain is in the heart.

For pilgrims like me, the Holy Mountain is in the legs.

CHAPTER 10

SPAGHETTI NIGHT AT ST. ANNA'S

Skete St. Anna may be located at the end of the earth, but it's not the most backward bit of rural Greece I've visited. From my post in the church courtyard, I look up at hillside dwellings called *kalyves* that resemble cottages I've rented on remote Greek islands.

Somewhere in my travels around Greece I must have encountered a church and tiny village that resemble the tableau here, for there is something very familiar about St. Anna.

An island scene, maybe. But not Skiathos, Zakynthos, or Corfu. Not Rhodes, Crete, or Kos. *Hmmm.*

The monks of Great Lavra explained that a skete is a monastic community established and administered by a ruling monastery; St. Anna is under the dominion of Great Lavra. They were quick to point out that the monks in a skete do not observe the same strict regimen or have the same visitation policy as the monks who live in the major monasteries.

Perhaps the Great Lavra monks were warning us; apparently, whatever regimen the monks of St. Anna do observe must not include welcoming guests. No one emerges to greet us from the church, the trapeza, the guest quarters, or the cottages.

After our long trek here, Spiro, unlike me, is too tired to complain about the lack of hospitality. He finds a shady spot to sit, leans against his backpack, and, almost before he finishes saying "Wake me up when the monks come," he falls asleep.

Rest up, Spiro. Tomorrow's the big day. Tomorrow we climb the Holy Mountain.

I, too, sit Spiro-like in the shade and close my eyes, but instead of quiet darkness I get a Mt. Athos map projected inside my head. I can't wait to get started. If it weren't an all-day hike to the peak, I'd like to tackle the Holy Mountain right now.

I open my eyes and try to visualize the trail on the map onto the distant mountain. The path snakes up the mountain to about the 5,000-foot level, then dead-ends in a cloud. Hope we have a clear day tomorrow. I'd hate to get a mile up the mountain just to look inside a cloud.

A low rumbling from offshore interrupts my thoughts. I rise, find a good coastal vantage point, and, to my surprise, spot a small ferry boat entering the small harbor located far below Skete St. Anna.

You mean instead of hiking all the way here we could have taken a ferry? This is what Spiro would say if he saw the boat.

But he says nothing. He's still snoozing.

Four men climb a steep pathway, as well as flight after flight of stairs, as they make their way up a ravine. They're not monks, but pilgrims, I soon detect. And they're traveling light—with small overnight bags.

They climb ever so slowly to the top of the bluffs and then, coughing and muttering in Greek, make their way to the church courtyard, greet me with a *"Yasou"* and trudge toward a long bench.

Breathing hard, they do what Greeks everywhere do after exertion: they sit down and light up cigarettes. After a few drags, a short mustachioed fellow of about thirty walks over to me. Introductions are made: Costas from Athens, Yannis from Santa Barbara, California. Goodness, *another* Costas, the second of the day, the tenth of the week. Since my translator is asleep and this Costas's English is pretty good, by mutual agreement we switch to English.

"How did you find out about St. Anna?" Costas inquires.

"From the guidebooks, the monks at Great Lavra, my map," I answer.

"Do other American Orthodox know about St. Anna?"

"Possibly, though I never met anyone who ever traveled here. What brings you here?"

Costas winces ever-so-slightly at the question. "I would ask the same as you."

Same as me? Costas and his fellow smokers aren't hikers, that's for sure.

Costas looks down at my wedding ring. "Did you tell your wife you were coming here?" he asks.

"Of course."

"Me too," he nods conspiratorially.

It's clear that Costas believes we share some secret, but I can't imagine what that would be. I look to Spiro, but my translator shows no signs of waking.

"My friends"—Costas gestures to the trio of smokers—"did not tell their wives they were coming to St. Anna's. One said he was going to a cousin's wedding. The other two said they just needed to get away with their friends to the beach, to a holiday hotel, for a few days."

Something isn't computing here. These guys lie to their wives that they're going to a beach resort instead of telling them the truth that they're going to a monastery? Wouldn't your basic deceitful male tell his wife that he's going to a monastery and go to a resort instead? What wife would prefer her husband hang with his drinking buddies at a seaside retreat with tavernas and topless Euro-babes versus a weekend of meditation on the males-only Holy Mountain?

"I don't understand why they didn't tell their wives they're going to the Holy Mountain."

"Maybe Greek wives, they don't understand like American women. The men can't talk to them about some things...."

A man needs...." Costas is working hard to get the right word, but it doesn't come. "A man needs...."

"To get away from the wife and kids once in a while?"

He shakes his head. "A man needs...we need...."

An unholy realization comes to me: the Greeks would rather have their wives worry that their husbands are playing in the company of other women at a beach resort rather than visiting an all-male bastion because...

...because these guys are playing for the other side.

I ignored the small amount of smutty speculation I heard about the homosexual activity on the Holy Mountain. Any time you get two thousand guys isolated from women, they're going to have some uncontrollable urges. It's probably a safe guess that there's at least the same gay-to-straight ratio among monks as there is in the general population.

Still, it's hard to believe that with all the lovely accommodating places in Greece available for liaisons, gay guys would pick the Holy Mountain for getting together.

And Costas and his friends sure don't seem gay. Having been around so many gay men in Hollywood, the arts world, and the publishing industry, I'm sure my gay detector, my gaydar, is at least ninety-five percent accurate.

These Greeks are not gay. But that still leaves the question of why they traveled all the way from Athens to Skete St. Anna. Pilgrims desiring only a short tour of Athos usually go to one of the big, easy-to-access monasteries that have decent guest quarters, regular services, and semi-regular meals.

"What made *you* decide to come all the way to St. Anna's from America?" asks Costas.

Well, if Costas isn't clear about the intent of his journey, I am about mine. I gesture to the top of the Holy Mountain.

"God?" Costas asks incredulously. "God told you to come here?"

"No, no, no. My friends invited me to visit the Holy Mountain with them. It was my idea to climb it."

"To what?"

"To climb the mountain."

Costas looks baffled, and even a little angry. "Why do you want to do this?"

Most Greeks, except for a few mountaineers in the Hellenic Alpine Club, never believe anyone would want to hike up a mountain just for the sheer pleasure of it.

"I love to walk. I want to get to the top."

"It's dangerous to go up there."

I've walked into this attitude before in Greece. In fact, everywhere I've hiked in Greece, from Crete to Corfu, and many other island and mainland locales, I've found it typical for Greeks to exaggerate the difficulty of any climb of any mountain. I've had a lot of time to think about this on the trail, and it seems to me there are three reasons for this anti-hiking attitude. First, Greeks lack the British and European tradition of alpinism. Even the other southern European countries such as Italy have parts of the Alps and some wonderful wilderness parks and mountain ranges. Second, Greeks are too closely removed from the countryside; although the ancestral village pulls at the heart of every Greek, rural life also has associations with picking olives and herding goats, poverty and backwardness. The mountain is the place you left behind in order to make your way in the world. Finally, Greeks are, to this day, one of the most hospitable of races, and it's a matter of national pride that visitors have a safe and pleasant time. Better to discourage guests from traipsing about the countryside so that they won't get hurt.

"I understood," Costas says curtly, "that you and your friend came here to see St. Anna." All of a sudden he seems angry and I don't have the foggiest reason why. Where's my translator?

Spiro stirs. The smoking Greeks have taken up a new position on the Aegean side of the courtyard, and now second-hand smoke, carried by the sea breeze, wafts over Spiro. His nose wrinkles, he sneezes, and he wakes. For a Greek boy growing up near Chicago, he sure is sensitive to cigarette smoke.

I turn back to Costas, but he's rejoined his countrymen, who are greeting a monk, who looks at least eighty years old. The Greeks greet him as *Gerontas*, or old one, a term of respect for an elder monk.

"*Paraklesis,*" announces Gerontas, as he makes his way to the church door.

"*Paraklesis?*" I ask Spiro.

"*Paraklesis,*" confirms my now awake and refreshed translator. "You know, the service of the names," Spiro says. "We're going to have it outside the church."

The old monk asks us to write down the names of our family members for mention in the prayers. Spiro tells me he is about to chant what Orthodox clerics call the Service of the Little Canon of Supplication to the Most Holy Mother of God and what Orthodox laity usually remember only as "that little service with all the names."

The most fully prepared of the Greek pilgrims unfolds a typed sheet, covered front and back with names, while Spiro, Costas, and the others quickly list their friends and family members on scraps of paper. I'm a lot slower with my list, since I can only print, not write, Greek. First I must translate some of the American names into Greek: father Jim becomes Dimitri; mother Helen, Eleni; cousin Diane, Artemis. Daughter Sophia is easy, just Sophia, but my dear wife Cheri...not a Greek name at all, so I improvise my phonetic best.

The old monk and the Greek men wait patiently while I conclude my labors. A faint smile crosses the monk's lips when I hand him my work. Probably hasn't seen such primitive Greek since he was in the first grade—about eighty years ago.

This service of the names originated in the then capital of Christendom, Constantinople, in the heat of August, which impressed chroniclers of Byzantium as a month of disease and pestilence. Prayers for the health and protection of the faithful were offered, and those who attended submitted their names and those of their loved ones, to be read by the priest in mid-service. The ancient practice survives among Greek Orthodox parishes in August, and on the Holy Mountain at some monasteries on weekday evenings throughout the year.

Oh Sovereign Lady, from all kinds of threats you save your servants, may we not abandon you.

What I have come to understand after my week on the Holy Mountain is how much the monks revere the Virgin Mary.

To all those embattled, you are peace, you are calm to those tossed by the tempest, the one protection of the faithful.

On Wednesday, we visited the Shrine of Panagia, where the Mother of God appeared on Mt. Athos. On her way to Cyprus, Mary was shipwrecked on the peninsula, found herself overwhelmed by the beauty of Mt. Athos, then asked her Son to make the mountain a place of prayer. In response, a voice was heard, saying: "Let this place be your inheritance and your garden, a paradise and a haven of salvation for those seeking to be saved."

In response to the doubters and pagans then residing on Mt. Athos, Mary performed a miracle. She asked Athanasius to lift a rock from the dry, barren mountainside, and a stream bubbled up. A cross in the rock in the streambed appeared and remains today.

Save your servants, from every danger, O Mother of God, for next after God we all fly for refuge to you as unbreachable wall and protection.

So if the Mother of God is so important to everyone around here, it follows that the mother of the Mother of God, St. Anna, is also admired.

Make known to me the way in which I should walk, for to you I have lifted up my soul.

My mind drifts from the Holy Mother to the Holy Mountain. Already I have summit fever. I can't wait to get on the trail. So many prayer services, so little sleep. And yet I'm energized. Anxious to leave behind the dusty-dusky churches for the alpine summit.

We pray for the servants of God who make this supplication, and for the servants of God Sophia, Mary...

Mary? How did we get from Cheri (pronounced *Sherry*) to Mary? Guess the monk did a little translation of his own. *Dimitri, Eleni, Yannis, Amalia, Yannis, Artemis....*

After the names of my family, Gerontas reads those of the Greeks who must have large extended families, because the chanting goes on and on.... Is the monk reading pages out of the Athens telephone directory? Why are eighty-five percent of all Greek men named Giorgos or Costas?

Lord have mercy, Lord have mercy, Lord have mercy.

For You, O God, are merciful and love mankind, and to You we give glory, Father, Son, and Holy Spirit, now and forever, and to the ages of ages. Amen.

Without missing a beat, the monk continues, and it suddenly comes back to me that "Amen" does not mean "The End," and that the roll call of names is only midway through the service.

From my youth up many passions make war on me: but you, O Savior, help me and save me.

Would it be wrong to pray for a good dinner? Good Lord, I'm hungry. We've got a mountain to climb, tomorrow. Spiro, especially; it looks like this 1500-calories-per-day- below-normal monastic diet we've been on does not agree with him.

All-holy Trinity, have mercy on us. Lord, cleanse us from our sins. Master, pardon our iniquities. Holy One, visit and heal our infirmities for Your name's sake. Lord, have mercy. Lord, have mercy. Lord, have mercy.

Ah, the Greeks look like they're packing up to leave. I think we're nearing the end.

Glory to the Father, and to the Son, and to the Holy Spirit; both now and forever, and to the ages of ages. Amen.

Amen. Let's eat.

It's Spaghetti Night at St. Anna's. We pilgrims sit at one very long table, with a sizeable gap between the Greeks and Spiro and me. After the lengthy dinnertime prayers we heard offered at the large monasteries, the blessing offered by a young monk in St. Anna's trapeza is remarkable for its brevity.

After his mercifully short blessing, the young monk ducks into the kitchen and soon returns with a huge platter of spaghetti. As he approaches the pilgrims' table, we can see the large Greek noodles glistening with a generous amount of olive oil. Ah, just the dinner we need before our trek to the Holy Mountain. Carbohydrate loading.

The monk puts the platter before Spiro, who forks a modest amount onto his plate. I do the same, and pass it over to the Greeks.

We watch, aghast, as the Greeks heap the remaining pasta onto their plates. Those pigs! Spiro and I should have taken more on the first round.

When the monk passes the plate of feta cheese to us, Spiro catches on quickly and cuts himself a nice thick wedge. I do likewise.

To our dismay, the monk serves the other courses—bread and red-dyed hard-boiled eggs—to the Greeks first. Perhaps because their plates are already so full, they each take only a slice of bread or two and but one egg per pilgrim.

After depositing our four-course dinner, the monk disappears. Apparently things are much more informal out here in a skete at the edge of the world. The monks don't eat with the visitors. And there's no religious reading accompanying this spaghetti feed. Without the monks around, we could probably even talk, but out of respect for tradition, we eat in silence.

The sound of forks scraping plates is positively unholy. You'd think the Greeks were getting their first meal in days. Hey, you Greeks, you're getting on the ferryboat in the morning and returning to your wives and having a home-cooked dinner by this time tomorrow. (Depending on the success of your fabricated stories and/or the gullibility of your wives, they'll either make your favorite dishes or throw them.)

Anyway, Spiro and I are the ones who need the nutrition. We're climbing the Holy Mountain.

A small icon of St. Anna looks down on our mastication. She appears appalled at our gluttony. Just as I suspected, the Greeks have seconds on what's left of the spaghetti and finish it off without offering Spiro and me any. One of them even tilts the empty platter so that the remaining olive oil flows onto his dinner plate.

I stare at the four red eggs in the bowl in front of me. I scan the room. No monks are in sight and the Greeks are paying attention only to their meals. I grab two eggs in each hand and thrust them into my jacket pockets. Alas, I am only half-successful with my mission. *Uh-oh.* Forgot about the water bottle in my left pocket.

Just then, the most organized of the Greeks, the young man with the typed list of names, looks over at us and gestures at the egg bowl. *Avga* (eggs), he mouths silently. I shake my head, as Spiro holds up the empty bowl, shrugging in insincere apology.

Meanwhile, as discreetly as possible, with my hands under the table, I transfer the eggs from left hand to right, extract the water bottle, squeeze it between my legs, switch the eggs back from right to left hand and deposit them in my left pocket.

The Greeks are trying to get our attention again, and appear to be pointing to the plate hidden behind the large water jug. *Psomi* (Bread), they pantomime. Oblivious to their request, Spiro polishes off the last of his feta. As I stand to reach behind the water jug for the bread plate, the water bottle between my legs drops to the floor with a thud, followed shortly after by the sound of eggs cracking as my jacket smacks against the side of the table.

I reach behind the water jug, and lift the bread plate only to find that…it's empty. *Hmmm…*there was nearly a half loaf there last time I looked. Spiro shrugs. I hold the empty bread plate up for the Greeks to see and shrug. They glare at me.

The young monk enters to pick up the dishes and tells us Gerontas will meet us in the church. Gerontas has something very special to show us, he reports.

The light inside St. Anna's church is dusty and old. Perhaps after services, when the candles are extinguished, some fraction of the smoke lingers. Forever. Outside the church the last of a happy Greek island sun radiates against the church walls and windows, but somehow by the time this light of splendid clarity reaches the inside of the church it has been dimmed to the most somber of illumination.

There appears to be no reason for such dusty light. No dusty carpet with dust mites. Windows and walls are clean.

I always suspected that dust just happens. During my bachelor days, I always thought dust was only a noun. Something that accumulated. Every so often—seasonally, perhaps—dust, the noun, could be sucked up by the old Hoover vacuum cleaner that Mom gave me when I moved into my first apartment at age nineteen. After a long and slovenly bachelor life I moved in with my new bride Cheri, who informed me, to my shock, that dust could be a verb—as in *dust the living room.*

But it's not really dust, in the dirty sense of the word—the kind of dust that makes you sneeze or puts a catch in your throat—that's visible in St. Anna's. It's more a smoky afterglow, hanging in the air for centuries, like the unceasing prayers of the monks.

Here come the bones. The old monk emerges from the dusky depths of the church with what looks like a huge serving tray.

Here we go again. Another evening. Another church. Another viewing of the relics.

As near as I can figure, in the Athonite view, great works of art, music, or religious scholarship are inspiring enough, but they do not elevate the soul to God as do the bones of a saint, which are truly an intercession. The bones of the saints demand constant veneration and thus must be exhibited and adored as frequently as possible.

Nowhere on the Holy Mountain have we pilgrims encountered any reluctance on the part of the monks to display the bones. After the evening meal at each monastery, I found myself back in church, watching a monk spreading out the monastery's prized bone collection on a long table. The nature of the exhibits and their miraculous properties was then explained at length. As to the genuineness of a saint's skeletal and/or digital remains, it is hardly necessary to add, no monk entertains the slightest doubt.

Considering the extent of the relic collections we've viewed, Gerontas puts forth a very modest display—only two exhibits.

"In the first case, observe the skull of the monk Nectarios. Asked by the Turks to renounce his faith, he refused and was axed. His skull was crushed, as you can see."

Yes we can see his crushed cranium. Nectarios really took one for the home team.

What stops me cold each evening about this osteo-Orthodoxy, what absolutely revolts me, is that I am expected to kiss each item as it passes. Even if the relics are in a glass case, it still grosses me out. The right hand of St. John Chrysotom, the thigh bones of Saints Marina and Isidoros, the skulls of St. Luke and St. Nicholas....

At vespers at Great Lavra, my imagination briefly started to get the best of me and I began conjuring, out of the candlelit darkness, an art film montage of skulls and jawbones, femurs and fibulas, desiccated hands and feet.

"And now we have here the left foot of St. Anna, mother of Mary."

There is a collective intake of breath among the Greeks as they press forward to venerate the foot, which is encased in an ornate slipper.

"You will notice that the foot has remained whole, and smells like myrrh," Gerontas narrates.

Of all the relics in all the monasteries I've seen presented, none of them have inspired the devotions of pilgrims quite like St. Anna has for these Greeks. After many kisses and exclamations, the Greeks finally retreat into the dim recesses of the church to regard the icons. I linger back and, to my relief, Gerontas closes up the case with St. Anna's foot.

"Where are you from?" Gerontas asks me.

"America. Santa Barbara, California."

"Cal-i-for-nee-a." He wraps his tongue around my native state as though experiencing a new—and not altogether pleasant—flavor for the first time.

"So faraway. What do the Orthodox of Cal-i-for-nee-a know about St. Anna?"

Maybe he should ask another Cal-i-for-nee-a Orthodox. A better Orthodox Christian. I can tell him all I know about St. Anna in two seconds. "The mother of Mary."

"Yes."

There is a long pause that seems even longer in the deep quiet of the church. The way the candlelight strikes the monk makes his gray, nearly white, beard seem brighter than his eyes. It's like talking to a bird's nest.

Clearly I am supposed to supply something more than a Sunday school answer to his question. But that's all I know about St Anna.

"Do you have any children?"

"A daughter, Sophia, three years old."

"Did you pray for her arrival?"

Yesterday morning at Great Lavra, with a team of translators and at a table of rather well educated monks and pilgrims, I labored to explain the technique of "Creative Visualization." I'm not going there again.

I look to Spiro, who nods, giving me my cue.

Arrangements with the Adoption Center, lawyers, count-less walks and talks with Sophia's biological mother, a few awkward phone calls with Sophia's biological father, inter-views by state social workers, counselors, health care workers and health insurance company representatives. Looking back, I must have prayed at least once that all those arrangements would work.

"Yes," I finally answer. Forgive my fib, O Lord.

He nods. At least I think he nods. I can't make out his forehead, but his beard appears to tilt in affirmation. "And now you've come to pray for another child?"

Huh? A monastery would be just about the last place on earth one would come seeking a child. "I came to Skete St. Anna to climb the Holy Mountain. St. Anna is near the Holy Mountain so—"

"Does your wife have trouble carrying babies?"

Trouble? Big time. "Yes," I affirm.

"And you, Yannis?" Gerontas probes.

Now he's really getting personal. Maybe if I stay silent, he'll think I don't understand his Greek and move on to another topic. The wisdom of the monks is no doubt consid-erable, but it seems to me the subjects of marital relations and procreation might not be their forte.

Spiro hovers nearby. I can see his unshaven chin in the dim light. I briefly imagine him as a monk. To my discomfort, he steps forward and begins to translate: "The monk wants to know if you have any trouble making babies."

Thanks, Spiro. "Spiro, what's with all the personal questions?"

"I don't know. All these monks have a specialty. The cook, the dentist…maybe this one is another marriage counselor."

The monk waits patiently for my answer.

"No problem with me," I tell him.

Actually, I reflect, I don't know whether I'm fertile or not, shooting live ammo or blanks. I managed—and the term is used loosely—not to impregnate anyone during my single days, by a combination of a little self-control plus a lot of birth control and more than a little luck. The near-religious practice of birth control was about the only religion I was practicing in those days. Call it responsible irresponsibility. A feckless horny bastard I was. But that was then, and this is now. Now, I would love to be able to make my dear wife pregnant. Certainly it would be a whole lot easier and more romantic than adoption.

"You and your wife want more children?" the monk asks. "And because of that you came to St. Anna?"

Am I the only one on the Mount Athos Peninsula with a trail map? Why is it so difficult for everyone on this peninsula to comprehend that St. Anna is the logical trailhead for a hike up the Holy Mountain? "I came here to climb *Agion Oros*. Tomorrow we'll walk to the top."

"Where else do you walk?"

"All over America. Europe."

"And you walk to holy places?"

"Sometimes," I allow. Sometimes it's all holy ground to me. However, this might be the wrong time to mention my Transcendentalist leanings.

"Yannis is the best writer about walking in America," Spiro interjects.

Gerontas seems taken aback. "This is his job? He is paid for this?"

"Yannis is a very popular writer and makes a good living," Spiro responds before I can find the Greek words.

Liar, liar.

"Why do you want to climb the Holy Mountain?" Gerontas asks me.

Not a hiker, this monk.

"I like to climb mountains."

"What do you hope to find on top?"

"It's supposed to be very beautiful there. And a great view from the top."

"May God be with you."

CHAPTER 11

HIKING THE HOLY MOUNTAIN

I awake from a fitful sleep, dress, lace up my hiking boots, and step into a gray dawn, into the same dim light that was inside St. Anna's.

From the dew-dampened courtyard I look toward Mt. Athos—or at least where Athos should be, for it is not yet illuminated by the light of the new day. It might be visible if I were observing it from the other side of the peninsula. Just about now, the daystar should be beaming its first rays at the outposts of eastern Orthodoxy on the other side of Mt. Athos, then sending its light traveling from the coast to the summit of the mountain.

We'll be coming 'round the Holy Mountain from opposite the morning sun, from what is now the dark side of the mountain. Theoretically, this side and our trail will be the last to get light, and will hold it the longest; so in the event our return to St. Anna is delayed, we'll be hiking with the last light of the day.

I don't want to set out until we can clearly see the trail, so I'll let Spiro sleep a bit longer before I rouse him. By my calculations, we should have plenty of daylight for the climb.

Bend at the waist. Reach slowly to the toes of my hiking boots. Hold for twenty seconds. My normal pre-hike ritual consists of three parts: stretching, visualizing the hike to come, and drinking coffee.

Such is the pleasure of my long-practiced ritual that for an instant I imagine I really smell coffee. Truly the thin rations and lack of sleep during my week in the monastic kingdom have only been minor deprivation. But even a day without my friend Caffeine is unbearable.

As I push my palms against the courtyard wall and stretch my legs, I conjure the Holy Mountain as depicted on the map. According to the map, the first few miles of the trail from St. Anna to Athos are a mellow contour around the southwest slope of the mountain. Then it gets challenging: a very steep northward ascent. The contour lines on the map are in increments of 100 meters, and the trail crosses a whole bunch of them in a very short distance.

With all that hiking around the Holy Mountain we did yesterday, the mountain is a familiar face to me now.

Standing on one leg, I pull the other up toward my butt. I face east, watching the upper ramparts of the Holy Mountain emerge in faint silhouette.

"Good morning, Yannis. Would you like some coffee?"

I don't believe my ears until I turn to see Gerontas standing behind me. An offer of coffee to a java junkie at the end of the earth. Proof positive that there is a God. "Yes. I would very much like some coffee."

"And your friend?"

"Spiro doesn't drink coffee."

The old monk beckons me to follow him across the courtyard.

By now, dawn's light illuminates deep piles of dark clouds offshore. I have no idea if these clouds are coming or going, whether these are the kind of normal morning low clouds that clear, or if an Aegean storm is brewing and headed this way.

"What is the weather today?" I ask.

Gerontas does not break stride. "Whatever God brings us."

Now there's a weather forecast appropriate for every day of the year. Still, I was hoping for a less cosmic and more practical prediction.

We enter a small anteroom off the courtyard to the rear of the kitchen. I smell the small propane stove before I see it on the counter.

"Do you think it's a good day to climb the mountain?"

"It's always a good day to climb the Holy Mountain."

Gerontas puts the old *briki*, the bronze coffeepot, over the high flame. "How do you like it?"

"*Metrio*," (medium sugar) I answer.

When the water boils, he adds sugar and stirs. Then when the water boils again, he adds the coffee. Lots of coffee.

Quickly he removes the briki and scoops a teaspoon of foam into each of the demitasse cups. Then he pours the remaining coffee, filling each cup.

Ahhh. I sip, slowly, enjoying the sensation of the warm cup against my lips, the Oh-my-God-this-is-strong black liquid as it rolls over my tongue, warms the roof of my mouth, flows toward my throat.

"We did not know if the eggs and bread you took from the trapeza last night would be enough food for your journey."

The coffee catches in my throat, stops at a critical junction. I gasp, as the coffee changes course in mid-swallow and diverts to the wrong passageways.

"We know you'll need strength for your walk." He places a plastic bag on the counter in front of me.

I involuntarily emit a weak strangling sound. The coffee that's infiltrated my windpipe is bad enough; worse is the coffee that made its way into my nose. Instead of spitting out the coffee, I must have inhaled, and the coffee, grounds and all, is assaulting my senses.

Busted big time. Did the Greeks rat us out?

"It's a long walk to the top of the Holy Mountain. Few who come to St. Anna climb the mountain, and those who do find it a very difficult climb."

I grow light-headed as the coffee mixes with my air supply. Despite my impaired breathing and java-jolted sinus cavities, I can smell what appears to be the world's strongest-smelling feta cheese through the plastic bag of goodies Gerontas has given me.

Gerontas suddenly picks up speed, leaving me and my tourist Greek behind.

"Up on the mountain…the Holy Mother…monks say… *Kyrie Eleison*…flowers… metamorphosis…white light…*Kyrie Eleison*….rocks…gospel…metamorphosis…rocks Christ… mountain…rocks…on the mountain…metamorphosis…"

A weak cough is all the response I can muster.

"Do you understand?"

"Some…," I gasp.

"God be with you."

The trail zigzags up the mountain.

I must have written these words hundreds of times in my descriptions of hikes. Even on this holiest of mountains, I can't stop practicing my profession. As Spiro and I head up the footpath, I can't help thinking how I will describe this trail.

No matter the number of miles of trail that have passed under my boots or that I have described so that others could follow in my footsteps, the first steps along a new trail still quicken my pulse and gladden my heart. Regardless of my pre-hike mood or condition, I'm immediately more joyful when I step into my hiking boots and lace them just so, and breathe in the faint smells of sweat and sage and pine that have become one with my daypack.

Nature's glory.

Twenty minutes along the trail to Athos, and I already feel a whole lot better about things. Spiro and I stop to look back at Skete St. Anna, now appearing as a small box perched over a distant coast. Our vista now is of more water than land, the Aegean shimmering all the way to a distant cloud bank that marks the end of the visible world.

When I returned to St. Anna's guest quarters and breathlessly announced that the monks had discovered we had purloined foodstuffs from the dining room, Spiro did not seem surprised. "They know everything," he muttered.

Spiro is looking good on the trail. His clothing—shirt, pants, and coat—are too heavy, but serviceable. At least Spiro won't freeze if the weather turns bad on the summit.

I'm uncharacteristically over-dressed. Hiking in Mediterranean climes should be done in hiking shorts; however, wearing them would severely violate the Holy Mountain's unwritten but strictly enforced "Pilgrim Dress Code," which calls for modesty in all visitor apparel. In fact, the friendly policeman in Karyes, while describing the challenges of law enforcement on Athos to me, politely pointed out that I should roll down the sleeves of my long-sleeved shirt to cover my bare arms.

Our chances of meeting a dress code–conscious monk seem slim to none. In fact, we're unlikely to meet anyone on the trail.

Spiro interrupts my trail-use analysis. "Look way down slope. See, we're not the only ones crazy enough to go hiking."

So much for my speculation that we two pilgrims will be the only ones on the trail. But wait…what we spy gamboling along the main coastal trail away from Skete St. Anna is not a hiker but a donkey.

A donkey.

Unlike all the other donkeys we've seen on Athos, this one is not being led by a halter. And neither is it burdened by cargo or a monk sitting sidesaddle. From our vantage point, this donkey appears to be enjoying a morning constitutional walk across the bluffs.

"What's the difference between a donkey and a guy who insists on hiking up Mt. Athos?" Spiro queries.

"I don't know, what?" I return, wondering what the punch line to this joke could be.

"Great! I'm following a guy 6,000 feet up a mountain who doesn't know the difference between a jackass and a hiker." He turns from the donkey to Skete St. Anna. "St. Anna looks a lot different from up here."

The way St. Anna is perched above the sea reminds me of a Greek island hotel. The Greek word for hotel is *xeno-thoheo*—literally a box for strangers. Or, in the case of these monasteries, a box for strangeness.

As we savor the coastal panorama, I double-bag, then triple-bag the industrial-strength feta cheese Gerontas gave us. Once the feta is neutralized, we can better enjoy the fragrances of the great out-of-doors. First to greet us is the smell of wet earth, a relief from the cloying incense and the rank odors of gone-too-long-without-bathing men.

"Spiro, how could the monks possibly have found us out?" I wonder, as we resume our climb.

Spiro smiles. "There's a special place in hell reserved for those who steal from a monastery."

"It must be double the crime and fine in a monastic zone. I guess there's only two ways Gerontas caught on to us: the Greeks tattled, or that young guest-master slipping in and out of the dining room has eyes in the back of his head."

"There's a third way."

"Yeah?"

"The monks know."

"The monks know what?"

"Yannis, they just know. The monks know things we don't. This is a pretty tight world up here. They're tuned in. They don't miss much."

Maybe so, but most monks have missed the hike up the Holy Mountain. Collectively, the monks from Iviron and Xeropotamou, Simonopetra, Great Lavra, and more have been a kind of Greek chorus of warning counsel. Opinion from the dozen or so monks with whom we shared our plan to summit Athos has ranged from neutral to negative.

The monks proved more conversational about Anna than Athos, perhaps because the skete represents the known limit of monastic civilization, and because few pilgrims—or monks—venture beyond it. As for the mountain itself, the monks appeared almost uninterested—it was mere earthly geography after all, just a backdrop for the real spirituality going on below in the monasteries.

The monks adjudged the trek up the Holy Mountain as a kind of religious penance; one called it "a reminder of the difficulty of the road to paradise." If we had to climb the mountain, we should do so with unceasing prayers. Several monks reminded us that pilgrims afoot are afforded ample opportunity for prayer along the way: at a combination mountain shelter/Chapel of the Virgin Mary midway up the mountain, at another chapel on the summit, as well as with each step along the trail.

Certainly for me, The Trailmaster, this pilgrimage up the mountain is play, not penance. If the Good Lord knows me at all, He'd better come up with worse punishment for my sins than forcing me to climb a mountain.

In contrast, my Santa Barbara friends have been consistently encouraging. From the moment I broached the subject of climbing Athos in a café in Thessoloniki, they have cheered my every effort.

Aside from my friends, the most encouraging pro-climb voices I heard during my week of travel about Athos were from a trio of Germans, the only pilgrims I observed who were well-shod, wore the latest in alpine outerwear, and carried the best in modern mountaineering packs. No doubt they could climb any mountain.

But Athos isn't just any mountain, and the Germans were frustrated that they weren't able to scale its heights. Devout Christians they were, but not Orthodox, and so were unable to obtain a visa to the Holy Mountain for more than the basic seventy-two- hour visit; thus time-constrained, they had no way of getting to the southernmost tip of Athos, climbing the mountain, and returning to Karyes before their visas expired.

Their genuine enthusiasm for my climb-to-come was tempered by more than a little envy.

We talked of the Athonite landscape and how unlike it was, compared to most of *Grichenland.* How vastly different Athos was from the Greek holiday isles where they had vacationed with their families. Compared to the austerity, to the near-barrenness, of most Greek islands, Mt. Athos is positively green. The mountainsides are cloaked with trees, actually enough trees to be called a forest. Most of Grichenland is not *gruen,* not green at all. But here on the Holy Mountain, greenery surrounds the monasteries and colors the coastal bluffs and mountain slopes.

The first part of our ascent of the Holy Mountain, which looks pyramid-shaped from a low-elevation vantage point, is on a very steep trail—way short of American national park standards in terms of grade or condition, but I've hiked worse. Spiro is keeping pace just dandy, and I'm starting to think that perhaps my fellow Santa Barbarans sold their hiking abilities short and might have been able to accompany me on this trail.

At least for the first few miles, anyway.

I'm in my zone. The Holy Mountain's Mediterranean flora resembles that of the coastal scrub and chaparral communities of my home mountains in back of Santa Barbara. I spy laurel and lots of heather. Scrubby-looking oaks frame vistas of the sea, just as they do on the slopes of the Santa Ynez Mountains behind my home.

The curse of the trail writer: I can't stop recording data about the natural world, noting trail conditions and directions. Some of my more rugged readers would really enjoy the trek from Skete St. Anna to the 6,756-foot peak. In my mind, my dispatch begins to take shape....

Hiking/ Mt. Athos

Holy Mountain Trail

Where: Athonite Peninsula.

Terrain: Steep peak cloaked in Mediterranean flora, pine, fir, oak, and chestnut woodland.

Highlights: Vistas of monasteries, Aegean, mainland Greece.

Distance: From Skete St. Anna to Agion Oros summit is 16 miles round trip with 5,800-foot elevation gain.

Degree of difficulty: Strenuous.

Precautions: Sketchy trail, volatile weather. Access to males only by permit.

MT. ATHOS, Greece—Any hiker whose first impression of the Greek landscape was formed by a visit to one of the country's sparsely vegetated islands will be astonished by the lush green landscape of Mt. Athos. Pine forests cloak the "Holy Mountain," and the spring wildflower show, highlighted by scarlet poppies, is spectacular.

The Holy Mountain, holy ground for the world's 270 million Orthodox Christians, is a self-governing monastic republic. In keeping with Orthodox tradition, women have not been permitted to set foot on Mt. Athos for more than a thousand years. In fact, visits, except by male religious pilgrims, are highly discouraged.

Still, the determined Christian hiker who manages to obtain the proper permits will find some great trails to trek on Mt. Athos. The Holy Mountain has several faces: an Aegean landscape of astonishing beauty; 20 monasteries of architectural genius that will not be seen again; and 2,000 monks living much the same as their brothers in Christ did 1,000 years ago.

My favorite trails included....

The way the Holy Mountain thrusts out of the sea reminds me of 4,087-foot King Peak, located just three miles from the ocean in northern California. The isolated mountains of the King Range towering over California's wild "Lost Coast" so inspired the great Catholic theologian Thomas Merton that he tried to establish a monastery there. He never did, but nuns did—the Cistercian sisters at Redwood Monastery.

Strong women these. When I met the nuns, I was impressed by both their faith and their efforts to save the old-growth redwood groves near their monastery from being toppled by huge timber companies.

Uh-oh. Perhaps I shouldn't be thinking about the rival Catholics on this bastion of Orthodoxy! Better stuff my ecumenical proclivities while hiking this mountain.

All Christians share the Holy Land (along with the warring Jews and Moslems), but only Orthodox possess the Holy Mountain.

I was born into Orthodoxy and, while it certainly has served me better than I've served it, my love of the natural world has often prompted me to muse about creating my own faith. Call me a Transcendental Orthodox or an Orthodox Transcendentalist. In my ideal church, the altar will be moved outdoors, and the Divine Liturgy will be celebrated—and I mean celebrated—in a beautiful place. Our Gospel readings will be from Mathew, Mark, Luke, John, Ralph (Waldo Emerson), and Henry (David Thoreau).

It's always been like this for me: closer to God in the Great Outdoors. In the city, under smoky skies, when surrounded by cars and people and all of creation appears to be covered by cement, I rarely feel God with me.

Out here, outdoors, at work and play in the fields of the Lord, I have been moved to thank God for whatever He did to get the universe started, for igniting the Big Bang, jump-starting the cosmos, for setting in motion an earthly evolution that has led to a planet that not only sustains life with its resources, but is dazzling in its diversity.

And praise God for the evolution of humans, some of whom have evolved sufficiently to occasionally remember to appreciate this place we call earth and other forms of life, and to become wise stewards of Creation.

We're more than halfway up the mountain, starting to emerge from the forest onto rockier ground. I look back at Spiro. He's struggling a bit but still doing very well. I had him in front, so that he could set a pace that was comfortable for himself, but sometimes reading a trail isn't so easy. In particular, trail-reading in this light and on this mountain is a challenge; the path takes a few unexpected twists and turns against the grain of the land. So I take the lead.

We walk into a cloud, but not a wet one, more like a cloud of white, as though we've stepped directly into the path of a priest's scenter, and its whole load of incense has exploded all around us.

But no incense smell assaults us; rather it's the sweet scents of wild herbage—rosemary and fennel—that perfume the alpine air.

"Metamorphosis, here we come," Spiro declares.

"Metamorphosis," I reply, pronouncing it the Greek way, like Spiro. "That's what Gerontas said."

"He said *what* about metamorphosis?"

"I don't know. His Greek was coming at me at warp speed and you weren't around to translate. Until today, the only time I've heard 'metamorphosis' used in a sentence it was about the change from caterpillars to butterflies."

"He must have been referring to the chapel at the top—the Chapel of the Metamorphosis."

We climb steeply. For a few minutes, the silence of the mountain is broken only by the scuffing of our boots over the rocks and our increasingly labored breathing.

Spiro, who seems to be conserving his energy by not speaking, suddenly intones: "Transfiguration."

"What's that?"

"A big feast day in the Orthodox Church."

"For what?"

"Metamorphosis means…transfiguration."

"It's not ringing a bell."

I can't remember a feast day, an epistle reading, anything related to the Transfiguration. My mind slips over the liturgical calendar the way my boots pass over the loose stones on the pathway. Transfiguration of the Cross? No that's near Easter. Anyway, that's the Elevation of the Cross, a completely different event. "When does this service or whatever take place?"

"August sixth."

August sixth. No wonder I have no recollection of any transfiguration. I can't remember saint's days or special observances in the best of times, and that week, for me, for our entire parish, is our weakest week of worship. Almost nobody in our parish goes to church on, or near, August sixth. It's either the Sunday of, or the Sunday after the annual Santa Barbara Greek Festival.

If Transfiguration takes place on Greek Festival Sunday, every parishioner is too busy bakalava-making, beer-pouring, gyro-slicing, dance lesson-teaching, cashiering, raffle ticket-selling or working at one of the hundred jobs necessary to make the weekend festival a financial success; therefore, no one goes to church. If Transfiguration is celebrated on the Sunday after the festival, everyone is recovering from festival burnout or leaves town on summer vacation, and is likewise absent from services.

Suddenly there's a blue hole in the sky over Athos and I'm able to glimpse its stony ramparts and the cross planted on the summit. The mountaintop looks fairly close to us, but I'm way too experienced a mountaineer to be fooled by outward appearances. We're sure to encounter rocky trails and a multitude of switchbacks before the summit is ours.

By the time I extract the camera from my pack, the blue hole, and the Holy Mountain, disappear.

Visibility worsens considerably during another hour of climbing that brings us to the Chapel of the Panagia, perched on a grassy saddle. As we approach, it appears like a summit hut, similar to those the Appalachian Mountain Club constructed in the 1930s in the White Mountains of New Hampshire.

Up close, though, it looks more like a house of worship, which causes me to reconsider our lunch plans. This is not a secular shelter, and it doesn't seem proper for us to eat our lunch inside a chapel dedicated to the Virgin Mary.

We're hungry, but nothing seems all that appetizing. Not the purloined foodstuffs from the St. Anna dining hall. Certainly not the pungent feta cheese Gerontas gave us. We settle on and share the last of my granola (home-made by Ernest's lovely wife Andriana, our choir director). And a package of Greek cookies.

We enter the chapel and almost immediately after crossing himself, Spiro finds a candle. No matches in sight, though.

My trusty day pack yields one of the Hiker's Ten Essentials—waterproof matches—and Spiro does the honors.

In the flickering candlelight, we stand before the icon of Mary. With so much of the Holy Mountain dedicated to her, it's altogether fitting that the Mother of God is honored with a chapel high on the shoulder of the mountain. It's a wonder Athos itself wasn't named after Mary as well.

We need not have worried about the possibility of an unholy luncheon inside the chapel, which is set up for both meditation and short-term habitation. A well offers drinking water for pilgrims, and wooden sleeping pallets offer overnighters a flat surface upon which to unroll their bedding.

Most pilgrims trek here to pray, and this is certainly as good a place as any—and better than most—for that purpose. The Chapel of St. Mary is probably the final destination for many of the pilgrims who come up here, and they likely feel quite content that they climbed this far. Not me, though. I've never started a climb with the thought I would only go halfway.

"Not much farther to the top," I cheer.

Spiro nods, lost in thought. Or prayer. Perhaps he's silently repeating the Jesus Prayer. For a few days now, he's had that special look of the monks of Athos, straddling the material and spiritual worlds.

As I watch him look into Mary's eyes, it occurs to me that Spiro, like the generations of pilgrims before him who have come this way, has already reached where he wants to go. A communion with the Holy Spirit. For a tenderfoot, he's been a fine, uncomplaining trail companion. While blessed with a great sense of humor, he's very devout as well, and takes his Orthodoxy seriously. A true believer, in the saints, their deeds, their icons. What is a hike to me is truly a pilgrimage to him.

This is Spiro's trek, too, I realize, momentarily a bit chagrined at my self-centeredness and compulsion to bag this peak. We've got plenty of time to reach the top of the mountain. I shouldn't be pushing him onward. Surely he could use time alone in this chapel, and probably a bit more rest.

I gesture that I'll be outside, and step out into a white cloud. My back tightened up in the cold chapel and, as I stretch skyward, I look north toward the summit of the Holy Mountain or where the summit should be, for visibility is now scarcely 100 feet.

I look at my Athos map, focusing on the tiny contour lines bunched up at the top of the Holy Mountain. Looks like we're at about 4,500 feet, with more than 2,000 feet in elevation to gain to the top of the mountain.

The top of the mountain.

Now it comes back to me. No, I don't remember any special Transfiguration service...but I remember the Transfiguration icon: Jesus all aglow, disciples falling off a mountain. The only icon I can ever recall seeing with a mountain in it.

And I remember the colors. The icon of the Transfiguration is a light and bright one, with warm hues of yellow gold, rose, hunter green, and copper—hues more characteristic of the early twentieth-century Arts and Crafts period than of Byzantine times.

The top of the mountain.

Christ stands upon a golden central summit, while the prophets Elijah and Moses occupy plainer promontories to the Savior's left and right. The two prophets each have two feet squarely on the ground, but Christ's disciples do not. The three are falling down the mountain. All but blinded by the Light of Lights, John and James are taking a header, literally falling face-forward down the mountain. Unlike his fellow disciples, Peter has arrested his fall and straightened himself out, but he still has a most tentative grasp on the rocks.

The top of the mountain.

The two prophets appear pretty casual about standing atop a precipitous summit; then again, mountaintops are where they had visions—Elijah on Mt. Carmel and Moses on Mt. Sinai, where he received the law of God.

The top of the mountain.

This is a Bible story, remembered from my youth, from the days of Captain Yannis, and a mountain story from Scout days, when I began to climb mountains to photograph them and remember their names and measurements.

Sometimes I forget people's faces and I often forget their names, but never do I forget the shape and size of a mountain.

"Yannis," Spiro calls out.

The mountain in the icon of the Transfiguration is Mt. Tabor, in northern Israel near Nazareth. I was disappointed to find out it stood only 1,900 feet high, this at a time when I was earning my hiking merit badge and had just climbed Southland high points Mt. Baldy and Mt. San Jacinto, both over 10,000 feet.

"Yannis. Let's go for it."

I step from the past back to the present, face to face with Spiro, who looks restored by his meditations.

Away we go into the fog.

I've hiked in so many fogs; in fact, I'm the only one in the twentieth-century to solo walk the whole darn California coast. All 1,600 miles of it. I know a thing or two about hiking in poor visibility. But this isn't like the many fog-outs I've experienced.

It's not a dark cloud engulfing us, but a very white one. In such intense light, my sunglasses do little to dim the glare. We zigzag up a ridge, dotted with firs, ragged sentinels on guard in the mist.

No wonder Father Nikon didn't take any photographs of his journey to the Holy Mountain. And he wasn't struggling with his English and confusing light and dark when he told me it was too *light* to take pictures.

I lead the way up the rocky narrow trail. Despite my summit fever, I try to check my speed, so Spiro can stay close at my heels.

Nature has bedazzled me by bright lights before. I have gazed into the white heart of the Mojave, at heat waves rolling across the sand dunes; I've been stopped in my tracks by sparkling sea shells of the Silver Strand; and I've stood awestruck before the white granite spires of the High Sierra. However, these were lights whose intensity could be explained by refraction and reflection, by the earth's surface and the sun's direction. Now I was experiencing an altogether different light, a light that always was and always will be, older than I can ever hope to comprehend, measure, or even imagine.

I blink, fighting the light.

Don't try to fool me, Holy Mountain. I've climbed higher mountains. Mountains twice your size. Mountains with way worse weather. Mountains with slopes made treacherous by layers of scree and ice.

To the top of the mountain.

The icon of the Transfiguration hangs on the wall of clouds in front of me.

The trail zigzags up the mountain. Jesus pauses on the turn of a switchback and waits for Peter, James, and John to catch up with him. "You're probably wondering why we're walking up to the top of Mt. Tabor, aren't you?"

Breathing hard, it's all the three disciples can do to nod.

"Remember last week when I told all twelve disciples that a few of you were going to see the Kingdom of God before you died? You're the three I picked to share that Kingdom. And that's why we're hiking up here."

It was quite a hike to the top for the disciples, but not for Captain Yannis, who had an easy time trailing them, but a more difficult time keeping out of sight of the apostles by hiding in the thin brush that dotted the shoulder of the mountain.

To the top of the mountain.

Jesus has to stop several times and wait for his apostles to catch up. "Peter, James, John, one more thing," Jesus tells them as they catch their breath. "You must be silent about what happens on top of this mountain. Say nothing until after I die and rise from the dead."

Finally, Jesus and his trio of followers reach the top.

Those disciples aren't like any summit-conquering hikers I ever met, Captain Yannis thinks. They aren't celebrating. They don't act happy at all. Or even relieved. Reaching the summit of the mountain should always be an occasion for celebration.

Given that they're hiking with Jesus, at least they might have given a prayer of thanks; but no, the disciples are so exhausted from the climb they fall asleep.

What's with these disciples? Captain Yannis wonders. It can't be more than three or four miles to the top. It's really not that hard a hike. Now, if we were doing Sinai, a long trail leading to a 8,651-foot peak, that would be a real hike, a reason to snooze on the summit.

Jesus isn't tired, though. He spends his summit time in prayer. As he prays, his body shines with a great light, and his clothing gleams bright white. And then—Holy Moses! And Holy Elija, too! Suddenly out pop these two old prophets on both sides of Jesus.

Captain Yannis draws as near as he dares without being seen. As he crouches behind a rock it occurs to him that Jesus, and probably the prophets, too, know he's there. He can't make out every word, but what he does get is that Jesus is telling the two old prophets about his upcoming crucifixion.

My God, what a light.

The intense light of the transfigured Christ, along with his conversation with the prophets, finally awakens the three disciples. Frightened, dumbstruck by what they are witnessing, they fall down. James and John go head over heels, landing face down, their backs to the summit and the amazing light.

Peter is on one knee, one hand on a rock, looking up the mountain. Unlike the brothers James and John, he's in the correct position to arrest his fall. True, he's got a hand in front of his face to shade the bright light, but he has two footholds and one handhold on the mountain.

From long practice, Captain Yannis presses close to the face of the mountain, as if taking cover from a rock-fall, but the mountaineers above him are not yelling "Rock!" They're not yelling anything; they're silent as the light.

Just after the disciples struggle to their feet, they get zapped by the Holy Spirit. Intense rays of light strike each of them.

Peter is shaking in his sandals, but he seems to be the only one to recover his wits, and he blurts out: "Lord, it is good for us to be here."

Good for who? For what? What's he talking about? Captain Yannis wonders.

That's all the response out of the disciples because a cloud covers them. It's a white cloud, as bright as the light from the Holy Spirit.

A voice comes out of the cloud: "This is my beloved Son. Hear him."

"Yannis."

Another voice from the cloud.

When the disciples look back toward Jesus, they see that his lights are out.

"Yannis, we're lost," Spiro tells me.

"No the trail is lost," I reply. "We're right here."

I swerve north. Must have missed one of those tight little switchbacks and continued contouring across the slope, instead of up it.

"Follow me to the cross, men," I command.

"What are you talking about?" Spiro yells back.

I cut sharply left and ascend on a steep trajectory, intending to reconnect with the zigzagging switchbacks that I presume will lead to the summit.

"How do you know which way to go?" Spiro demands.

"This looks like another mountain I climbed, a long time ago."

The cloud curtain begins to part and we find ourselves hiking amidst the great limestone formations that form the bulk of the peak. The cross atop the summit comes into view.

As we rejoin the trail, the cloud cap over Athos tears and blows away and we file past a great scattering of cracked marble. The rock formations suggest a temple, an acropolis, the ruins of an ancient Greek city.

And finally the summit, marked by the mighty cross. The wind whips clouds past the peak. Spiro and I exchange high-fives, then hang onto the guide wires holding up the cross.

Just below the cross is the Chapel of Metamorphosis. We'll go in to get out of the wind, but right now we're content to let the wind whistle through us and savor vistas down the length of the Athos peninsula, and of mainland Greece and an Aegean that rolls to the far horizon.

"I'll ask you again," Spiro calls into the wind. "When we were in the cloud, and we got off the trail, how did you know the way?"

"The terrain, the rocks—it looked like a mountain I climbed when I was a kid."

"In California?"

"I don't know where. I thought it was a real mountain, but maybe it was just my imagination."

CHAPTER 12

THE RETURN OF CAPTAIN YANNIS

In flight from Caesar's Army, the persecuted Christians retreat from the seashore. Women, children, and the Saint cross a shallow river near its mouth at the sea, while a small band of sword-wielding guerrillas under the command of Captain Yannis fight a valiant rear-guard action to slow the Roman soldiers. On the other side of the river is a small village, abandoned by the townspeople when they realized the fighting was coming their way.

Captain Yannis quickly strategizes. A steep mountain rises from behind the village, thrust up from the sea like a fist. Atop the peak of this mountain is a church with a cross atop it. "Through the village to the top of the mountain!" Captain Yannis commands. "Climb to the cross!"

The Saint tips his beard in approval. Captain Yannis nods back, glad to have the Saint at his side. The Saint always appears to the captain in moments of crisis and battle, to encourage, advise, and lend strength.

"Follow me, men!" shouts the captain.

"To the cross!" echo the Christians.

The Romans are many and the captain's men brave, but few. Fighting by the captain's side is his loyal lieutenant, the huge Tashi the Impaler, who sticks enemy soldiers with an oversize spear and flings them as hay from a pitchfork. Through the narrow streets of the village they battle the pursuing idolaters. Sending the women and children on ahead, the Christian guerrillas retreat, but their swords cut like scythes through wheat, laying out rows of soldiers as the village streets run red with Roman blood.

The Romans halt midway up the mountain to regroup as the Christians scurry up the hill to the church.

Clouds darken the sky. With a lull in the fighting, an unearthly silence settles over the land. Only a baby's cry and the sobs of a woman who has lost her husband break the stillness.

The wounded are carried into the church. Robes are ripped into bandages. An earthen jug with the last of the water makes the rounds, offering scant relief to the parched throats of the Christian soldiers.

Captain Yannis assembles what's left of his bloodied band. "Brave men, we have fought for three days. We have made the legion of Caesar pay for each step they have taken onto our God-given land. As you can see, there is no more retreat. We must hold our ground."

"Captain Yannis, is there no hope of reinforcements?" a young soldier asks.

The captain shakes his head solemnly. "It is true we are few," he admits. "Fewer now that we have lost brave comrades—the brothers Panos and Alexandros, Phillip, Simon, Haralambos of Cyprus...warriors for Christ."

"But we must have help," the young soldier insists. A murmuring spreads through the ranks. "Perhaps the rebels from Tiberias.... If no Christians help, then we know what will become of us when the Romans attack."

"Who among us knows for certain?" counters Captain Yannis. "Does an archer know if his arrow will find its mark before he lets it fly? Does a fisherman know if he will catch a fish before he casts his net? And who knows if this day we will prevail against the dark forces of evil?"

"God knows." The Saint's voice silences the soldiers, silences the whole mountain. "Pray with me," he commands. "The Lord is my shepherd, I shall not want...."

Captain Yannis and a few stalwarts join the Saint. "Yea, though I walk through the valley of the shadow of death, I will fear no evil; for You are with me."

Soon all the men, women, and children on the mountain recite the psalm in resounding chorus: "Surely goodness and mercy shall follow me all the days of my life; And I will dwell in the house of the Lord forever."

When the psalm concludes, the Saint lays a hand on the Captain's shoulder and says quietly, "The hope of Christendom is upon you, Yannis."

"The Romans!" shouts the lookout.

"Positions, men!" Captain Yannis commands.

As the Saint ushers the women and children into the church, and the men make ready for battle, a second shout comes from the sentry. "It's just an advance party. Their leader."

"Plutonius," mutters Tashi the Impaler, brandishing his mighty spear. "I'd like to toss that pagan to hell."

"He'll be going there soon enough," Captain Yannis replies.

The centurion and three of his soldiers, holding a white flag, march up to the captain at his position below the church. "Captain Yannis, I have come in peace," greets Plutonius. "This day can end without further bloodshed."

Captain Yannis stares down at him. "Did you walk all the way up this mountain to tell us you're returning to Rome this afternoon?"

Plutonius smiles. "You and your men surprised us with your valor and your skill at arms. When other Christians revolted, we slaughtered them like sheep. I have fought the Goths and the barbarians on the empire's frontiers, and can attest that you are a worthy enemy."

"Should I be thanking you for the compliment, Plutonius?" spars Captain Yannis.

Some of the Christian guerrillas laugh, with Tashi the Impaler laughing the loudest.

Plutonious smiles again. "But as you can see, you are badly outnumbered, and your rag-tag guerrillas are no match for the army of Rome. Lay down your arms. Pledge allegiance to Caesar and King Herod, and I shall spare your lives."

"We have a king."

"Jesus? King of the Jews? He died on a cross."

"He rose from the dead and lives with us now."

"Don't tell me stories of ghosts," Plutonius retorts. "Already you have severely tried my patience and that of the empire. Surrender now or you shall pay dearly. After your men are all killed, your women will be handed over to my troops for their pleasure and your children will be sold into slavery."

"Plutonius, you are slaves to fear and to Caesar, a false god. You and your idol worshippers will never defeat us."

"Brave words, Captain Yannis, but foolish," replies Plutonius as he starts back down the hill. "Better make an offering to your god; no one else on this earth can help you now."

The Romans return in force just moments later, marching in tight battle formation up the mountain. The fighting is furious, and though the Christians give more than they get, they're forced to retreat back toward the church.

Captain Yannis is in the midst of the melee, swinging his sword with deadly precision. At his side is Tashi the Impaler, who skewers Roman soldiers like so much shish kebab. But no matter the courage of the Christian guerrillas, the Romans remain in their deadly formation and continue their advance.

We must break the Roman ranks, get them fighting us one on one, thinks Yannis. *The hope of Christendom is with you.* The words echo in his ears, overwhelming the din of battle.

Out of time, out of room to maneuver, the captain knows with full certainty that this is the last stand, and the time to implement his final battle stratagem, a well-rehearsed but never battle-tested plan.

"Make your cross!" he commands the Christians.

The dispersed Christians gather at the base of the church steps and, as one, raise their right hands and make the sign of the cross. This has the effect of unnerving some of the

Romans, as does the Christians' shout: "In the name of the Father, the Son, and the Holy Spirit!"

The guerrillas form a cross formation, with the top pointed down the mountain toward the Roman army. At the top stand Tashi the Impaler, Captain Yannis and a few of his bravest lads. The front ranks of Romans attack as predicted, and as the legion advances, those Christians at the top of the cross give way, retreating up the church steps. Meanwhile, the men making up the long body of the cross move quickly to support both sides of the bar of the cross.

Thus, the Christians envelop, surround, then crush the Roman formation, forcing them to break ranks. Vicious hand-to-hand combat ensues.

Plutonius, a smirk still on his face, seeks out Captain Yannis. The smirk remains, even when Captain Yannis buries his sword to its hilt in the centurion's chest.

Seeing their fallen leader, the surviving Romans flee the field, running down the mountain toward the sea. As the dust clears, Captain Yannis and his exhausted men watch the sun struggle against the clouds. A spectacular sunset it is, with low purple rays of light slanting against the church. The devout soldiers fall to their knees, turn to the light, and give thanks. The women and children emerge from the church and join the soldiers.

Captain Yannis stares up at the church and notices the Saint looking out the window at the ethereal light. He glows in the twilight, framed by the window like a living icon. He appears wise and holy and serene as ever, as though he knew all along that God would provide and prevail.

CHAPTER 13

LOST DONKEY

Everything looks so ordinary in the morning light.

In its second hour after rising, the sun peers over the low south shoulder of the Holy Mountain and bathes Skete St. Anna in pleasant but unremarkable light. The blue sea is calm, the blue sky cloudless.

In contrast to yesterday's ascent through the transcendent ether to the top of the Holy Mountain and our descent, first through the whitest of clouds, then through the Athos alpenglow, this morning's walk will be lit by the most common daylight.

Beginning my pre-hike stretches in a light as flat as St. Anna's courtyard, I bend at the waist, touch the top of my hiking boots, and take comfort in my familiar ritual. Yesterday was TWFW.

Too Weird For Words.

When we returned to St. Anna's at sunset the skete appeared emptied of all humanity. No overnight guests. Not a monk to be found.

Someone, perhaps the young guest-master, left dinner on the table for the returning mountaineers. It was an exact repeat of the previous evening's repast: slices of feta, bread, and spaghetti. The pasta was cold, but we didn't mind, for we were ravenous and so pleased that we didn't have to share with the piggish Greek pilgrims.

After the longest hike of his life, Spiro felt simultaneously exhausted and exhilarated, very much the conquering hero. For him, good Orthodox boy that he is, the spiritual glow generated from scaling the Holy Mountain was better than anything he might have received in climbing a 14,000-foot peak in the Rockies.

After a week on the Holy Mountain and the realization that I lack the kind of Christian virtues and practices that earn you points around here, it made me feel good to use one of my earthly skills—trail-finding—to lead a true believer to the top of the Holy Mountain.

I was exhausted, too, but not from hiking—after all, it's my job. I felt drained, zapped by the Holy Mountain.

Spiro and I decided it was okay to talk in the dining hall. As we wolfed down our late dinner, we talked about how lucky we were to see something that few pilgrims had ever seen: a part of Greece like no other, a view through the clouds of heaven and earth, and maybe even a bit of heaven on earth.

And more.

"Metamorphosis," Spiro said when we finished recounting our hike to the top.

Walking into an icon, a very strange light, a surprise meeting with Captain Yannis after all these years.

Metamorphosis indeed.

"Metamorphosis," Spiro repeated.

We finished eating in silence, as though the monks had suddenly appeared in the dining room to shush us, and went to bed.

Now, in the plain light of the morning after, I have difficulty believing what transpired yesterday. Some kind of heightened awareness, perhaps a hallucination, brought on by the ultra-low-calorie diet. Followed by that crazy dream, that vivid fantasy from my youth, "Captain Yannis and the Fighting Christians."

I push my palms against the courtyard wall, stretch my legs, and conjure the walk to come: an easy day's hike west along the coastal trail to the Monastery of Gregoriou, then on to the Monastery of Simonopetra, where Spiro and I will rendezvous with the Santa Barbarans.

Unlike my pre-hike regimen of the previous morning, today's exercise fails to summon any monks. Or coffee.

I had been looking forward to telling Gerontas we made it to the top of the Holy Mountain, and to thank him for the provisions. As for what happened near the summit, I don't know what to tell him. Or anyone else.

Spiro stirred while I was getting dressed and I told him to sleep in if he wished. Off for a morning stroll, I whispered, as though we were in church.

From the courtyard I climb to meet the footpath and walk north, turning back to regard St. Anna and an Aegean that, in this clear light, appears as wide as any great ocean.

I contemplate my next hike, another one for my *Los Angeles Times* hiking column, along the Halkidiki, the distinctly secular portion of the peninsula adjacent to Athos. I'm certain the coast walkers among my readers will enjoy an account of Halkidiki, which beckons with some 300 miles of shoreline, as well as little-known resorts and beaches that are among the cleanest and most tranquil in Europe.

On the bus ride from Thessaloniki to Ouranoupolis, I looked out at fields, vineyards, olive groves, and pine forests and at coastal bluffs bedecked with scarlet poppies. Heavenly hiking.

My research had revealed that Halkidiki hoteliers are among the most enlightened in the travel industry—at least when it comes to hiking. The Halkidiki Hotel Association has designed and way-marked more than a dozen trails, and I look forward to following the footpaths, signposted with red circles on boards, from resort to resort.

Suddenly, I'm very hungry. And I left my pack back in the guest quarters. This is just not like The Trailmaster. Really, set out on a hike, even a short one, without my trusty daypack? I have nothing in my pockets. Except three figs. I pop one in my mouth and continue along the trail.

I plan my first big meal off the Holy Mountain Mortification Diet. First some really good red wine, no more monk vino. And enough already with the hunks of feta; bring on a full complement of hors d'oeuvres, *mezedes* fit for a king: calamari, pita bread with lots of dips like *tahini* and *melatzana*, plus *a horatiki*, a village salad with tomato and cucumber and olives. And *tyropita*, those fabulous cheese triangles toasted just right with the filo dough crispy. And *keftedes*, Greek meatballs, just like Mom makes them. And after the mezethedes, bring on the main courses with…. Oh, wait a minute, this feast has to take place at a seaside taverna with a view of a beach.

A beach with women on it. Lots of women on the beach. Frolicking at water's edge. Sunbathing topless. Scandinavian babes, Greek girls—no, the Greek girls rarely go topless, so make that Italian girls. After such a long time without glancing at the feminine, even the German women will look good. Even the super-sized East European women with their unshaven armpits and scanty swimsuits that cry out for the arrest of the boutique owners who sold the thongs to them….

My reverie of wine and women ends abruptly when I spot the donkey.

And a monk. Riding sidesaddle.

I'm flustered. As though the monk can read my thoughts from fifty meters away.

God knows, and perhaps a monk knows, how quickly a man's mind can travel from the Holy Mountain and its denial of sensual pleasure way down to earth and full indulgence of the appetites.

Spiritually speaking, caught with my pants down.

Keep those donkeys on the trail, I say. As long as donkeys are used as beasts of burden, the trails of the Holy Mountain will be crucial transportation links and no more roads will be built. Besides, what could be more Biblical, more spiritual than a donkey? You can't have a proper pilgrimage when sharing the way with a bus.

The monk draws close and halts his donkey. With his long beard and wire-frame glasses, he could be a revolutionary from the days of Czarist Russia; make that the studious sort of revolutionary, the kind who writes manifestos rather than lobbing Molotov cocktails.

"I saw your donkey yesterday morning," I greet the monk.

Now there's a spiritual how-do-you-do. What am I thinking? My mind races to recall the traditional way for a pilgrim to meet and greet a monk.

The monk smiles. "A good animal, but he runs away sometimes. He likes to eat the grass on the hills near the Monastery of St. Paul."

The proper Athonite greeting pops back into my head. Better late than never.

"*Evlogeite.*" Your blessing.

"*O Kyrios.*" The Lord (blesses you), he returns.

"Where were you walking when you saw my donkey?" the monk asks.

"Above Skete Anna, on the way to the Holy Mountain."

"Why did you come to St. Anna?"

"To climb the Holy Mountain."

The monk is silent for a time. From his perch atop the donkey, he looks up at the Holy Mountain, then scrutinizes me. "And did you climb it?"

"Yes. All the way to the top. To the cross."

"And what did you see up there?"

Light. Light like I have never seen before.

I feel the holy man's hands reaching out, but his soft hands are motionless. And yet we are connected now. From inside of the monk, coordinated with his breathing, comes the Jesus Prayer. He transmits to me.

Lord Jesus Christ, Son of God.

"Clouds," I answer. The Jesus prayer fills me, too, and it is hard to breathe. "Many white clouds."

Have Mercy on me.

The donkey snorts, edging sideways toward a tempting clump of grass at the edge of the trail. "Clouds. And?"

The monk shifts on the donkey to look at me. No, not at me, through me. Sunlight glints off the monk's wire frame glasses, flashing into my eyes.

I squint back at the monk.

Lord Jesus Christ, Son of God.

Metamorphosis.

Yesterday I saw an icon hanging on a cloud.

Have Mercy on me.

"Between the clouds, Spiro and I could see the Aegean and faraway to Greece."

The monk nods politely. "Where are you going next?"

"To Simonopetra. To meet my friends."

Mercifully, the monk speaks Greek slowly and we are able to converse at a speed, and at level that matches my tourist grasp of the language. The journey up the mountain was with my friend Spiro from Chicago, I explain. Three more friends traveled with me to the Holy Mountain from Santa Barbara, California.

The monk wants to know all about my family. When I married Cheri. How many children? And about Sophia. Beautiful name, Sophia. Do you want more children?

He seems particularly intense about this question.

Lord Jesus Christ, Son of God,

I nod slowly.

"You should have more children," he advises.

Or maybe he said *you will have more children.* Greek grammar is impossible.

Have Mercy on me.

"When are you leaving St. Anna?"

"Today."

"So soon. With all our talking…your name…?"

"Yannis."

The donkey lunges for some fresh grass, rips it from the side of the trail. The monk steadies himself on the animal's back and gives it an affectionate pat. "Daniel."

Daniel the Donkey. One of his now-famous predecessors carried the Holy Virgin and witnessed Christ's birth. Donkeys are everywhere in the gospels.

"And you, Father are…?"

"A woodchopper."

A what? Where's Spiro to translate? Wood-something.

"Wood—?"

The monk pantomimes holding something in his left hand while hitting it with the right. He's axing wood. Splitting logs?

Odd. This monk has none of the ruddy complexion of a woodsman. And he has delicate hands, appropriate to a supplicant from the Eastern Church, not a sawyer from the North Woods.

Maybe he's not exactly a woodchopper but a part-time teamster. That must be it. He leads Daniel the Donkey over to the wooded part of the peninsula, loads the animal up with firewood, and transports the wood back to St. Anna's to warm the cottages and chapels scattered on the hillside above the skete. Instead of the crack of the whip and the traditional cursing of the teamster, the monk urges on his animals with a prayer rope and the Jesus Prayer.

Just after I figure out the monk's profession, Spiro wanders down the trail to greet us. "I recognize that donkey," he tells me.

"Same one we saw yesterday: Daniel the Donkey. Belongs to this monk, whose name I didn't catch. He just told me he's some kind of woodchopper or woodcutter or something."

"*Evlogeite,*" Spiro greets the monk.

"*O Kyrios.*"

As one, Spiro and the monk's Greek quickly accelerates past my poor powers of comprehension. *Holy Mountain… wood…Skete St. Anna…food…Spiro…Yannis…he's a nature writer…children…donkey…Daniel…more children?…Daniel…donkey…icons…metamorphosis…Anna…*

I am left to watch them gesture, from the top of the Holy Mountain to the donkey to me to Skete St. Anna. After several minutes of rapid-fire engagement, Spiro chuckles and the monk smiles.

Somehow I amuse them.

"Yannis, the monk is named Daniel," Spiro explains. "The donkey is just donkey. Father Daniel is not a woodcutter, he's a wood sculptor. He's an icon-maker, who works with wood."

No mirrors on the Holy Mountain, but I know my face is reddening in embarrassment under nine days' worth of beard. "It's an impossible language. I'm never going to learn Greek," I mutter, in English, to Spiro.

"My Greek is very bad," I tell Father Daniel.

As if he didn't know that.

"Father Daniel has invited us back to his cottage to see his icons," Spiro reports. Interested?"

Father Daniel continues transmitting.

Lord Jesus Christ, Son of God,

"Yes, of course."

Have mercy on me.

Spiro nods in satisfaction. "Good. I told him how much you like icons and that we'll follow him back to his cottage."

CHAPTER 14

"Name Him Daniel"

When we reach his retreat, Father Daniel dismounts and leads his donkey into a pen behind his isolated hillside cottage. The creature regards us with that baleful expression only a donkey can make. With its worn boards and funky gate latch, the donkey's corral cannot be considered high-security confinement. No wonder the donkey is always breaking free and going on walkabouts.

But maybe this is by design, I consider. Perhaps the monk and the donkey have an arrangement: in exchange for good works and doing what it's told, albeit stubbornly, the donkey is allowed to stray. But the donkey must not stray too far. Must not stray too often.

Maybe that's how we seem to God. Like donkeys, not too smart, very stubborn. Do what we're supposed to do with frequent complaining.

What did you learn atop Mt. Athos, John?

Men are like donkeys...

As we follow Father Daniel to his front door, I tell Spiro my "We're-All-Just Donkeys-in-the-Corral of God" revelation.

Spiro's eyes roll heavenward. "Deep thinking, Yannis. Be sure to write that one down."

We pause just outside Father Daniel's magnificent door, an amazing example of the wood-carver's art, featuring a half-dozen saints (none of the more common, recognizable to the layman ones). The detail in the face and clothing is astonishing.

Inside, I am disappointed to find only a few examples of the monk's iconography.

As if reading my mind, Father Daniel tells us that all his icons are one-of-a-kind and that as soon as he carves them they're shipped straight to those who commission his work.

He seats us near his workbench and offers his portfolio for review. Spiro is impressed and, as we turn the pages of photographs of the monk's work, is quite complimentary. I concur. It must be quite an artistic challenge to make each of the saints look distinct from his fellows without the use of color.

When I find a St. Nicholas in Father Daniel's portfolio, I get an idea. I was underwhelmed, to say the least, by the quality of icons in the Karyes souvenir shops and beginning to despair that I would ever find a quality Nicholas to take home to my godson.

Even diminished by the small color photographs in the monk's album, Father Daniel's carved icons have a special quality. Perhaps I can bring something unique back to my godson. Provided I can come to terms with the icon-maker.

He must do a lot of Nicks, I think. Nick is nearly as common a Greek name as Giorgos or Costas; it's got to be on the list of Top Ten Male Greek Names.

Most icons are still painted, Father Daniel explains. But he really likes to work with wood. The challenge is to add that third dimension missing in painted icons and still be true to the Byzantine tradition. He carves deep enough to make the saints' features stand out, but not so deep that the work becomes sculpture instead of iconography.

My only hesitation is the medium itself. A moment of doubt when I think of the reaction of George Scarvelis, my godson's father, to a *wooden* icon. George knows the Byzantine world, from his studies in college and his reading and travels, from chairing the iconography committee for the new church. What's this purist going to think?

Maybe the icon's origin—bringing it back from the Holy Mountain—will make up for the not-quite-kosher medium.

Maybe not.

"Your work is beautiful, and I would like you to make a St. Nicholas for my godson Nicholas," I tell Father Daniel.

"I would be pleased. That will be...." He scribbles figures on a piece of paper, then stops abruptly. "In dollars: three hundred fifty," he says firmly. "Half now and the rest due after I send the completed icon in six months."

In Greece, from Athens gift shops to village marketplaces, it's traditional to negotiate for handicrafts. I feel my Greekness coming up and the way this deal should go down: *Father, this is lovely work, but your turnaround time is six months, and then there's delivery costs; I'll go two-fifty. Yannis, I can take twenty-five dollars off; three-twenty-five. Father Daniel, let's meet at three hundred dollars out the door. Deal?*

What am I thinking? Just an hour ago, the monk zapped me with the Jesus Prayer. I can't negotiate with someone who's taken a vow of poverty.

Spiro looks slightly aghast at my hesitation. He nods at me.

"Thank you Father, I am so pleased you will make an icon."

The deposit pretty well wipes out my funds, but I can't imagine needing any more money on the Holy Mountain. Credit cards are accepted everywhere in Greece off the mountain, and I can hit an ATM back on the mainland.

I agree to the monk's terms and ask if I can take his picture. Spiro gives me a you've-got-to-be-kidding look. Father Daniel agrees to my request with a faint smile and obliges by taking the tools of his craft and posing, as if working on a small wooden icon.

As I gaze through the camera viewfinder and compose Father Daniel's portrait, it occurs to me just how Byzantine, how icon-like the monk's face appears. The long face and beard.

Long, but not large nose. Behind his small glasses are large eyes, taking in God's glory. As I take the picture, I write its caption: *Father Daniel, Master Iconographer-in-Wood of the Holy Mountain, Skete St. Anna, The Holy Mountain, Greece.*

"I carved a St. Spyridon once," Father Daniel tells Spiro. "But if you want a good one, go to Corfu."

Spiro nods. "Corfu."

I smile. The memory of St. Spyridon that eluded me at Father Nikon's Chapel of Spyridon returns. "St. Spyridon died way back in the fourth century but his body never decomposed," I explain to Spiro, who translates into Greek. "He's in a silver case in a church on Corfu. He delivered the island from the Turks. I was there on one of the special days when the islanders parade him around. People with diseases kiss his slippers and pray to him and get miraculous results. Anyway, half the male population of Corfu is named Spiro."

"Pretty good recall for a guy who's grossed out by bones and stuff," Spiro tells me, in English.

Father Daniel directs us to wooden chairs around a small table near his workbench. "Yannis, are you named for St. John the Evangelist or John the Baptist?"

"The Baptist."

He nods with satisfaction. "The voice in the wilderness."

"And your name, Father?" Spiro inquires. "The prophet Daniel?"

"Daniel and the lion?" I add. A Sunday school lesson remembered. Mrs. Lambros would be so proud.

Father Daniel shakes his head. "*Ochi, ochi.* I am honored to have the name of another Daniel, Bishop Daniel from my home island of Zakynthos. And Daniel the Greek of Mt. Athos. Ever hear of him?"

We don't have a clue.

After a moment of silence, a half-minute burst of Greek to Spiro.

"He's going to tell us the story of Daniel the Wilderness Monk," Spiro tells me. "And I'm going to translate as best I can."

About two hundred years ago, a Greek boy by the name of Dimitri came here by boat. He resolved to attach himself to the first monk he met to be his spiritual guide.

He met Elder Herman, a very stern monk, who constantly corrected the novice and frequently beat him. Dimitri learned much from his elder and was tonsured as a monk and took the name Daniel.

One day Daniel was baking bread for Elder Herman. He stirred the fire with the poker and the iron bar fell off the wooden handle into the flames. "Forgive me, Elder," Daniel cried out. "The poker has fallen into the flames."

"Reach in and get it," Elder Herman commanded.

"Bless me," said Daniel.

"God bless you."

Daniel thrust his bare hand into the oven, right into the embers, and pulled out the poker. Without burning his hand!

Everyone on the Holy Mountain soon heard of this miracle and wanted to see Daniel and his hands. But Daniel, being modest, wanted no part of this so he left Father Herman for a time to live in seclusion.

After Elder Herman died, Father Daniel moved into a cave above St. Ann's Skete, in the mountains high above the sea. It was a small cave with room for some icons on the eastern wall alongside the skull of Elder Herman. And books, lots of books. Father Daniel read and studied a great deal.

For the next thirty years, he mostly kept to himself. Near the end of his life, the monk was visited by learned men, who wrote down some of his wisdom. Father Daniel taught that when we are spiritually challenged or tempted, we should thank God for this because He sends this for our benefit, and He won't allow us challenges beyond our strength. If we complain, our temptations are likely to increase. Father Daniel the Wilderness Monk said, "When someone resists a trial or thinks to run away from it, he is sure to encounter a worse trial."

Spiro looks wrung out. "Thanks for translating," I say, in English to Spiro. I sneak a grin at my friend, but Spiro's expression is completely serious.

Father Daniel loses the faraway look he had while telling his story, and glances about the room as if he's misplaced something. "Excuse me for being such a poor host," he apologizes as he disappears through a doorway.

Spiro watches the doorway, edges his chair closer to mine. "Yannis," he whispers conspiratorially. "Father Daniel has some very special things to tell us."

"And some very cheerful things. It's bad enough to be out in the world and know if things can go wrong, they will go wrong. Now a monk tells us that if things go wrong, and you run away, something even worse will happen."

"Yannis, you're not getting it. Father Daniel is a very special monk."

"No doubt. Carving icons in wood when all the other monks paint—"

"No, not his art, that's not why he's special. He's one of those monks who knows things. Knows us. Knows you, especially."

"Knows me? We just met."

"He's one of those monks that gets it."

"Gets *what?*"

"*Sshhh.*"

"They all get it. Or think they do. That's why they're up here in the middle of nowhere."

Spiro shakes his head. "I told him a little about our hike up the Holy Mountain. About the white light. Metamorphosis. He knows about us, about what really happened up there."

"What really happened? I don't know what really happened."

"He does. He knows what you experienced, even if you wouldn't tell him about it."

"Spiro, hallucinations are accepted practice around here. To the monks, any vision or weird flashback you have just indicates some saint at work. It was just a weird climb."

"Yannis, don't you see that climbing the mountain is just part of our pilgrimage? The monks know why we really came, especially why *you* came to St. Anna's."

"I'm not keeping secrets. I've told them over and over. We came to climb Mt. Athos."

"Nobody believes that because—"

"*What?*"

Spiro glances at the doorway. "*Sshhh.* We came all the way out here to St. Anna's because...."

Father Daniel returns with the traditional tray of refreshments: loukoumi, ouzo, and water. He carefully serves us pilgrims, and joins us at the table.

"Daniel isn't a very popular name anymore," Father Daniel relates. "The Greeks—and it's mostly Greeks I meet on the Holy Mountain—rarely name their sons Daniel."

Spiro's lips appear sealed by the Turkish delight and he does not translate, but I think I'm getting it, so don't ask for help.

"You know the Greeks," the monk continues. "Once they have a name, it goes on and on."

"Giorgos, Giorgos, Giorgos," I return.

I feel the warm glow of the ouzo, which descends rapidly to my empty stomach and radiates back to my heart and lungs.

Father Daniel nods.

Tradition is everything with Greeks, I muse. While a popular name like Giorgos could multiply exponentially, a not-very-common name like Daniel could all but die out in a generation or three. Once a Greek name, like a gene, gets thrown out of the pool, it cannot continue to replicate.

"On the Holy Mountain, the names we have are different from the ones we get at our birth," Father Daniel explains. "When a novice becomes a monk, he takes on a new name."

That would explain Father Seraphim. And Father Cherubim. And Erastos, Christodoulos, Theodisios, and all the other monks whose names wouldn't cut it in the secular world, but seem perfectly appropriate in Monk-Land.

In contrast, Daniel is a fine name, serviceable in both the secular and sacred worlds.

I look down at what should be an empty glass of ouzo and find it full. A miracle. No, not a miracle at all; Spiro isn't one for distilled spirits and did a switcheroo, exchanging his full glass for an empty one. In trade, he took the loukoumi, relieving me from attempting to swallow that sickeningly sweet stuff.

Leaving his ouzo and loukoumi untouched, Father Daniel sips only from his water glass. *He's one of those monks who knows things.* A buzz. From…the ouzo? No, from the monk. The WiFi connection again. I can feel Father Daniel inhaling and exhaling with the Jesus Prayer.

Lord Jesus Christ, Son of God.

"Yannis, have you ever thought…that if St. Anna were to answer your prayers and give you a son, what you would name him?"

Have mercy on me.

Not really. Cheri and I considered Alexander when an early sonogram of our daughter in her biological mother's womb mistakenly predicted Sophia was to be a boy. We discussed *Alexander James* in honor of the Greek tradition of giving the boy the middle name of his grandfather.

Father Daniel's intense gaze ignites the ouzo in my chest. John flambé.

Lord Jesus Christ, Son of God.

Wait a minute. St. Anna? What prayers? For what son?

Have mercy on me.

"Yannis, do you understand?"

"My wife Cheri and I have not talked much about baby boys. Or about boy's names."

Lord Jesus Christ, Son of God.

"Pray to St. Anna for a son. And name him Daniel."

Have mercy on me.

CHAPTER 15

THE MIRACLES OF ST. ANNA

Not a monk in sight. Not a cassock to be found around the kitchen, the trapeza, the hallways, the guest quarters.

"Don't you understand?" Spiro asks, as we cross the church courtyard. "St. Anna is the best place in the world to ask God's help for children."

Spiro halts. He takes off his backpack and leans it against a stone bench.

"Men from all over the world come here to pray to Anna, mother of the Virgin Mary, for kids."

"So, you're saying—"

Spiro steps in front of me, rests his hands on my shoulders. "You have your darling little Sophia. That's it, the one child. You've talked about adoption."

We shared only fragments of small talk as we packed our bags and departed the guest quarters. And now it appears Spiro will not leave until he speaks his mind. He lifts my backpack from my shoulders and stands it next to his on the bench.

"The monks think adoption is a great idea," Spiro continues. "And of course they think it's natural that you would want more children."

"I doubt monks are authorities on what's natural behavior. Did you tell them I wanted more children?"

"No."

"Did I tell them I wanted more children?"

"No. But it's not your words; it's your actions. You traveled all the way from Cal-ee-for-nee-ah to St. Anna's, presumably to ask the monks for help and to pray to her icon."

"The monks can't really believe somebody would travel eight thousand miles just to see an icon."

"This is not just any icon. And from the monks' point of view, taking a pilgrimage to a holy icon makes a whole lot more sense than traveling six thousand miles to climb a mountain. There are mountains everywhere to climb. But only one St. Anna."

"But I told them flat-out, over and over, I was just going to St. Anna's because it was on the trail to the top of Athos."

"That is what you said, yes."

"So we're supposed to believe men come here from all over the world to pray to St. Anna for help in fathering children."

"All over the world might be an exaggeration," Spiro backs off. "Who's heard of the power of St. Anna's icon back in the U.S.? But from all over Greece might be correct."

The four gluttonous Greeks. I feel a pang of sympathy for them. Here they are embarrassed as hell to be talking to the monks about their fertility, and I'm going on about how the only reason I'm here is to climb the Holy Mountain. It must be hard, coming from a macho culture, from a society that adores children, to have trouble producing them. A blow to the *philotimo*, to a Greek man's pride, that's for sure.

"I eavesdropped a bit on the Greeks," Spiro admits. "They all had different issues. Last time I checked, women were at least half responsible for making a baby. So the wives have problems, too. But of course women can't come here, so the men have to do all the talking about the relationship."

"Now that's a switch. Okay, these guys visit St. Anna, a quick prayer, a return engagement with the wife, and nine months later—*Yasou!*—another Giorgos."

"From what I overheard when Gerontas was counseling the Greeks, it's a little more complicated than that: the monk blesses holy oil that they've brought from back home. He gives them prayers and some other regimen."

Suddenly I am aware of the hot sun on my neck and the perspiration on my brow. How could I be so slow on the uptake? Why didn't I track why the monks kept probing into my family life? All those highly personal questions about babies and making them...The monks were connecting the dots between my small family (who could be happy with just one child?) and my journey to Skete St. Anna.

And all the while, the monks were certain my stated mission to hike up Mt. Athos was just a cover-up for infertility.

I'm thinking: *I came to conquer a mountain.*

The monks are thinking: *He came to Mt. Athos to ask for God's help.*

"Didn't you hear what Father Daniel said?"

Spiro has that look. That look of the true believer. He has the fiery eyes of Dean the novice monk when tested about his faith. I find it hard to meet his gaze and look instead up at Mt. Athos.

"Didn't you hear what Father Daniel said?" Spiro repeats, louder this time. "About praying to St. Anna for a son?"

Maybe I lost something in translation. My own translation. When Spiro was breakfasting on Turkish delight.

Spiro puts an arm around my back and gently but firmly turns me—and my attention—from the ramparts of Mt. Athos to the doors of St. Anna's.

"Yannis, go pray."

"Spiro, the church is locked."

"No, it's not."

Spiro sits on the stone bench. "I don't think you ever got a good look at that icon of St. Anna."

No, I didn't get much of a look at the icon of St. Anna. I got a little distracted, repelled actually, when the monks brought out her...left foot. I hesitate. Spiro and two backpacks stare back at me from the bench. The Holy Mountain and the church doors both seem about the same distance away from me.

"Hey, praying to St. Anna isn't just my suggestion. You heard what Father Daniel said."

At the mention of the monk's name, I feel that buzz again, though Father Daniel is nowhere in sight. Likely it's the two ouzos I had for breakfast. In fact, two ouzos instead of breakfast. I float across the courtyard to the church door.

Spiro is right. The door is unlocked.

I step from the bright morning light into the somber, smoky interior of St. Anna's, into air thick with incense. A dusky light it is, a merging of sunlight and candlelight, a light that resembles day's end at the moment when the sun hasn't quite set, minutes before the streetlights are lit.

A blind man's holiday, they used to call such light.

I make the sign of the cross. Once. Twice. Three times. Each time I touch my fingers to my forehead my head feels lighter. With each breath, I draw more incense, more smoky light inside of me. A gentle warmth fills my chest.

The prayer stalls are empty of monks, but not of their essence. When I close my eyes for a moment to help them adjust to the darkness, I hear the monks chanting:

Kyrie Isou Christe.

The Jesus Prayer in Greek.

Eleison me.

As harbor lights beckon the sailor, those icons illuminated by candles invite the pilgrim. St. Anna, with the most candles illuminating her, draws me near.

As portrayed in the icon, Anna is a mature woman, with shadows beneath her eyes and creases in her neck. I peg her in her early forties, but ageless, really. An older mother, and a wise one.

Underneath her large halo is the faint suggestion of dark hair, and a face that is every inch the stoic's. In the Byzantine style, her eyes are large, her nose long, her lips sealed tight.

She sits on the simplest of thrones, a wooden chair, gold-colored and ornate, but not over-the-top regal. The furniture-gold pales compared to the golden light behind her, the light of the Son of God to come.

Anna wears a floor-length black dress, nearly covered by a red cloak. Anna's hands, both her right, blessing hand and her left, which holds her daughter, are extraordinarily long.

Her feet…a relief to find her feet covered by the folds of her cloak. What happened to her body after death, anyway? How did her left foot come to reside in this church at the end of the earth?

After viewing so many interpretations of the revered Theotokos on the Holy Mountain and hearing the monks voice so many praises to the mother of Christ, it's odd to view Mary as a mere child in the arms of *her* mother.

Seated on Anna's lap, Mary appears to be the size of a two- or three-year old, but there's nothing toddler-like about her; she's depicted as a miniature adult, with scale-model Byzantine features and a face wise beyond her years.

Mary's head, too, is halo-surrounded, and she's garbed like her mother: long black dress and red cloak. Her bare toes extend out from the bottom of the dress; this barefootedness returns a bit of the child to Mary's lost youth.

Mary's left hand is held up in front of her, palm forward, as if she is calling a halt to something or issuing a warning. Her right hand, also palm forward, is off to her right side, in the kind of gesture a teacher makes when making a point.

Hey, quiet down, pay attention, we've got something important to discuss. The point I'm making is.…

The point is…pilgrims believe in St. Anna, believe in her power, believe she can intercede in their lives and give them children.

Apparently St. Anna rewards the faithful.

What is remarkable about the icon of St. Anna is not the icon at all, but what is stuck in the frame surrounding it: pictures of babies.

Lots of photographs of babies. Some studio portraitures of the little ones, but mostly snapshots of babies, newborns to toddlers, wedged in and under the icon frame, all around St. Anna. Each photo a testament to…

Prayer?

Faith?

Luck?

A few babies have pink complexions, but most are very Greek-looking, with dark eyes and dark hair, and as olive-hued as their parents. The bambinos wear the cutest of baby clothes, particularly the little girls, who are frou-froued up the way Greek mothers and grandmothers like to dress their darlings.

Except for a few cradling arms or steadying laps in the photos, it's just the babies in the photos.

Perhaps St. Anna's message is: "Parents, I'm not doing this for you, but for the kids."

Apparently, the grateful parents get the message.

I extract the photo of a baby girl from the icon frame and admire the little cutie with the big smile. I turn over the photograph and read the one-word message written on the back: *Efharisto.*

Thank you.

I return the baby photo to the icon.

Men from all over the world come here to pray to Anna.

When a Greek man prays to St. Anna, he must ask her to correct a problem: in his reproductive system or his wife's, or in their very union.

What can I pray to St. Anna for?

Nothing wrong with my plumbing needs fixing.

And how can St. Anna help Cheri? Never in the two thousand year history of Christendom, has there been recorded a single instance of praying to a saint who has reversed a hysterectomy.

Does St. Anna do adoptions?

Dear God.

Please St. Anna, hear my prayer.

I make the sign of the cross.

Kyrie Isou Christe.

My wife Cheri and I would like a son, to raise, to love, to mother, to father.

Please God. Please St. Anna.

Eleison me.

My step is as light as my head. The whole mountain vibrates beneath my feet.

Lord Jesus Christ, Son of God.

Marching to a different drummer now.

Five minutes up the trail from St. Anna and quite suddenly I'm awash with a feeling of loss. That gut feeling a journalist gets when he spends too little time getting the story or doubts he got the right one.

Have mercy on me.

Not four hours before I couldn't wait to get off Athos and partake of the pleasures of a Greek feast and of observing the latest in European Union swimwear. Now, curiously, I feel reluctant to leave the Holy Mountain.

Spiro stops at the top of a hillock for a last look back at St. Anna. I notice a loose strap on Spiro's pack and tighten it.

"Thanks," Spiro says, adding a light comradely pat on my shoulder. "You look a little pale. Did the icon of St. Anna upset you?"

"Why should it?"

"Father Daniel's words?"

"Father Daniel's words?"

"What Father Daniel told you. You did understand what he was telling you?"

"Yes. First the story you translated about the Father Daniel of old and his solitary life. And then there was the current

Father Daniel complaining that nobody names their son Daniel anymore."

"And?"

"And then he said, 'Pray to St. Anna and if you have a son, name him Daniel.'"

I look back toward Skete Anna and, at the far limit of my vision, spy a monk standing on the crest of a low hill.

It could be Father Nikon.

It could be Father Daniel, the Icon-maker.

It could be Father Daniel, the Wilderness Monk.

"No, Yannis, that's *not* what he said. He said, 'Pray to St. Anna and you shall have a son. And he will be named Daniel.'"

It could be any monk on any day of any year of any century. All I can discern is a black cassock backed by the blues of the Aegean Sea and the brilliant Greek sky. I wave goodbye to the monk, but the monk does not wave back.

"Yannis!"

"What? Say that again."

"'You shall have a son. And he will be named Daniel.'"

PART II

SANTA BARBARA

CHAPTER 16

A Match Made in Heaven

We ascend Jesusita Trail into the Santa Ynez Mountains behind Santa Barbara. On the weekend after St. Barbara's Day, I told my son the story of hiking the Holy Mountain. Now it's time to tell him the rest of the story, the part that takes place in Santa Barbara, the part that's about him. His story.

The boy—young man, really—hikes with long, easy strides and travels a mile of trail with a minimum of steps and effort. He can keep this pace mile after mile. As for his reaction to my account of hiking the Holy Mountain, he expressed more interest in the "hiking" than the "holy" aspects of the story; that is to say his questions and comments were directed to the topics of trails, and how one's hiking—and thinking—abilities might be affected by the monastic diet, long nights of prayer, and a couple of glasses of ouzo.

We are a long way from the Holy Mountain, but not far removed from thoughts of it, and we're hiking in a land of rocky hills and Mediterranean flora that closely resembles parts of Greece. Jesusita Trail leads along the west wall of Mission Canyon. At the mouth of the canyon stands the Santa Barbara Mission, above the head of the canyon rise Cathedral Peak and La Cumbre Peak, and in the middle of the canyon lies a collection of cascades hikers call Seven Falls.

We leave the trail at its first crossing of Mission Creek and pick our way up-creek. After a bit of boulder-hopping, ducking under tree limbs, and dodging poison oak, we find an agreeable place to sit, atop large rocks in the middle of the creek. It's been a dry December and the creek flows slowly, the famed falls slender cascades indeed; still, sufficient water flows to fill shallow pools and burble loudly enough to drown out all sounds from the city below.

As we break out the water bottles and power bars, sunlight finds the dark recesses of Mission Canyon and warms us. It's almost winter solstice, this clear and cool Saturday nearly the shortest day of the year. The light will not linger long in the steep and shady canyon bottom.

"Your mom and I get the call about noon at the house," I begin. "From Virginia, head counselor at the Adoption Center. She wants to talk to both of us. So we both get on the line. We're in the kitchen on cordless phones. Cell phones were the size of bricks then.

"Virginia says: 'A birthmother, Lisa is her name, has a baby boy she wants to place. She picked you.'

"Now we're not immediately jumping up and down with happiness. Reason being, we started trying to adopt three years ago and a couple times, we were in—I hate to use this word, but it's true—*competition* with other couple for babies. So maybe this Lisa picked us and we're like in the semifinals, the Final Four bracket or something.

"Your mom is holding her breath. I say, 'Tell us more.'

"Virginia tells us about Lisa. She's not a flaky teenager, like a lot of birthmothers; she's twenty-eight, so that's good news. A healthy pregnancy, no drugs or alcohol, all the prenatal checks. An uncomplicated delivery and a healthy baby. Lisa's mom and dad, David and Monika, are solid, a good Catholic family. They live fifty miles away, in Ventura County.

"'When was he born?' your mom asks.

"'About two weeks ago,' Virginia tells us.

"*Uh-oh.* Red flag. If this Lisa really wanted us to be the parents, how come she didn't pick us *before* the baby was born? Or at least right after. Your mom and I are exchanging looks, like this isn't going to work.

"And then Virginia says: 'The baby's name is Daniel.'"

"I've never been so surprised, so shocked by anything in my life. I look out the kitchen window. La Cumbre Peak—partly hidden behind a cloud."

Daniel looks north up at the summit ridge of the range, and points to its most prominent peak: "That La Cumbre Peak?"

"Yeah, *that* La Cumbre Peak, only I'm not seeing our local peak, I'm seeing the Holy Mountain. And I hear the monks chanting, echoing in my ears. I can't believe my eyes, can't believe my ears. So I ask Virginia: 'So this Lisa, she's *thinking* about naming the baby Daniel, right?"

"'No,' she says. 'He's already officially, legally, Daniel. Got a copy of the birth certificate right here: *Daniel.*'

"Mom sees me react, and then she remembers, too, me telling her the story of my trip to the Holy Mountain, St. Anna, and Father Daniel.

"And then comes another shocker.

"'Daniel James to be exact,' Virginia goes on. 'His middle name is James.'

"*James,* that's your grandfather's name. Greek tradition and all, you give the middle name of the grandfather to the first boy in the family. So we would have picked James for you anyway."

"Daniel James," says Daniel with a smile.

"Daniel James. I'm looking out the kitchen window into the cloud over the peak, into the white light, and my heart is pounding. *Kyrie Eleison. Kyrie Eleison. Kyrie Eleison.* At that moment, though, the James part of it doesn't register with your mom—she's Italian after all, and doesn't remember about the Greek tradition of middle names. But then, wham!—it's her turn to be overwhelmed.

"Virginia says: 'And Cheri, Daniel was born January 25th.'"

"'On my birthday!' Now your mom is beyond happy, practically dancing around the kitchen.

"What are the odds?' Virginia asks. 'I have a good feeling about this. A match made in heaven.'

"Your mom can't speak at this point. I blink, take some deep breaths, and come back to the present. The Holy Mountain is La Cumbre Peak again, the monks' chanting fades away, and there's a long silence over the phone.

"I walk into the living room and over to the corner with our icons. Mary and Jesus, St. Anna, that poster of the Holy Mountain.

"'If it's okay with you,' Virginia says, 'I'll set up a match meeting for tomorrow morning.'

"I'm overwhelmed. By the realization that we are about to have a son named Daniel, that we're about to have a match meeting that seems to have been arranged a long, long time ago. I make a quick sign of the cross before the icons and hurry back to the kitchen to be with your mom.

"'Yes!' Mom and I tell Virginia. 'Make the arrangements. We can't wait to meet Lisa, her family, and that baby boy named Daniel.'"

Resuming our hike, we scramble down-creek to rejoin Jesusita Trail and follow it on a switch-backing ascent out of Mission Canyon. For many years this non-Spanish-speaking gringo hiked this trail and assumed that its name, Jesusita, was the diminutive of Jesus, "Little Jesus," given to the footpath by the padres from the nearby Santa Barbara Mission. Later I learned the name Jesusita means Virgin Mary, and later still that Jesusita is urban slang for a super-Christian, one always ready to share the faith.

The trail leads west onto a ridge, and then turns ocean-ward. We take a seat atop a cluster of boulders and admire the view: the city of Santa Barbara, the beautiful harbor and coastline, the Channel Islands and the wide blue Pacific.

"A match meeting?" Daniel inquires. "What's that?"

"That's adoption talk for a meeting with the birthmother and adoptive parents. Just what it says—a meeting to see if it's a good match. If it is a good match, the adoption is on; if it's not, the adoption is off, or at least delayed until any big issues are resolved.

"Next morning we head over to the Adoption Center offices on upper State Street. We're early. And in they come. Lisa, pretty, about the same size as your mom, her parents, Monika and David, very nice people. And Baby Daniel, asleep in the infant carrier. We really want to get a good look at you, hold you in our arms, but you're sleeping away and no one wants to wake you. They put you, still in the car seat, on a big stuffed chair near the conference table.

"The Adoption Center runs these match meeting with a strict format. First the birthmother and adoptive parents spend as long as it takes getting to know each other. Then there's a break for lunch. After lunch, birthmother Lisa will talk to the counselors and your Mom and I will talk to the counselors; by then, we'll all know if it's a good fit. After all this, and a specific amount of holding of the baby, the birthmother is supposed to declare: 'I want you to be the parents of my baby.' This is a powerful thing for her to say. She's not giving up her baby; she's making a conscious decision to place her child with a mother and father of her choosing.

"We talk and talk, and it's easy to talk with Lisa and her parents, about serious things, like the value of a college education, and silly things, too, like the best way to burp a baby. Yeah, it's pleasant conversation, but parents who want to adopt can't help feeling a match meeting is like a job interview. You don't want to sell yourselves too hard, but at the same time you want to get in your points that you're super-qualified for the job of parents. Your mom is great at this—she connects with everyone on an emotional level, draws Lisa out. We all talk about Sophia, and her potential new role as big sister. I answer practical questions from Lisa's father about things like health insurance. They want to know about our work, your mom the editor, and all about The Trailmaster, my unusual job, and my favorite hikes. We don't really talk much about religion. Roman Catholics and Orthodox are really pretty close, so raising you Orthodox isn't any big deal to them.

"Mom and I want to know all about Lisa, and it's her father who fills us in. She was an absolutely brilliant child, David explains, but a brain injury from a car accident left her slightly impaired. She's still smart, but her focus is off, which you don't really notice at first, but as the conversation gets more and more detailed, you see that she drifts off track. To be a good mother, you really have to be there, really be there, all the time for a child. She knows she's doing the right thing with this adoption. But it's hard, very hard.

"Less than an hour into the match meeting, we learn from David how we were picked. He's a business consultant, Mr. Super Organized. Early in the pregnancy, when Lisa and her family decided to place the baby for adoption, he made a questionnaire for adoptive couples. He tells us we were the only couple to get a perfect score: thirty questions, thirty correct answers. God knows what the questions were, or how we got all thirty right. And I'm certainly not going to ask at this point.

"He started his evaluation system before there was a sonogram—in fact, Lisa didn't want one—and so no one knew whether Lisa was going to have a little girl or a little boy. We stipulated on all our paperwork: we wanted to adopt a baby *boy*. Anyway, David, who is absolutely compulsive about making arrangements, wanted to button things up as early as possible, so he encouraged Lisa to choose another couple, the second-place finishers, who didn't specify the gender of the child they want to adopt.

"Then you were born and…for reasons we never understood at the time, and still don't understand, the other couple dropped out of the picture. Decided they didn't want to adopt you. So Lisa is back home from the hospital with a baby she's named Daniel. David gets into his files, contacts the Adoption Center again, and asks if Cheri and John McKinney still want to adopt a baby boy.

"I can see your mom is relieved by this explanation. I'm relieved too, but not as much. But for once in my life I'm smart enough to stop asking questions, to take something on faith.

"And I'm not any kind of businessman, like Lisa's dad, but I know this: if you've made the sale, don't keep selling. So I nod to your mom and we relax, keep the conversation light. But there's one question I *must* ask: How did Lisa come up with the name Daniel?

"Lisa said she went through a lot of names. And it just came to her one night. She remembered the story of Daniel and the Lion's Den from Sunday school. Daniel was a strong person. Daniel sounded like a strong name for a boy.

"And then all of a sudden Lisa goes off script. She stands up, looks across the table at us and asks: 'Will you be the parents of my baby?' This is way early in the meeting for this question, but we don't care. 'Yes, yes!' we say, and Mom and I stand up and hurry around the table to join her.

"Lisa asks your mom: 'Will you be Daniel's mother?'

"Lisa asks me: 'Will you be Daniel's father?'

"'Yes! Yes!' It's hugs all around. We're thanking her, thanking her for her courage, thanking her for trusting us. She's thanking us, for stepping up, for giving you a home, for wanting to raise you, to love you.

"This goes on for some time, and it's pretty wonderful, her parents jumping in and saying they're so happy. Never mind how the match meeting is supposed to happen, this is going great. Virginia encourages everyone to go with the flow. More hugging, and we're all crying, Lisa, your mom, Monika. David and I choke up, and even Virginia, who's arranged dozens of adoptions, is crying.

"The only one in the room not crying is you. Babies your age don't smile yet, but somehow you look as happy as can be."

A faint smile crosses Daniel's face. With eyes as blue and brilliant as the sky, he tracks a red-tailed hawk as it soars over Inspiration Point. Before the hawk captured his attention, his eyes were on uptown Santa Barbara, where nearly eighteen years ago something called a match meeting took place that forever altered the course of his life.

No matter how vividly I recall it, no matter how clearly Daniel imagines it, the Holy Mountain is located six thousand miles away from us. The Santa Barbara Adoption Center lies just a few miles below, amidst the clusters of white-walled, red-tile-roofed buildings that line State Street.

It must seem all so real to him now.

Back from the Holy Mountain to his hometown.

Another faint smile, and he nods. My cue to continue.

"After Lisa told us she wanted us to be your mother and your father, Virginia started to make arrangements to…bring you home."

The hawk glides away to the west and disappears into the sun, a great ball of orange fast-setting into the ocean. Daniel's gaze turns to the southeast, to the Santa Barbara Mission, to our home.

"Home," he says softly.

The only home he has known since he was two weeks old. I remember the day he came home as if it was yesterday.

CHAPTER 17

THE SPIRIT OF ADOPTION

At noon we stand on the front steps for a photo, our last as a family of three: Cheri, John, and Sophia. Our friend Leopold "Bink" Goncharoff takes the picture, just after returning with Sophia from a romp at Kid's World, a nearby park.

"What a good-looking family," says Bink, as he aims the camera.

An old-fashioned-looking family, I think, as I put my arm around my wife and daughter. Cheri wears one of her classic Mom outfits, a simple black jumper. All morning she wondered aloud about whether she should wear jewelry: on the one hand, she wants to wear earrings and a favorite necklace, to feel pretty, to make a good impression; on the other hand, this is really Motherhood Redux, and she shouldn't wear anything sharp or pointed that can scratch a baby. Still, the little guy won't be pulling on her earrings for a while longer, so why not look nice while she has the chance? Sophia, who looks cute in anything, wears one of her church dresses, while I turn out in khaki slacks, a white shirt, and black vest.

"You guys look kind of stiff standing there," Bink observes. "Why don't you sit?"

We sit down on the steps. Background for the photo is our old Craftsman home. It occurs to me that nothing in this picture looks modern: not the porch, not the front of the house, and not our family. Perhaps the original owners of the house took a similar picture when they moved in circa 1912.

"Smile," Bink coaxes.

Nobody is smiling much.

"This is a happy day," Bink reminds us.

Sometimes you're too happy to smile, I reflect.

Or too blown away.

In a few hours, we will have a son.

A son named Daniel!

A miracle from the Holy Mountain.

Cheri plucks at her hair—gathers a wavy lock behind her right ear, pulls it straight, and releases it. Telltale sign that she's nervous.

A son, born January 25, on her birthday.

Expressing our heartfelt thanks, we wave goodbye to Bink. Cheri and I each take a hand and walk with Sophia back into the house.

I remember when I first held newborn Sophia in my arms. A tiny bundle, she was. Just six pounds, two ounces. All Girl. And all feet, long feet with long toes.

Sophia Rose with the Amazing Toes, I called her.

Daddy's girl.

We worry about her now. She had complained that her head hurt just before we took our family photo. The arrival of a new baby could bring up issues for her, about where she came from, how she ended up with these strangers she calls Mom and Dad.

Always Cheri and I have been open about discussing, in age-appropriate ways, her adoption. But it's one thing to talk about something of which she has no memory and another to see an actual adoption, of a child who will be her baby brother, acted out right before her five-year-old eyes.

Sophia scampers off to her room, Cheri busies herself in the kitchen, and I return outside to sweep the front porch.

Certainly this part of the adoption, the *baby delivery* or *child transfer* or whatever it's supposed to be called, is supremely stressful for adults. It is the strangest of procedures, even when third parties coordinate it, when the passage of the infant from birthmother to adoptive parents is facilitated by nurses, doctors, social workers, lawyers, and Adoption Center counselors. Usually such transfers take place at third-party locales—in conference rooms at adoption agencies or in lawyers' offices. The neutral settings and the sober professionals help reduce the high emotional charge of birthmother and adoptive parents alike and increase the odds of a successful adoption.

But Lisa and her family wanted to come to our house. On a Sunday afternoon. Meet family to family.

Absent attorneys, counselors, and health care professionals, we are on our own. "You and Cheri are veterans; you'll know what to do and what to say," Virginia assured us.

We do know what to *do*.

Only forty-eight hours to get ready for Daniel and the time flew by in nervous but joyous preparation: shopping for an infant car seat and all the baby supplies; cleaning the house, painting the nursery, assembling the crib and bassinet that we saved from the time Sophia outgrew them, retrieving the changing table, and all the other baby furnishing stored in the attic with the hope that one day we would be able to use them again.

Our Baby Delivery Plan calls for a home-and-garden tour. Then same-sex bonding—with Cheri, Sophia, Lisa, and Monika spending time with the baby in the nursery while David and I talk business in my office. Lemonade, iced tea, decaf coffee and cookies in the living room. Finally a closing prayer circle, led by me.

We know what to do. But what to *say*?

Lisa already said, "I want you to be the parents of my child." Cheri and I already said "Thank you for trusting us." Surely something more must be said when the mother of the baby you're going to adopt actually places the infant in your arms and leaves him with you—perhaps never to see him again.

Porch swept, I walk back through the front door, imagining Daniel's arrival. The family will step right into our living room—big beams, lots of windows, wood floors, old furniture and fixtures. An American bungalow with…

Byzantine icons. In the Holy Corner. That's what we call the nook by the stairs where a cross hangs and our icons are displayed. Just ten feet from the front door. You can't miss the icons: the Holy Mother and Jesus, St. Sophia, John the Baptist, the Baptism of Christ, the Transfiguration of Christ and more. Plus a framed poster of the Holy Mountain, and a towering figurine of St. Francis, Cheri's favorite saint.

Let the Sacrament of Adoption begin.

If only there were one.

Adoption should be a sacrament. Baptism, Chrismation, Eucharist, Confession, Holy Orders, Marriage, Anointing of the Sick, *and* Adoption. If there is a sacrament uniting two adults who love each other, why not one for uniting children with adults who promise to love them?

If Adoption were a sacrament, we would all know what to do and what to say.

But there is no sacrament of Adoption. No Adoption ceremony. No Adoption service. Not even an Adoption prayer. Not a clue in a book or a hint to be found online about what to say when a mother entrusts her baby to another mother, another father, another home.

For you did not receive a spirit that makes you a slave again to fear, but you received the Spirit of Adoption. The verse from Romans, given to me by the monks from the Holy Mountain, that has to be part of my closing prayer.

After that, all I have are notes, lots of them, assorted verses and prayers as well as a gathering of my own thoughts and observations. It occurs to me that my notes are much like those I brought back from the Holy Mountain: stories about icons, favorite psalms and passages from scripture, wisdom from the monks, and a lot of disconnected expressions of my fumbling faith.

I watch Cheri rearrange the cookies on the serving tray. She wanders into the nursery and inspects it for the umpteenth time.

We're running late, that's what Lisa's father told me, when he called at twelve-thirty, a half-hour before they were supposed to arrive. David is a man punctual, business-like, in all life's appointments. Likely it bothers him to be late, however justified, however unusual the circumstances.

The baby had a fussy morning. That's the way he put it. "Lisa and Monika thought it best the baby napped," he said.

"Never wake a sleeping baby," I chimed in with a show of support that I hoped hid my own nervousness.

Now they are almost two hours late. I know what Cheri is thinking, that somehow Lisa or one or both of her parents had a change of heart, that Lisa is having a hard time letting go.

What is Lisa thinking right now? I can't imagine. And David and Monika. What is going through their minds during the drive to Santa Barbara? What in your life could possibly prepare you for driving your daughter over to the house of strangers so she can place her son, your grandson, in the arms of a woman and a man they hardly know?

When we hear a car drive up, Cheri joins me at the living room window and we watch the family get out.

How normal they look: mother, father, daughter, and a three-week-old baby out for a Sunday drive.

Lisa and Monika wear nice dresses, while David is clad in blue slacks and a button-down white shirt that screams for a tie. The baby is dressed simply, definitely not in his Sunday best.

"He's in a onesie," Cheri breathes, softly, as though the family might hear her words pass through the window, down a flight of stairs, out the front gate, across the sidewalk and parkway, to the street, to their car.

Lisa extracts the baby from his car seat, gathers him in her arms, and looks down the street: a mile away is the palm-lined shore and the wide blue Pacific. Carefully, Lisa climbs the steps and makes her way under the pergola draped with climbing roses, and through the front gate. Her parents follow, lugging boxes and sacks. Baby supplies, I assume.

I want you to be the parents of my child.

Lisa pauses again, this time looking in the opposite direction from the sea, to the Santa Ynez Mountains in back of Santa Barbara.

The ancient doorbell rings, buzzes really, and suddenly the living room is full of hugging people. Within a minute, before I even close the front door, the handoff is made. Lisa places the baby in Cheri's arms. I see the tears in my wife's eyes, but Lisa appears not to notice.

Our Baby Delivery Plan works well: house tour, girl talk, guy talk, fussing over the baby. And despite our worries about Sophia, she's having fun, reaching into the big bags of baby supplies the family brought and pulling out items one by one. Judging from the circle of crumbs around her mouth, Sophia has gobbled more than her share of cookies.

Lisa strolls from the nursery into the living room and over to the icons. She has something in her hands, in a plain brown paper bag.

"This is a really strange picture," Lisa says when I join her in the Holy Corner.

The picture is a framed poster I brought back from the Holy Mountain. Beloved Mary, Mother of Jesus, hovers atop Mt. Athos, as though rising from a volcano. Clad in a royal red cape fringed with gold, a blue robe, and red slippers, she extends her right hand heavenward while her left holds a gold scepter topped with a Byzantine cross.

"It is an unusual perspective," I agree. "I bought it when I went hiking in Greece—to some monasteries."

The Holy Mountain's twenty monasteries are each smaller than Mary's hand, and the summit of the Holy Mountain itself reaches only to Mary's hips. Deep blue sea borders three sides of the Mt. Athos peninsula; its border with mainland

Greece is a boundary line in the form of a scroll, held fast by the sharp teeth of two prehistoric-looking leviathans. The scroll lists the name of the monasteries in service to Mary.

"The mountain in the picture—it's a real place?"

"Yes. It's called the Holy Mountain."

Lisa appears not to hear, for she opens the brown bag and extracts a needlepoint. "I made this," she declares, holding it up.

The needlepoint is of Jesus in the field with a flock of sheep. *The Lord is My Shepherd* is stitched in red.

"I made this for Daniel," she adds, handing it to me.

"It's beautiful," I say, admiring the fine stitching. I know nothing about needlepoint except that it must be very time consuming to get all that colored yarn into a pattern.

Cheri glides over with the baby. "Lisa made this for Daniel," I tell her.

"It's beautiful," Cheri affirms. Cheri is quite the seamstress herself, so "beautiful" from her means a whole lot more than it does from me, and somehow Lisa seems to know that, and beams.

I turn and place The Lord is My Shepherd on the mantle, next to an icon of St. Sophia.

"Do you want to hold him?" Cheri asks.

Lisa doesn't seem to hear. She looks out the window into the branches of the old oak tree. Cheri and I exchange glances. Maybe Lisa doesn't want to hold him one last time.

"Sure," I say quickly. Cheri places the baby in my arms and I cradle him close. A long time since I held a small baby. Five years, to be exact, since Sophia was this small.

I remember to support the baby's little head. Actually, his head isn't so small, I observe, as I peer closely at my new son. Daniel is one big baby.

Lisa's father drifts over to us. "He's a big guy," David comments, as though reading my mind. "Ten pounds, four ounces when he was born. And always hungry."

Daniel is almost part of our family. A more perfect family than I ever imagined. A girl and a boy. A squirmy boy. Reflexively, I tilt him upward and pat him on the back. Cheri smiles, and I return him to her arms.

It's time for the Sacrament of Adoption.

"Please make a circle, right here, near the icons," I ask the assembled.

I should have added, "around Cheri and the baby."

No, everyone knows that.

We gather around in front of the icons, three Catholics, three Eastern Orthodox, and a baby yet to be churched.

I have the sudden urge to be outdoors. In a meadow, bedecked with purple lupine and gold poppies, with lots of people, forty or fifty or more, holding hands, in a great circle, with Cheri and the baby in the center.

"Dear God, we ask for strength, and for Your blessings for those gathered here for baby Daniel: for Lisa, Monika, David, Cheri, Sophia, and John. Help us to remember that in some ways we are all adopted, children of God, adopted by Your grace. Help us walk as children of light."

I look around the circle.

Sophia is doing fine. This is like pre-school. Circle time.

Hands folded, eyes shut tight, Lisa prays along with me.

Her father looks comfortable. Social contract completed, business done, let's close the monthly Christian Businessman's Breakfast with a prayer.

"I have a verse I'd like to share that I got from monks while I was hiking in Greece, around a place called the Holy Mountain: 'For you did not receive a spirit that makes you a slave again to fear, but you received the Spirit of Adoption.'"

Tears roll down Monika's face. She would have been a terrific grandmother.

"It's Romans 8:15, and the verse is about adoption. I like to think the Spirit of Adoption applies to adoption like... we're doing here. It's only natural we all have some fears to get over about adoption. It's a very hard thing to do. But in this case...."

I look up at the icon of St. Anna. The Spirit of Adoption is very strong.

In Cheri's arms, baby Daniel lies quiet, awake, peaceful.

"He was given the name Daniel. Daniel, in the lion den, showed us his courage, his faith. And Daniel the Prophet in the Book of Daniel, tells us of his revelations. In 2:21, Daniel writes: 'He changes times and seasons; he deposes kings and raises up others. He gives wisdom to the wise and knowledge to the discerning.'

"From the Book of Daniel 7:13, we learn: 'In my vision at night I looked, and there before me was one like a son of man, coming with the clouds of heaven. He approached the Ancient of Days and was led into his presence.'"

So far, so good, but now I can't find the next passage. Ecclesiastes is next and I can't find the verses. Deep breath. *Wing it, Yannis.*

"If we have faith, we know there is a time for everything. And that's why the third chapter of Ecclesiastes tells us that there is a time to every purpose under heaven.

"A time to be born and a time to die,

"A time to plant, a time to reap,

"A time to kill, a time to heal,

"A time to laugh, a time to weep..."

Reap. Weep? Does this passage really rhyme? Am I forgetting something?

"A time to..." I look at Lisa and momentarily stall. She opens her eyes and looks back. What must she be feeling right now? Her time as a mother is almost up. She is looking at Cheri and the baby. No, she is looking past them. At the icons.

"A time to build up, a time to break down,

"A time to dance, a time to mourn,

"A time to cast away stones,

"A time to gather stones together."

Cheri holds tight to the baby, looking into the infant's eyes, praying.

"For everything, turn, turn, turn,

"There is a season, turn, turn, turn,

"And a time to every purpose, under heaven."

Turn, turn, turn? That can't be right. Oh, Lord, no. I'm not reciting scripture, I'm rocking with a parishioner, Chris Hillman, a member of that classic rock band, The Byrds. Ecclesiastes has vanished, and all I can conjure is Chris Hillman in his choir robe, singing from the loft of St. Barbara Greek Orthodox Church. I am off the pages of the Old Testament to…*A time to…oh, what is it time for?*

There is another Bible verse I want to recite, that is supposed to form my closing, but it has completely deserted me. Another one gone missing in my jumbled notes. What can I substitute?

"Kyrie eleison," I say, playing for time. *"Kyrie eleison. Kyrie eleison."*

"Lord have mercy. Lord have mercy. Lord have mercy."

Flashback to the Boy Scouts. I'm eleven years old, drafted as troop chaplain. At the end of our hike, back at the trailhead, all of us Scouts in a circle holding hands and little Johnny giving the closing prayer:

"May the Great Master of all Scouts be with us until we meet again."

CHAPTER 18

INSPIRATION POINT

O n a warm Saturday afternoon in May, Daniel and I hike Jesusita Trail again, this time from west to east. The path leads through rustic San Roque Canyon, crisscrosses an all-but-dry creek, and meanders past a meadow, a ranch, and an avocado grove. We switchback out of the canyon, ascend to the crest of a ridge, and gain a far-reaching view.

The saints—or at least their names upon land—surround us. To the south lies the city named for St. Barbara and to the east and west the mountains named for St. Inés. The islands of Santa Cruz, Santa Rosa, and San Miguel float on the far horizon. To the west, across San Marcos Pass, on San Antonio Creek Road, stands St. Barbara Greek Orthodox Church.

My son and I hike in companionable silence. Earlier today, we talked a lot, when a letter from Greece arrived in the mail.

The first thing Daniel noticed is the top two lines of the return address:

Monk Daniel
The Holy Mountain

We smiled at the wonderful simplicity of such an address.

As simple as Monk Daniel's address is, it was no simple task to locate him after all these years, I muse. I began by writing a letter asking for help to locate Father Daniel, and my friend

Alex Trigonis saw to it that it was delivered to his brother, Father Ephraim, now a monk at Xeropotamou Monastery on the Holy Mountain.

At about the same time, we enlisted the help of Alex's other brother, Father Michael, also a monk, at St. Anthony's Monastery in Arizona. The monks at this American outpost of Orthodoxy are known to have a close connection to their brothers on Mt. Athos. After Daniel McKinney played three days of baseball with the Grizzlies, a Chicago Cubs scout team, in a tournament near Phoenix, he and I drove 100 miles into the desert to St. Anthony's, located near Florence, Arizona.

We left a letter for Father Michael, who was unavailable because of his duties with Elder Ephraim, the very same monk from Philotheou who, when I arrived on the Holy Mountain, had just set out to establish Orthodox monasteries in America.

Mission accomplished. St. Anthony's is an authentic Athonite monastery in design, and in monastic practice, but there's one major difference between it and the twenty monasteries on the Holy Mountain: women are permitted to attend select services, walk through the garden, and browse at the gift shop.

We attended vespers at a beautiful church of Byzantine design and twenty-first-century construction. It was Daniel's first visit to a monastery, and he was impressed, listening intently to the chanting and taking pictures with his iPhone.

In the days and weeks that followed our visit to St. Anthony's my thoughts turned to St. Anna's and I tried to picture Father Daniel: in his early sixties now, beard gone gray, a few steps slower, but even spiritually even stronger, the Jesus Prayer vibrating in the air around him.

Months passed without word from the Holy Mountain, and I began to nervously speculate. Might Father Daniel be older than I remember and...gone to visit Our Heavenly Father? Could he have moved into town, so to speak, into Karyes, where other monk artisans live? Could he have adopted the lifestyle of the nineteenth-century Daniel the Wilderness Monk and retreated to a remote hermitage? And as silly as it sounds, I couldn't help wondering what had become of Father Daniel's donkey. I reminded myself that donkeys live longer than horses, and hoped I would learn the wayward beast was still alive and kicking.

Three months after contacting Father Ephraim, good news arrived from the Holy Mountain: Father Daniel still lived near Skete St. Anna and still made wooden icons. After another month, (young) Father Ephraim relayed a phone number for Father Daniel. I enlisted Spiro to help and he called again and again, getting nothing but static on the line. With more sleuthing I located a phone number for St. Anna. Spiro called this number many times, day and night, and lo and behold, a Father Yannis answered the phone. Spiro told Father Yannis the story, and the monk offered to help. Not only would he help, but—hallelujah!—he spoke English.

Father Daniel does not do email but Father Yannis does, and he and I emailed back and forth in English. He printed out my emails and translated them for Father Daniel. Father Yannis also emailed me back on behalf of Father Daniel, who was very happy to hear about young Daniel and would be pleased to make a carved wood icon of the Prophet Daniel in time for Daniel's graduation from high school.

Phew! In retrospect, I might have made a quicker connection by writing him a letter and addressing it:

Monk Daniel
The Holy Mountain
Greece

Inside the envelope is a short note from Father Daniel (translated into English by Father Yannis I presume).

Dear Yannis,
I am very glad I hear news from you after 20 years.

Regarding the icon of Prophet Daniel, I am going to make
it normal size, that is 23 x 32 cm. Don't worry about the
dates. You will have it before the end of June as you wish.

As Daniel and I continue our ascent on Jesusita Trail, I
recall more of Father Daniel's letter:

You make me very happy with your news. You adopted a
boy named Daniel, so I can say your prayers to St. Anna
have been heard. A miracle was done and you part of it.

A miracle. It's been a very long time since I last thought
of St. Anna, of my awkward prayers to her, or of a miracle.

Shortly after we adopted Daniel, we started to calculate,
tried to figure the odds.

I've never had a head for mathematics, much less statistics,
but Cheri and I have friends who are so inclined, including a
high school math teacher. By their reckoning, the probability
of an American couple adopting a baby named Daniel James
by his birthmother and born on his adopted mother's birthday
is about one in one hundred million. Adding certain variables
could increase the odds to one in five hundred million.

A miracle.

Maybe. As Cheri and I learned, a "miracle" means different things to different people.

The rationalists among us, then and now, claim that with
so many people in the world, and so many opportunities for
odd happenstance, a one-in-a-million or even one-in-a-hun-
dred million occurrence is no big deal. A "miracle" like this
happens every day to someone, somewhere in the U.S., and
many times over around the world. The "miracle" of St. Anna
can be explained by statistical probability and the further
coincidence of a note-taking observer present on the scene to
record these random events.

As for the monks on Mt. Athos, a miracle is a miracle is
a miracle, and their frequency is really not all that surprising.

If you have faith, stand before an icon, and pray for a saint to intervene on your behalf, your prayers will be answered.

And what about those Greek pilgrims who journeyed to the Holy Mountain to pray to St. Anna for assistance to overcome their difficulties in making babies? When their babies were born, did they believe the infants were answers to their prayers to St. Anna? Miracles?

Those Greek pilgrims who prayed to St. Anna with positive results credit her. At Skete Anna I saw, surrounding the icon of St. Anna, the photos of the babies sent from grateful fathers who appreciated the intercessions of the Holy Mother of the Holy Mother. When Daniel came to us I knew that I, too, must send a photo of our baby to the monks at the skete and ask them to place it next to the icon of St. Anna.

Jesusita Trail, as with so many trails on so many mountains, leads to more than one "inspiration point." Only one official, capital-I-for-Inspiration, capital-P-for-Point, Inspiration Point exists on the ground and is marked on the map; however, the hiker finds inspiration at many vista points along Jesusita Trail.

Inspiration is where you find it.

Or where it finds you.

Lord Jesus Christ.

The Jesus Prayer starts up again. It sometimes comes to me in church from an icon; more often it begins deep inside of me when I'm in nature, on the trail. Sometimes I initiate the Jesus Prayer myself; at other times, like right now on Jesusita Trail, I just hear it—feel it, really—a transmission from someplace far away.

Son of God.

"Daniel, remember I told you that it's the custom for a father who's been successful with his prayers to St. Anna to send a photo of his new child to Skete St. Anna? The monks put the pictures up around her icon."

Have mercy on me.

Daniel nods. "You sent St. Anna my baby picture?"

"I did. A very special picture. When you were about six months old, your mom and I dropped Sophia off at kindergarten and decided to go for a walk along Carpinteria Beach. It was a cool morning, so Mom put a little knit cap on your head before she tucked you into a front pack, and off we went. Happy times. You were a baby who just loved being outdoors. It was low tide, the beach long and wide. The wet sand at the shoreline glistened with a magical light. We were walking east, into the sun. But the sun was hidden by clouds. What amazing clouds! Big and powerful, the mists of heaven.

"We just had to take a picture of those clouds. Of you in those clouds. Mom held you high above her head and I took a picture. I kneeled down on the sand and shot the photo from a low angle: your mother's arms, this baby in his little cap, and those dramatic clouds. And it turned out a beauty. Depending on how you look at the picture, you see a baby boy getting launched for a flight into the clouds or a baby descending from the clouds into the outstretched hands of his mother.

"'Daniel in the Clouds,' we called the photo, and we used it on the invitations we sent out for your baptism. And that was the photo I sent to the Holy Mountain, to Skete St. Anna, to be placed by the icon of St. Anna with the other photos sent in by other happy fathers whose lives had been changed by the works of this saint. *'Efharisto Ayia Anna,'* I wrote in Greek on the back of the photo. Thank you, St. Anna."

I see the flash of a smile cross Daniel's face as he takes the lead and heads up the trail.

As I fall into step behind Daniel, I wonder if any grateful fathers who have benefited from her wonder-working have ever sent St. Anna photos of their children at four, or fourteen, or as young adults, with a note that says "You made our family possible, and we are forever grateful."

St. Anna. Who *else* to thank for this blessing of a son named Daniel?

The Santa Barbara Adoption Center closed long ago. Its business model—creating families with personal connections, lengthy counseling, and carefully arranged match meetings—was far too slow and labor intensive to survive in the Digital Age. It could not compete with online matchmaking services, the trend toward overseas adoptions, and lawyers, lawyers, lawyers.

Only the Spirit of Adoption remains.

Maybe I'll start a trend and send St. Anna a photo of Daniel at eighteen years old, a handsome young man now, his beard growing in strong, the last of his freckles fading away.

No, there's a better way than sending pictures for father and son to connect with St. Anna. Father Daniel suggested that way in his letter:

You are invited, both you and your boy to come to St. Anna, to my place any time you want. It is an opportunity to know each other better and discuss about spiritual issues, the need to have faith.

"Hey Daniel, let's go hike the Holy Mountain."

"Where?" He stops in his tracks and turns around, giving me that *Are you out of your mind?!* look that only teenage boys can give their crazy fathers.

"We'll hike over to St. Anna, meet Father Daniel and pick up the icon he made for you."

Daniel is incredulous. "Are you serious?"

"Father Daniel invited us. He said in his letter 'come any time.'"

"People always say things like that, just to be polite," Daniel objects.

"Not monks. When they something, they mean it."

My mind races over the obstacle course of logistics: we need airplane tickets, new backpacks, a good map of the hiking trails, and pilgrim permits, very hard to get, to visit the Holy Mountain, and reservations to stay overnight at each of the monasteries...but it will all work out because...

Spiro will join us.

"When would we go?" asks Daniel, still in shock.

"Next month, after you graduate."

"In four weeks!"

"Father Daniel said come any time and this is the right time. It's time for you to meet Father Daniel."

Daniel tugs at his baseball cap and looks below at his hometown. "I don't know. I'm not super-religious and to be stuck on an island with guys walking around in robes and praying all the time—"

"Daniel, it's not like that."

"You haven't been there in twenty years," he snaps. "How will I even talk to anyone?"

"Spiro is going to be in Greece for a big family wedding. He'll come with us to the Holy Mountain for sure. And Spiro's godson Zachary will be in Greece, too; most likely he'll come along, too, so you'll have another young person to hang with."

Daniel shakes his head and takes a step back, as if stepping out of the batter's box to contemplate the next pitch. "What if we hike way out in the middle of nowhere to stay with Father Daniel—does he even have a house?—and he expects us to pray in Greek with him all day long?"

"Father Daniel lives in a little house and he'll be happy to see us," I assure my son. "This wonderful icon-maker, this wonderful man, this wonderful monk is making an icon just for you."

He shakes his head in disbelief and steps back onto the trail.

"Think how happy he would be to meet you," I call out after him, "and give the icon to you in person."

We continue our hike. Inspiration Point draws near, and if we walk another six thousand miles east on Jesusita Trail we'll reach the top of the Holy Mountain.

I wish you the best. God bless you and your family.
With Jesus Christ's Love,
Monk Daniel

PART III

RETURN TO THE HOLY MOUNTAIN

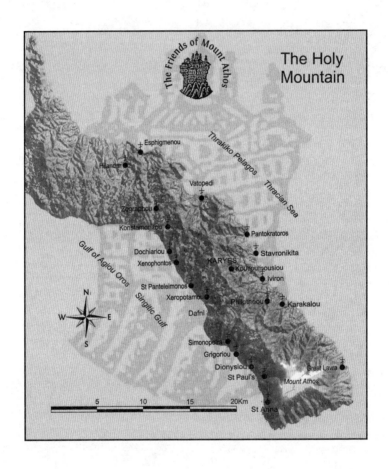

The Friends of Mount Athos

The Holy Mountain

Esphigmenou

Hilandari

Vatopedi

Thrakiko Pelagos

Thracian Sea

Zographou

Konstamonitou

Pantokratoros

Dochiariou

Stavronikita

Xenophontos

KARYES

Koutloumousiou

Iviron

St Panteleimonos

Gulf of Agiou Oros

Singitic Gulf

Xeropotamou

Philotheou

Karakalou

Dafni

N

W E

S

Simonopetra

Grigoriou

Dionysiou

St Paul's

Great Lavra

Mount Athos

5   10   15   20Km

St Anna

CHAPTER 19

SPLASHING IN THE DRY RIVER

"We have no record of any reservations," Xeropotamou's young guest-master tells Spiro and me once more.

The tall, thin monk has a more than passing resemblance to Spiro's godson Zachary Deligiannis, who sits with my son Daniel on a bench in the cool entry near the guest-master's office. Were Zach to go on the monastic diet and allow his college-student beard to grow wild, in six month's time he might easily double for the guest-master.

The young men—twenty-three-year old Zach, a recent graduate of college and nursing school, and eighteen-year-old Daniel, a recent graduate of Santa Barbara High School—are blissfully unaware of our predicament. Between the two, they know ten words of Greek that are not words for something to eat or drink.

Spiro and I stand with the monk just outside of the door of his office, where the *archontaris* repeats the bad news: "We received no letter or fax about your arrival."

Through the open door of the office I can spy no paperwork whatsoever on the desk. Or any evidence of a fax machine. The only communication device in sight is a land-line phone, a vintage instrument manufactured well before Daniel, Zachary, and the guest-master were born.

From the ferry landing at Dafni, we were fortunate to catch a ride in a van for a few miles up the dusty road to the bottom of the long entryway leading to Xeropotamou. And (we thought) we were fortunate to arrive at the monastery just after midday and to catch the guest-master at his station, at a time when most monks are sleeping.

However, once we set down our backpacks and Spiro and I engaged the guest-master, we became less certain of our good fortune. It is disheartening, to say the least, to travel 6,000 miles to the Holy Mountain, and then to be told you have no place to stay on the first night of your journey.

I had planned this trip and midway through Day One it is not working. I was certain that we had a place to stay at Xeropotamou.

If not, though, where else can the guest-master send us? It is highly unlikely any of the nineteen other monasteries on the Holy Mountain has a room at the height of visitor season for four American pilgrims without reservations. Moreover, on Mt. Athos, more so than in most places on earth, the rules are the rules and, as the always spot-on Friends of Mt. Athos web site warns, *"No reservation, no accommodation."*

"Perhaps our friend Alex Trigonis sent a fax?" Spiro suggests.

Back to fax. Twenty years earlier (at the dawn of the Early Internet Era of dial-up modems and primitive email) facsimile transmission was still high tech and a crucial communications tool for the pilgrim seeking to secure permission to visit the Holy Mountain and to book overnight lodging with individual monasteries. We faxed and faxed and faxed.

(And mailed letters, too. To secure a passport for more than the usual three-night pilgrimage, we had to write formal letters months in advance to the Patriarchate in Constantinople— *err* Istanbul—in order to establish our credentials as devout Orthodox, and then send our request and support documents to the Mount Athos Pilgrims' Bureau in Thessaloniki.)

Our friend Alex—Dr. Trigonis—is an orthodontist with a large and successful practice. Even today, healthcare

professionals fax, so when he promised to contact Xeropotamou on our behalf, I figured it would be by fax.

Spiro explains again in Greek so clear and so slow that I
can easily understand: Alex Trigonis is a parishioner at Saint
Barbara and a friend of (he gestures to me) Yannis. Spiro
details how far we've come from home—Chicago (Zach),
Hong Kong (Spiro), Santa Barbara (Daniel and John).

Indeed we journeyed far, and after long days of travel to
and across Greece rendezvoused the evening before at the
Capsis Hotel in Thessaloniki. Spiro bused in from a cousin's
wedding held in a village located halfway between Athens and
Thessaloniki; Zach took a ferry from the isle of Santorini back
to the mainland and a bus from Athens; Daniel and I took a
flight from Amsterdam to Athens and another from Athens
to Thessaloniki.

In Thessaloniki, we met another of Spiro's godchildren,
Marina, a bubbly college sophomore on a month-long Classical Studies tour. We walked the waterfront and stayed up
talking until 2 a.m.—not the best idea, considering that our
schedule required us to get up at 4:30 and taxi across town
to a bus station in order to board the 5:15 bus bound for
Ouranoupolis (The Heavenly City). We boarded the 9:30
a.m. ferry for the two-hour voyage (with stops along the way
at coastal monasteries) to the little port of Dafni.

Plan A is for us to stay Night One at Xeropotamou. We
do not have a Plan B.

Our basic Pilgrim Visa allows us only four days and three
nights on the Holy Mountain. My co-conspirator Spiro and
I intend to "burn" our allotted nights with stays at the big
established monasteries until our permit expires and thereafter wander off into the wilderness at the remote end of the
peninsula, staying several more days at St. Anna's or with
Father Daniel (if he invites us to stay with him). Our ratio-
nale is that the big monasteries may be sticklers for the rules,
whereas out where God left his shoes, the monks are less likely
to inspect the dates on our visas.

"*Endaxi,* I understand," the guest-master assures us. "You have traveled a long way. We remember Alex and his visits to Xeropotamou."

"Alex contacted Xeropotamou and said we—the four of us—were coming," Spiro labors on. "Under the name 'John McKinney.'" He gestures to the boys on the bench. "His son, Daniel. My godson Zachary Deligiannis, and myself, Spiro Deligiannis."

"Endaxi. Endaxi." All right, All right.

"Alex's brother is Father Efrem," Spiro points out.

"I understand, I understand."

On this second go-around, the guest-master repeats his answers to our inquiries, perhaps to emphasize that he is *doubly* sure he has no record of any reservations.

I have the distinct feeling that the guest-master, devout soul that he may be, is not comfortable working in the hospitality business.

The monastery leadership drafts the youngest (or newest) monks to serve as guest-masters, probably assuming that these men have been most recently "in the world," and are thus more likely to be better educated and multilingual than the older monks; therefore they should be able to relate to the passing pilgrims. Not every young monk, though, has the temperament to deal with tourists, even devout, respectful, and religious ones. But you don't say no to the Abbot. Doubtless monks in a thinly staffed monastery such as Xeropotamou must toil in guest services when their temperaments might be better suited to gardening, incense-making, or archiving medieval manuscripts.

"Alex said he would contact Xeropotamou for us," I tell Spiro in English. "He was sure he would remember our arrival date, because June 30 is his anniversary. His wife is named Alex, too—Alexandra. So I'm sure Alex got the date right."

"Yannis, I'm not sure this is relevant...."

We have name-dropped our only name. We have played the "We are friends with a monk's brother" card. Twice.

"There is no reservation for you to stay this night," the guest-master says with more than a trace of finality.

"The guest-master says there's no reservation," Spiro announces in English, loud enough for the boys to hear.

As the guest-master begins to retreat, I step between him and the office, and launch a last-ditch pitch. "My friend is Alex Trigonis," I begin in Greek. "Alex and I are from Saint Barbara Church, from Santa Barbara, America, California."

"Yes, yes," nods the guest-master.

Spiro looks at me as if I've lost my mind. "Yannis, I already told him—"

"Alex Trigonis comes to Xeropotamou," I continue. "Many times, to visit his brother. Spiro and I came to Xeropotamou twenty years ago. We stayed one night. We talked with the brother of Alex. He was a novice. Now he is Father Efrem."

"Yes, yes, yes," repeats the guest-master, upping his responses from twice to thrice.

"After Xeropotamou, we walked to the Holy Mountain. It was a good walk. We walked to St. Anna. We walked to the top of the Holy Mountain."

"Yes, yes, yes," the guest-master interjects, urging me on in triplicate.

Daniel and Zachary join us. They look amused. Perhaps it's the spectacle of me speaking Greek. Spiro smiles faintly; either I amuse him as well or he realizes his friend's tactical maneuver.

"Now Spiro and I return," I plod onward. "To walk again. To St. Anna. To see Father Daniel." I gesture to the two young men. "This time with Zachary, godson of Spiro, and Daniel, my son. We are very happy. To walk the Holy Mountain. To return to Xeropotamou. We would like to talk to Father Efrem. Again. And—"

"Endaxi, endaxi, endaxi," the guest-master repeats, clasping his hands together as if he is about to pray for me to stop. He appears to have the same faint smile—or is that a grimace?—as Spiro. "Please wait," he tells us before striding into his office.

"What were you telling him?" Daniel asks.

Before I can answer, the guest-master returns with a brief pronouncement:

"You are welcome to stay one night. Please accept our hospitality."

Hospitality arrives moments later in the form of a tray brought by another young monk, who directs us relieved pilgrims to a small table. It's the traditional monastic welcome: glasses of water, shots of *tsipuro,* and pieces of loukoumi.

We quench our thirst with the water and regard the loukoumi, known everywhere around the world, except by Greek speakers and proud Hellenes, as Turkish delight.

Spiro, I remember, loves the chewy candy; for me, the rubbery, gelatinous, and way-too-sweet treat is an acquired taste, one I failed to acquire on our last trip to the Holy Mountain, when I nearly always gave Spiro my allotment of loukoumi.

Under a liberal dusting of powdered sugar lie four pieces of loukoumi, two tinted pink and two green. The boys go for the green ones and Spiro the pink.

The green ones are mint-flavored and almost tolerable. The pink ones, most popular among loukoumi gourmets like Spiro, are flavored with rosewater. Pink loukoumi tastes to me like a mixture of sugar and cornstarch saturated with old-lady perfume and provokes a gag reflex.

Zach savors his slice of loukoumi. Like godfather, like godson.

Daniel shakes his head after his first bite. Like father, like son.

Suddenly I am filled with the warm memory of reading Daniel, seven or eight years old then, the first book in *The Chronicles of Narnia,* by C.S. Lewis and later watching the movie version of *The Lion, The Witch and the Wardrobe.* Edmund betrays his siblings to the White Witch in part because he is heavily under the influence of Turkish delight.

I recall trying without success to explain to Daniel how delicious this candy must be for Edmund to lose his senses.

"Remember Edmund?" I ask the group.

Daniel and Spiro look blankly at me.

Zach brightens. "Narnia."

"Yeah, in the story the witch gave Edmund the candy and he lost his mind. She gave him boxes of Turkish delight, the sweetest and most delicious candy ever, and Edmund kept shoveling it in his mouth."

Daniel shakes his head. "He went crazy for *this*?"

"What Edmund didn't know was that the Turkish delight was enchanted. Anyone who tasted it had to have more and more and more, and, unless stopped, would continue eating it until they killed themselves. Even when Edmund realizes the nice lady giving him candy is an evil witch, he can't stop craving it."

You'd think Edmund could have got a better price for selling his soul, I muse, as we turn our attention to the tsipuro. While loukoumi, a.k.a. Turkish delight, has Ottoman origins, tsipuro is Greek from the start—a creation of a group of fourteenth-century monks on Mt. Athos. The monks produced a variety of tsipuro flavored with anise that came to be called ouzo.

Where did my little boy go? In the ten years since I read him *The Chronicles of Narnia* he has grown from a little over four feet tall to a little over six feet tall. By the way he bends his elbow with the Greek brandy, I have to think this is not the first time Daniel has picked up a shot glass. Perhaps those high school graduation parties were not the alcohol-free gathering we parents liked to imagine.

Spiro parts with his dose of tsipuro in exchange for the last piece of loukoumi, a more than fair trade from my perspective. But before I reach for more tsipuro, Zach and Danel split the last shot and send it down their hatches. Hardly have we put down our empty glasses when the guest-master appears and tells us to make our way to the church.

I have drilled Daniel and suggested to Zachary that we follow Spiro's lead in all areas of Orthodox protocol, and so we closely trail our spiritual leader as he regards the high-profile and even scary scenes of the apocalypse in the narthex. We are close at his heels as he enters the church, crosses himself, and kisses particular icons. Soon we come to a halt. The monk (the one who brought us the welcome tray) has brought out a few of the monastery's treasures for us to venerate.

Among them are "the largest piece of the original holy cross," the monk tells us, with Spiro translating. This is impressive to all of us. Daniel and Zach look closely, touched as the monk points out the nail holes. "You can see the holes left by nails that held Christ to the cross."

"Xeropotamou is dedicated to the Forty Martyrs of Sebaste," explains the monk, showing us another ornate case, this one displaying multiple relics. "And now, here are the bones of the Forty Martyrs."

We follow Spiro's lead, making the sign of the cross and kissing the cases holding cross and bones.

Daniel and Zach handle their first venerations like veterans. Way to go, boys.

I wonder if Daniel remembers the story of the Forty Martyrs of Sebaste. It seems to me I told my son this strange tale when he was a little guy, about the same age as when I read him *The Lion, the Witch and the Wardrobe*.

What must he be thinking? I muse. The stories of his childhood coming to life. With illustrations. Jesus nailed to the cross, the Forty Martyrs frozen in a lake. And his own story, in progress. Tomorrow we will begin our hike to St. Anna's, and in just three days Daniel will meet Father Daniel.

Zach and Spiro are already on monk time—that is to say they, like the monks, are sleeping in the middle of the afternoon. Not five minutes after the guest-master showed us our modest room, Zach selected a bed, plugged his phone charger into the one and only outlet, and fell asleep as soon as his head hit the pillow. Spiro walked with us to a vista (meditation?) point just outside the monastery walls. Under a shade ramada is a picnic table with a long bench, evidently a bed to his liking, for Spiro was snoring within seconds.

In contrast to the Deligiannis boys, Daniel and I are buzzing. For Daniel, his first twenty-four hours in Greece have been a flurry of firsts: first authentic gyro, first Greek coffee, first Greek taxi ride, first Greek bus ride…. He and I discuss more "firsts" as we meander down the monastery's landscaped entry road to another shady spot with a view.

And then there's Greek politics and the Greek economy that have us pilgrims—or at least me—on edge. Greece is out of money, and if no agreement is reached with its European creditors by midnight tonight, the government will default on its loans. There are mass demonstrations in Athens against the austerity measures demanded by lenders. The unemployment rate among young people is twenty-five percent and the economy is in shambles.

Spiro, who has followed the news of "The Crisis," as it's called in Greece, had calming words for us on the ferry ride over to Mt. Athos: "We're going to the one place where there aren't constant worries about money. We don't have to pay for our food or lodging. If there's a general strike and they stop ferry service, we'll just hang out on the Holy Mountain for a couple of months. No problem."

"And then there's all the new stuff here," Daniel continues. "Tsipuro, loukoumi…and I'm kissing icons and…bones. Forty of those guys. Who were they?"

"The Forty Martyrs."

"This one of the strange stories you told me as a kid?"

"I think so."

In fact, I know so. "The Forty Martyrs of Sebaste." Inexplicably, the story comes back to me in a rush from my last telling a decade ago, fills me to overflowing with all its gory details, and I am compelled to let it out.

Once upon a time in Sebaste, an Armenian town in what is now eastern Turkey, there lived a group of forty Roman soldiers who were Christian. It was 320 AD and a dangerous time to be a Christian—particularly a Christian soldier. The eastern half of the Roman Empire was ruled by one of the last pagan emperors, Licinius, who, fearing insurrection, was determined to rid the ranks of the military of Christians.

The garrison at Sebaste was under the command of Agricola, who shared the emperor's distaste for Christians and Christianity. However, Governor Agricola was a practical man, and he admired the forty devout Christians as brave, battle-tested, and highly skilled soldiers, valuable in the defense of the empire against Barbarians and Persians.

"I hear that you refuse to make the sacrifice ordered by Emperor Licinius," he began. When the Christian soldiers affirmed this was true, Agricola gave them a choice: "Make sacrifices to the gods, and continue your rewarding careers with all honors and privileges...*or*... refuse this command, be stripped of your military rank, and face court martial and the potential consequences—ranging from disgrace to the death penalty."

When the soldiers refused to make sacrifices, Agricola threw them into jail overnight to think about it. But what the soldiers thought about was the words from Matthew 10:2: "Good is the beginning of your resolve, but he who endures to the end will be saved."

The next day things did not go better with Agricola. The crafty commander tried flattering the stubborn Christians by telling them how handsome and brave they were, and how misguided they were to even think about giving up the good life as elite soldiers for just one god. When the soldiers remained unmoved by flattery and threats, Agricola threw them back into prison, this time for a week.

During their confinement, Cyprion, a brave veteran, reminded his brothers-in-arms how God had protected them in battle and would surely assist them as they battled this enemy. Meanwhile, Agricola consulted with higher authority and was told to be firm, even ruthless, with this quiet (so far) insurrection.

The soldiers marched to their hearing singing the psalm "O God, in Thy name save me," as they always did before they marched into battle. Agricola told them they were a disgrace to the legion. "You have no lord but Caesar," he roared.

"Nothing is more dear or honorable to us than Christ our God," replied another brave soldier. "We are soldiers of the Lord, now and forever."

After that, the command stirred up the local pagan citizenry and ordered the townspeople to stone the rebellious Christians. However, as the mob hurled stones at the Christians, the stones U-turned and struck those who threw them. One stone struck the face of a Roman soldier and knocked out his teeth.

When stoning didn't work, the Christian soldiers were led to a lake. It was winter and a bitter wind was blowing. The soldiers were stripped naked and ordered to stand through the night in the freezing waters. "You will stay in the icy lake until you freeze to death or agree to sacrifice to the gods!" Agricola told them.

In order to tempt the suffering soldiers of Christ, the guards set up warm baths on the lakeshore. Any Christian who agreed to sacrifice to the idols could exit the frigid waters to revive—indeed survive—in the baths. In the first hours of darkness one soldier succumbed to temptation. However, when he entered the warm bath, the temperature change shocked his frozen system. He convulsed and died.

In response to the defection, the remaining soldiers maintained their solidarity and Holy *esprit de corps* and ramped up their prayers. Their prayers were soon answered. An extraordinary light warmed the holy soldiers and melted the ice. One of the Roman guards named Aglaius looked upward to see thirty-nine radiant halos slowly descending onto the heads and literally and figuratively saw the light. He threw off his clothes, and dashed into the lake, shouting "I am a Christian too!" Aglaius brought the number of martyrs once again to forty.

Early the next morning, Agricola and his cohorts came to the lake and were furious to find the Christian soldiers still alive—and that one of the guards had joined them. The forty captives were dragged back to prison and tortured. Roman henchmen crushed the bones of their legs with sledgehammers.

The bodies were carted to the edge of town, thrown in heap, and burned. After the funeral pyre burned out, the charred bones were collected and that night thrown into the river. The Romans took this action in order to prevent the Christians from gathering the relics, displaying them, and making heroes of the forty traitors to Caesar.

However, there was no stopping the forty men on their path to martyrdom. Three days later, the holy martyrs appeared in a vision to the local bishop, Peter of Sebaste, and directed him to recover their bones from a bend in the river. The bones of the martyrs shone like stars in the water, and were easy to collect as they floated by.

And so it came to pass that the relics were distributed throughout Christendom; in this way, veneration of the Forty Martyrs became widespread, and numerous churches were erected in their honor, including this important one at the Monastery of Xeropotamou on Mt. Athos.

"Are you kidding me?" Daniel sighs. "This is as crazy a story as the one you told me about St. Barbara."

"I guess—"

"Maybe more crazy."

We gaze down at the port of Dafni, as still as the waters around it. Not a vessel coming or going. "And the monks?" he asks sharply. "They really believe these stories?"

"I don't know about the monks," I answer. "But it's natural for the rest of us to have doubts."

Daniel looks from the sea up to the mountains. When he's in a new place, his internal navigation system is always recording. I marvel at his amazing sense of direction—better even than my own. In fact, it was Daniel who led Spiro and me out of the monastery, turn after turn, down passageways, across courtyards, and out a side gate. He just *knew* which way to go.

"It's just so…strange here, as weird as the stories."

The Lion, the Witch and the Wardrobe. The Forty Martyrs of Sebaste. And his own story: The Mountain, the Monk and the Icon. Weird stories indeed.

I nod. "Too weird for words; that was my reaction to this place."

"It's not…just the place," he replies, wrestling with his words. "It's what all these monks are…doing, what we're all doing here." He looks up at the Holy Mountain, stark and rocky, a two-day hike away. "Science…," he starts in again. "If you believe in science…it's hard to believe this stuff."

"Stuff?"

"The stories, all those saints."

"I know what you mean," I say. *No wonder he has doubts,* I muse. The story I told him about my first trip to the Holy Mountain was all about doubt. Doubts at the start. Doubts at the end. Doubts all along the trail.

I vaguely considered the likelihood that Daniel, too, would have doubts, even serious questions of faith, during our journey. But I never guessed my teenaged son, not one to easily talk about his feelings, would let his doubts out after only four hours on the Holy Mountain.

"Daniel, it's okay to be skeptical," I reassure him. "Especially at your age. And it's okay to have questions and doubts here on the Holy Mountain. We're not the first guys to come here with doubts."

"We have to go to church before we get anything to eat," he says, looking accusingly back at Xeropotamou. "What's with that?"

Perhaps it's Daniel's body, not his spirit, that is most unsettled, I consider. More than eight hours have passed since breakfast in Ouranoupolis.

"You bonking?"

He shrugs.

"Want a power bar?"

He nods and I retrieve a chocolate-flavored protein bar for him from my pack. "Let's hike," I urge. We walk in silence for a few minutes along the monastery's entry road to meet the main road from Dafne to Karyes.

At a tight bend, where the road turns away from the coast, I spot a bright red trail sign with white letters in Greek and an arrow pointing to the monastery Panteleimon. At the bottom of the sign is a stick figure of a hiker, with backpack and walking stick, and the English letters FOMA. Blessed be the Friends of Mount Athos for this trail sign, as nice as any in the U.S.—or in England, where the Friends are headquartered.

"Where's this go?"

"Along the coast to Panteleimon, the Russian monastery."

"The big green one?"

"That's the one."

Daniel and Zach were wide-eyed when the ferry approached Panteleimon, which resembles a small town with many buildings and churches. Roofs, onion domes, and bell towers are painted green. Everything is super-sized about this monastery, which has a capacity of one thousand monks and is said to have the largest bell in Greece; when it rings on Easter Sunday and on the Feast Day of St. Panteleimon it can be heard all over the Holy Mountain.

We were surprised to find that more than half the pilgrims aboard the ferry were Russian. Most disembarked at the harbor at Panteleimon and walked to the gigantic monastery, located very close to the waterfront.

"We don't have time to visit Panteleimon today, but we should be able to get a good look down at the monastery from the trail."

Daniel looks relieved.

We step along the trail, which contours around the coastal slope and affords us fine views out to sea. We are not far along when we join a length of pathway paved with flat stones.

"Daniel, this trail might be a thousand years old. It's a mule track. They used lots of mules back then. And still do. Tomorrow we'll probably see mules on the trail."

"Don't they use trucks now?"

"There are places on the mountain trucks can't go. Places without roads—only trails."

I hope.

After a chocolate power bar, a drink of water, and ten minutes of hiking, the worry is gone from Daniel's expression and the spring has returned to his step. He hikes ahead of me on the coastal trail for some time, then abruptly stops, and when I catch up with him, he blurts:

"That piece of the cross, with the nail holes. You think it's real?"

Before I can answer, he continues. "I think it's real, the piece of cross. But…you know…where Jesus went after? I…I…"

His words hang in the still air. It's so quiet. But not entirely silent. We hear something, but can't quite recognize the sound.

Daniel takes a few more steps along the trail and stops again. "When are we meeting Father Daniel?"

Before I can answer, we hear the sound again, stronger now, and Daniel takes off at a brisk walk down the trail. It's the sound of running water.

We hear it before we see it: Xeropotamou. "The Dry River," not dry at all.

We descend a leafy corridor to a bridge over the river. Xeropotamou, this fork of it anyway, is not a mighty river, but would be if it filled its banks to overflowing. A river optimist would say the gorge is half full; a river pessimist would say the gorge is half empty.

In the second week of summer in a dry year Xeropotamou remains vigorous. Its waters cascade over rocks, swirl around boulders great and small, and pour into pools. The sound of falling water is amplified by the narrow gorge through which it flows.

"Xeropotamou, means 'The Dry River,'" I tell Daniel.

"They sure got that name wrong."

Perhaps the river was named in the dead of summer after a ten-year drought. I'm certain Xeropotamou swells to a torrent in winter and early spring, when abundant rains fall on the Holy Mountain. At times of high water, the river would be impossible to cross without this bridge.

The bridge is as beautifully situated as it is useful, and we take advantage of an obvious photo opportunity to take a father-son selfie: two pilgrims on a bridge with the rushing river in the background. Daniel reaches out a long arm with his smart phone to capture us, and an abundance of blue. I wear my favorite button-down blue hiking shirt; Daniel a blue synthetic T-shirt, upon which, centered on his chest, rests his silver cross and chain, glinting in the sun. Behind us is the blue river, below us the blue sea, above us the blue sky. And Daniel's blue eyes and mine, sparkling in the moment.

The sound of the river brings me happy memories. Of hiking with my little boy, a sign at the trailhead, a footpath into the mountains, a stop at a stream, snapshots of happy hikers, a snack and a story.

A story. What's the story with Xeropotamou? Was the river dry when the monks arrived? Even if it weren't such a misnomer, the name would be an oddity. Most monasteries and most natural features on the Holy Mountain are named for holy men, not earthly geography.

Surely there is a story behind the name Xeropotamou, but I can't think of one.

Or can I?

We linger at the stone railing of the bridge and watch the river flow. "There's a story about Xeropotamou," I say.

Daniel shakes his head. "And let me guess, you're going to tell it." He helps himself to another power bar from my pack. "Okay, let's hear it."

"It took many days to sail from the Holy Land to the Holy Mountain, and the desert monks were exhausted when they arrived on these shores. But they had faith and trusted in their leader, Elder Cosmos, who had a vision and knew exactly where on the Holy Mountain to start a new community. Elder Cosmos directed his brother monks to build a trail from the boat landing up the bluffs, then higher and higher up the shoulder of the mountain.

"It was hard work shoveling rocks in the hot sun. It was the middle of summer, and there was little shade to be had from the low brush on the hillsides. The men were always thirsty, and water had to be carried from far away. The monks began to grumble: 'This is madness. Why not build the monastery on the slopes of the mountain where there is water? Why are we digging a trail along a ravine as parched and dry as anything we left behind in desert?'

"'Pray and dig on,' Elder Cosmos urged his tired men. 'Have faith, brothers.'

"Finally, after many days, one of the men cracked a rock with his pick and the barest trickle came from the ground. A bird landed on the rock and it was hardly enough for the creature to drink. But Elder Cosmos gathered his brothers around him to pray, and because of their strong faith, the trickle became a spring, the spring a stream, the stream a river, until the river carved a great gorge into the Holy Mountain. The monks sang the praises of the Lord: 'Hail the water. Heaven has blessed this land with a river sent from God's own hand.'"

"Ha-ha. You just made this up, right?"

I smile. "How did you know?"

"It's not crazy enough."

We both laugh.

"I'll remember that if I ever try to make up another one."

And I must keep in mind he's not eight anymore; he's eighteen, with a BS Detector that's extraordinary for one so young. "You know, there's another story, a *true* story about another spring on the other side of the Holy Mountain. We might hike past it day after tomorrow. One day long ago Father Athanasius was walking on a trail like this one when—"

"Nooooo! Not another crazy story," Daniel cries, throwing his hands in the air in (not altogether) mock exasperation and scampering below the bridge and down to the river bank. Leaping from rock to rock, he heads downriver.

I descend more slowly amidst the rocks and into the gorge. The story I was told twenty years ago when hiking around Great Lavra rushes into me, fills me to overflowing. I might as well try to stop the river from flowing than the recall of this story.

One day in 963 AD, St. Athanasius the Athonite was out for a walk along a trail on the south side of the Holy Mountain. He was troubled. The founder of Great Lavra faced resistance from longtime ascetics, who were first to settle on the mountain and very reluctant to leave the solitary life, join a community with lots of rules, and help build an enormous monastery. Food was running out and monks were deserting.

Athanasius himself was contemplating packing up and leaving, when the Theotokos suddenly appeared on the trail.

"Where are you going?" the Mother of Our Lord asked.

Athanasius started to explain his rough go getting Great Lavra built and staffed.

"God told you to build a monastery here, and you're giving up just because you're running out of bread and a few weak monks are quitting."

"Well, there were those two assassination attempts."

"Be strong, Athanasius, I will help you."

"Oh dear God," Athanasius replied. He realizes he's talking to a *woman*. There aren't supposed to be any women on the Holy Mountain.

"Uh, who are you?" asked Athanasius.

"I am the Mother of the Lord," she answered.

Puzzled, he rubbed his forehead. "Forgive me, I am often visited by demons who try to trick me. How do I know you are who you say you are?"

"Athanasius, truly I am the Mother of the Lord," she replied with heavenly patience.

Athanasius still had his doubts.

"Athanasius, bang that big rock with your walking stick."

He did, and water flowed from a new spring.

The rock and spring are still there for pilgrims to see today. As for Athanasius, the Theotokos appeared again to encourage him, and happily he recognized her on later visits.

By the time the story ends, my head is as clear as the waters of Xeropotamou and I'm boulder-hopping downriver. I climb to the top of a tall outcropping located in midstream and see Daniel, two cascades down from me, splashing water on his face. I turn on the GoPro and record some video: Daniel on the rocks. Daniel zigzagging from bank to bank. Xeropotamou frolicking to the sea.

Later this summer Daniel will hike the John Muir Trail, 225 miles from Yosemite Valley across the High Sierra to Mt. Whitney. It will be a challenging trek for him but I know he's ready for the high peaks and steep passes with a new backpack, plenty of freeze-dried dinners, and his great sense of direction. And the good company of his buddies Peter and Huck, also trail-wise far beyond their eighteen years.

Daniel climbs to the top of another ledge, where a slender waterfall no taller than he drops to an emerald pool. He looks to the mountain and raises his arms high overhead. In triumph? In joy? In praise?

This is our Xeropotamou. Our river of hope and healing and grace.

It's time for vespers. We shall gather at the river at day's end and give thanks.

For waters still and waters wild, let us praise the Lord.

God is the Mountain, the pines are His fingers, trails the creases in His hands.

God is the River, glorious waters flowing free from the headwaters of His heart.

CHAPTER 20

Forty Martyrs, Four Pilgrims, and a Priest

O God, save Thy people, and bless Thine inheritance. Look upon Thy world in mercy and compassion. Exalt the horn of Orthodox Christians, and send down upon us Thy rich mercies, through the intercessions of our all-immaculate Lady, the Theotokos and Ever-Virgin Mary....

By the time vespers begin, we are all refreshed: Zach by his nap in our room, Spiro by his siesta in the shade, and Daniel and I by our time at the river. Fortunately we are revived, for this is not a sit-and-watch service, but a time to stand up for Jesus, and for all the saints, too.

Monks in motion. They light candles, kiss icons, make the sign of the cross—everything but sit still. Icons, icons everywhere. The monks, a half-dozen laymen (workers at the monastery), and a husky pilgrim from Athens who walks with a limp make the rounds to the icons. Hoping to identify Father Efrem, I look carefully at the faces of the monks, but fail to identify anyone who, age-adjusted, might resemble the novice I met twenty years ago.

Of the holy, glorious Forty Martyrs, of the holy and righteous Forebears of God, Joachim and Anna; and of all the Saints, we pray Thee, O Lord.

Spiro decides that we, too, should make a circuit around the church, and we follow him, looking where he points, venerating what he venerates. As we soon observe, there is veneration and there is Veneration, there is Orthodox and there is Very Orthodox. Our simple cross-making before the icons is no match for the expressions of faith shown by the other worshipers. Zach and Daniel, attending their first church service on the Holy Mountain, are particularly surprised to encounter practices rarely or never seen in their home parishes.

Some monks cross themselves three times in a row and finish with a flourish by sweeping their right hands to the floor. A pilgrim crosses himself twice, bowing each time with his right hand to the floor, then kisses the icon, then crosses himself and bows again. Right next to Zach, a young worker makes a full prostration. He kneels, places his hands on the floor, and touches his forehead between his hands.

"Again we pray that He will keep this holy church and every city and country from wrath, famine, pestilence, earthquake, flood, fire, the sword, foreign invasion, and from civil war, and from sudden death...

Back in the States, we practice a Westernized version of Orthodoxy. By tradition we stand a lot and we kiss a few icons, but we also sit, facing forward, Protestant-style, in pews. Often our priests give sermons that might be delivered from Episcopalian or Presbyterian pulpits, with references to popular culture, business, and football.

Daniel and Zachary exchange *Can you believe this?* looks. By any measure, we are a long way from Saint Athanasios Greek Orthodox Church in Aurora, Illinois, and Saint Barbara Greek Orthodox Church in Santa Barbara, California.

From the way an older monk looks at Zach as he passes by, something tells me Zach's earring is going to get him into trouble on the Holy Mountain. The small silver hoop on his left ear is but the smallest punctuation of style, and would pass unnoticed in most cities and on most college campuses, but here....

Lord have mercy. Lord have mercy. Lord have mercy.

Following Spiro, we pass wall paintings of the saints, medium- and large-sized icons, and regard what is an overwhelming display of more than two hundred portable icons arranged in the sanctuary, the choirs, and all around.

Daniel and I stop—more accurately, we are stopped in our tracks—before a very old and very odd icon of the Forty Holy Martyrs of Sebaste. Measuring about two feet high and a little more than a foot wide, it's divided into two scenes separated by braided rope. The small top scene depicts the *Epitaphios*—the dead Christ lying supine on a pale pink tomb slab. The larger lower section shows the Forty Martyrs in a frozen lake. Above their heads are their gold crowns of impending martyrdom.

Hear us, O God our Savior, the hope of all at the ends of the earth.

Spiro and Zach move on while Daniel and I peer at the details of the work. So much story told by a relatively small icon! The one Christian soldier no longer able to endure the cold heads for a warm bath, while the Roman soldier standing watch prepares to take his place in the icy waters. Up top, archangels Michael and Gabriel fly across a starry sky.

I wonder if the icon paired with the tale of the Forty Martyrs makes the story more—or less—real to Daniel. A powerful merger of ancient art and oral tradition or a crazy illustration to go with a crazy story? Judging by the look on Daniel's face, he's leaning toward crazy; his expression reflects what he has already put into words: *"It's just so…strange here, as weird as the stories."*

I hear the voice before I recognize it. Like earlier this afternoon, when I heard the sound of the river before I sighted it. It's a voice from long, long ago.

For thou art a merciful God, who loves man, and to thee we send up glory, to the Father, and to the Son, and to the Holy Spirit, now and ever, and unto ages of ages.

The voice belongs to a monk standing in the dim light by the altar screen. Middle-aged, his chestnut beard going gray. Oh my God, it's Alex's brother, Dean Trigonis. Make that Father Efrem. Now a full-fledged monk. And not just any monk, but a *hieromonk*, a Priestmonk, an ordained priest who conducts services.

"Father Efrem," I whisper to Daniel, tilting my head toward the altar.

"Chill." He grins. "The one in charge."

I smile and nod. A secular way to put it, I suppose, but spot on. I'm delighted we found him. I knew, just knew, I must begin my second journey to the Holy Mountain where I began the first. At Xeropotamou. With the first monk I met. Father Efrem. It was to Father Efrem I turned for help in order to locate Father Daniel. I poured out my heart in a letter that Alex forwarded to his brother:

> *Dear Papa Efrem,*
>
> *Twenty years ago on a visit to the Holy Mountain I met a monk who changed my life—and eventually the lives of many more people. That monk was named Daniel, he carved icons from wood, and he lived near Skete St. Anna. With your help and blessings, I would like to find Father Daniel, tell him the story of our meeting, and ask him, if he is able, to make an icon of the Prophet Daniel for my son Daniel. Here is a short account of a long and wonderful story....*

Months later, Father Efrem got back to Alex, and he to me, with the briefest of messages: Father Efrem remembers your visit, and there is a monk named Daniel, who still lives near the Skete St. Anna. No other details were forthcoming, but that was enough for me to gain a foothold, as it were, on the Holy Mountain, and buoy my hopes that I would soon locate Father Daniel.

Monks and all the faithful bow their heads as the priest,
Father Efrem, prays in a strong voice:

*"O Master, great in mercy, Lord Jesus Christ our God, through
the intercessions of our all-immaculate Lady Theotokos and
Ever-Virgin Mary, through the power of the precious and life-cre-
ating Cross, of all Saints, make our prayer acceptable, grant us
forgiveness of our trespasses, shelter us under thy wings, drive away
from us every enemy and adversary, give peace to our life, O, Lord."*

Spiro and Zach drift over to join us. "Surprise," Spiro
whispers to me. "Father Efrem's the priest, right?"

"Right," I whisper back as we watch Father Efrem read
by candlelight, sending prayers laden with incense across the
church and around the world.

*"Have mercy on us and on thy world and save our souls, for
thou art good and love man."*

With the shared hope of Father Efrem soon discovering us,
Spiro, Zach, Daniel, and I wait in the courtyard between
the church and refectory in the most conspicuous spot we
can find—next to a ten-foot-high arcade of red marble that
shelters a fountain. As if four Americans, perhaps the only
Americans and native English-speakers on the entire Mt.
Athos peninsula, weren't themselves conspicuous enough.

At dinner, Father Efrem ate with his brother monks while
we and a Greek pilgrim from Athens dined at a separate table
on the opposite side of the refectory. As meals must be eaten
in silence, we couldn't very well talk to him. And unfortunately Father Efrem was seated in such a way that he was
looking away from us, making it difficult for us to make eye
contact with him and for him to notice us. I briefly considered waving at the monk, but remembered that the trapeza is
considered a holy place and my gesture would be judged not
only uncool, but blasphemous as well.

We give glowing reviews to our first meal of the journey,
a dinner highlighted by a hearty and delicious dish of spinach

and orzo, accompanied by white wine and bread, and topped off with a dessert of canned peaches. In quality, the dinner far exceeded my expectations—and made my dire warnings to Daniel about monastery food seem unfounded. He raves about the "spinach-rice thing" and vows to ask his mother to make the dish when he returns home.

"Where do monks go after dinner?" I wonder aloud. Before I can speculate, out of the corner of my eye I see a monk moving briskly across the courtyard toward us. "John," he calls out. "Yannis."

I turn to find Father Efrem. "Father," I greet him happily and with some relief, and beckon my friends and son to draw near. "Father Efrem, this is my friend Spiro, who came with me on my first trip."

"Evlogeite, Father," Spiro asks humbly.

"O Kyrios," replies Father Efrem.

Evlogeite (Bless me). *O Kyrios* (the Lord). I remind myself of the proper pilgrim-monk interchange. Lord knows I forgot this greeting so many times on my previous trip to Mt. Athos. And here I go again, forgetting the ancient greeting at the first opportunity to use it.

"And Spiro's godson, Zachary Deligiannis," I continue.

"Hello, Father," Zach puts in.

"Zachary," Father Efrem says slowly, as if he likes the sound of this name. He turns to Daniel and smiles. "And this must be Daniel. Daniel James."

A bit startled, Daniel smiles back. "Hello, Father."

"Let's take a walk," Father Efrem suggests, and he leads us across the courtyard toward the monastery's main gate.

"A big Greek community in Chicago," Father Efrem begins, talking while we're walking, and directing attention to Spiro. "Spiro, what's your work there?"

Spiro explains how, many years ago he left his big Greek family behind in Chicago to take a job with United Airlines in Hong Kong. But he didn't leave his faith behind, he assures

Father Efrem, who is intrigued to learn that Spiro attends Saints Peter and Paul Orthodox Church located in a suite on the seventh floor of a high-rise office building.

"Are you married?" Father Efrem asks.

"No," Spiro answers. "And neither is my brother. It's very upsetting to my mother."

"I understand. We can't always please our mothers."

I think of Father Efrem's mother, Catherine Trigonis, for more than twenty years a regular at Saint Barbara Greek Orthodox Church. Her oldest son became an orthodontist, her middle and youngest sons became monks. Her husband, in the last months of his life, decided he wanted to die a monk and moved to St. Anthony's Monastery in Arizona. After he died, the widow Catherine moved to the monastery and became a nun. Six months ago I spoke with her after vespers at St. Anthony's.

"I saw your mother at Saint Anthony's," I begin. Almost immediately I regret setting foot on this conversational trail. *He hasn't seen his mother, now a nun, in more than twenty years,* I realize. "She remembered me from church and greeted me very warmly," I say, with a trace of finality, as if there was nothing more to say.

Before things get really awkward, Spiro jumps in with a question: "Father Efrem, why did you become a priest? Not many monks do."

A slight smile crosses Father Efrem's lips. "The short answer is the Abbot asked me to. The assistant abbot is a priest, but very old and no longer able to serve. My only hesitation was my Greek—it's not high level, but the Abbot said my American accent is fine. And he reminded me that we have few monks and much work to do at Xeropotamou."

I think of the monastery's beleaguered guest-master. Likely the Abbot has assigned him many tasks, all more important than dealing with pesky pilgrims without reservations.

"Zachary, what are your plans?" Father Efrem asks.

"I just graduated from college and nursing school," Zach replies. "I'd like to get a job as a traveling nurse. Work three or four months at a time in different places around the country."

"And would you like a family one day?" the monk inquires.

"I don't see myself ever getting married or having kids," Zach answers.

Maybe I'm just imagining this, but Father Efrem's gaze fastens on Zach's earring. To the monks, Zach's earring might be saying "feminine," not "fashion." In a word, "gay."

"Never?" Father Efrem follows up.

"Well, not any time soon," Zach replies, modifying his stance and perhaps mollifying the monk.

We exit the monastery and to my surprise join a dirt track ascending north into the mountains. All of a sudden it seems like we're taking a hike.

Father Efrem turns from Zach to Daniel. "And you Daniel, what are your plans?"

"I just graduated from Santa Barbara High School. I'm going to take what's called a gap year. A year off before I go to college—to work, travel, figure out what I really want to do."

Father Efrem nods his approval. "And you are beginning your gap year with a trip to the Holy Mountain. And a visit to Father Daniel."

"That's the plan."

He nods knowingly at Daniel. "When I came here, a few months before your dad visited, I guess you might say I was on a gap year. The Abbot wanted me to think and to pray for a year, to be certain that becoming a monk was the right decision.

"And Yannis, you're still hiking?"

What a ridiculous occupation I have. But a memorable one. Even a monk who hasn't seen you in twenty years remembers your line of work.

"Yes, I'm still hiking trails and writing about them," I reply.

Father Efrem picks up the pace. The boys soon fall far behind while Spiro and I have to work to stay even with the monk. "The Crisis," Father Efrem says suddenly. "What's your experience of it, traveling around?"

"The Greek people are hurting," Spiro answers. "Especially in the big cities. Especially the young people, who have no jobs."

"The Crisis," Father Efrem repeats. "It's about more than loans and debts and interest rates. More than the way rich countries treat poor countries. Money is all that matters to so many."

All of sudden Father Efrem's words become a torrent, rushing past us, like Xeropotamou after a winter storm. Satan takes many forms, he suggests, and these days may be a secret global conspiracy of corporations and political leaders who want to establish a new world order with centralized economic control. Under such an order, countries will be no more, and the men in control will try to wipe out Christianity. But Orthodox, the most traditional and faithful of Christians, will stand and fight in the battle to come. And right now we must fight against the forces of radical Islam and against creeping ecumenicalism, which might seem like a good idea but could be a trick to bring Orthodox Christians under control of the Church of Rome.

As quickly as it began, the deluge of words stops. And we stop, too, at a bend in the track that offers a grand view of the sea. Here we are, four American hikers in outdoors-wear in various shades of blues and greens and khaki and one American expat in a black cassock, watching the sun sink into the Aegean.

Father Efrem calmly and quietly asks about my family—to my astonishment remembering my wife Cheri and daughter Sophia by name, as if he were a parish priest who sees us every Sunday instead of a monk who last inquired about my family twenty years ago.

"Thank you for writing to me," Father Efrem says.

"Thank you for helping me find Father Daniel," I reply.

"I was very moved by the story of Daniel. And the blessings you received from St. Anna. A miracle."

Zach and Daniel hike up to join us. Father Efrem turns his back on the setting sun and looks into our eyes. "Spiro and Yannis, Zachary and Daniel, may the Lord bless you on your visit to Agia Anna and to Father Daniel, and on your hike around the Holy Mountain."

CHAPTER 21

FELLOWSHIP ON THE TRAIL

As we hike into the hearty heather, my heart soars ever higher. I'm in a zone.

The Mediterranean Zone. Blue sky above, blue sea below, a gray-green flora of high shrubs and low trees all around.

Mt. Athos has the look of the land I love, the brush-covered hills back home. It's as if Daniel and I hiked six thousand miles east on the Jesusita Trail, contoured 'round the world from our home in Santa Barbara at 35 degrees north latitude to the shores of the Mediterranean Sea at 35 degrees north latitude, all the while staying in the same zone.

The Mediterranean Zone. Buckthorn, myrtle, and scrub oak, here, there, and everywhere. We've hiked from the chaparral of the New World to the maquis of the Old World, from Cathedral Peak to the Holy Mountain. We left behind our city in the very rare part of America with a Mediterranean climate of short wet winters and long hot summers and arrived at another Mediterranean land of similar temperature and temperament.

I am Mediterranean by nature, half Greek—the bottom half for sure, with goatherd legs. And I am Mediterranean by nurture, born and raised in the coastal sage.

I am a drought-tolerant hiker, ready to cross any *xero-potamou* (dry river) and trek across any *xero*-scape (dry landscape).

Our trails meander amidst great thickets of lentisk, small trees with small red flowers, deep green leaves, and dark red berries. Also called mastic, it's prized for its ivory-colored resin, harvested by making cuts in the bark. For the last 2,500 years or so, it's provided a smoky-flavored chewing gum (an acquired taste indeed) for the peoples of the Mediterranean.

We hike past arbutus, easily identified by its red peeling bark. Back home we call it madrone. When the trail leads us alongside laurel, I remind my fellow pilgrims that winners of the ancient Olympic Games were given wreaths of aromatic laurel leaves.

I'm fond of the wild olive, the oleaster, a feral form of the domestic olive tree. It rubs up against other plants, a full-fledged member of the coastal scrub community, and distinct from the cultivated olive. It tickles me to imagine olive trees escaping centuries of cultivation efforts and adapting to life in the wild. Other wild olive trees appear to have been wild all along, never drafted, grafted, and pressed into domestic service.

Spiro, Zach, and Daniel are in the zone, too, captivated by the sights and sounds and aromas of Athos. The birds sing and the monks chant, stories are told of holy men and miracle icons, and the sun rises over the Holy Mountain and sets over the Mediterranean Sea.

We hike trails on three sides of the Holy Mountain, from monastery to monastery. Monasteries of the Rocks Trail will deliver us to St. Anna's.

Lord Jesus Christ, Son of God, have mercy on me.

And to Father Daniel.

The footpaths leading out of Karyes and along the east side of the peninsula, like the coastal trails extending along the west side, have been upgraded and are more hiker-friendly (re-routed farther away from roads) now than they were twenty years ago. This pleases The Trailmaster. And trail signage has improved remarkably, thanks to the Friends of Mt. Athos. FOMA trail signs point the way at crucial junctions.

When I return, I shall tell the Friends I appreciate their trail signs and let them know their stern advice posted on their web site about the need for advance reservations for overnight lodging is indeed accurate.

Trail traffic is very light: a half-dozen young Russians and a priest bound for the summit of the Holy Mountain, and two well-equipped Greek hikers heading for Great Lavra. No monks on the trail, that's for sure.

When I was the *Los Angeles Times* hiking columnist, I was quite the exacting trail critic. I reviewed hikes in the ways an art critic reviews a gallery opening or a film critic a new movie. What are the hike's highlights? Shortcomings? What about this venture into nature is worth two or three hours of a hiker's time?

My job is different now: to guide my son and Spiro and Zachary along the trails of the Holy Mountain.

Lord Jesus Christ, Son of God, have mercy on me.

And to lead them to Father Daniel.

And yet once The Trailmaster, always The Trailmaster. When something bothers me about a hike, I just have to let those who may follow in my footsteps know about it. And so it is with the Mt. Athos map I purchased in a Dafni souvenir store just minutes after stepping off the ferry. The cover of the map captured my heart and six Euros with its title and graphics: "Holy Mountain" it reads in Greek and English; "HIKING" it reads in capital letters in English; and hiking bootprints lead across the bottom of the map.

Alas, the map and I got off to a bad start. The map does not show the excellent trail that extends from Xeropotamou to Paneteleimon. I remembered the footpath from twenty years ago and, even had I not, the trailhead was marked by a bright red sign posted by the Friends of Mt. Athos. Hardly a secret pathway, it's been here since Byzantine times, for heaven's sake. Daniel and I had a wonderful time on the trail and it made me angry that other hikers might miss out because it's absent from the only map for sale on the Holy Mountain.

My irritation at the map increased when I examined the map's legend, which appears to have been lifted from a map of some heavily touristed Greek isle such as Santorini, and lists features the Holy Mountain never had and never will, such as an Ancient Temple, a Museum, and a Medical Center.

Why include features in a map's legend when they do not appear on the map and do not exist on the ground? No lakes, ponds, or estuaries are to be found on Mt. Athos. No named or numbered highways, no railways, no bus stops. Cartographer and traveler alike have no need for the icon of knife and fork (restaurant), a bed (hotel), or a red cross in a box (hospital). The only truly necessary icon on a map of the Holy Mountain is a square topped with a cross (Byzantine Monastery).

My rant about the map does not reach sympathetic ears; my companions think me a crank and suggest I forget paper maps and instead use a mapping app on my mobile phone. But no, old-fashioned hiker that I am, I retreat to the 1990 "Holy Mountain" map that served me well on my first hike here. Better an old map that illustrates trails that have faded away than a new map that leaves out trails that can be hiked in the here and now.

From our trailside view of the humongous monastery, we have to wonder: Was Iviron designed as a castle? A fortress it is, with great walls and defense towers. The mighty citadel occupies a bluff next to a brook flowing down into an attractive cove.

We step off the trail and pose for a photo: the four hikers shouldering our backpacks, with bigger-than-life Iviron in the background. Daniel reaches out a long arm to take a groupie. He has the arms for the job—better than any selfie stick—and I can easily edit his arm out of the group picture on my iPhone.

Inside the high walls, Iviron is no less impressive, a mighty compound with a bell tower and sixteen chapels. Surrounding a large courtyard are the cells of monks, a library, guest quarters, a reliquary, and a gift store.

Everything about Iviron is large scale. We are the only visitors to the reliquary in St. Nicholas Chapel, where more than 200 relics of saints are kept in cases. This monastery has the relics of more canonized saints than any other on Mount Athos, and truly it would be an all-day task for a pious visitor to venerate them all. Among them is the lower leg and foot of St. Fotine (pronounced Fotiní), the Samaritan woman whom Jesus met at the well. I shall report this sighting of the saint to my dear godmother Fotine, my most enthusiastic supporter for trips to the Holy Mountain. *Nouna, I saw your saint's left foot and part of her leg.* Maybe I should find a more delicate way to describe my look at the relics of St. Fotine to a classy lady of eighty-five, but maybe not, for she has quite the wry sense of humor.

The gift store offers an overwhelming number of icons in all sizes, half of them with Greek writing, the other half with Russian. I'm pleased to note the store has hiking sticks for sale. For eighteen Euros, the pilgrim can get outfitted with a sturdy wooden staff that is curved shepherd-like at the top. I briefly consider the photographic possibilities of a hiker with a Lord-Is-My-Shepherd–brand hiking stick. Good, but not worth the cost in ridicule I would suffer from Zach and especially Daniel, who would remind me that I should step into the twenty-first century with collapsible titanium hiking poles.

Iviron reminds me of one of those castles in England so popular with tourists. I half expect a National Trust volunteer tour guide, an older gent in a blue blazer, white shirt, and tie, to appear and escort us around.

Instead, we get a middle-aged monk, Father Gabriel by name, who greets us in the church and asks who we are and where we're from. Spiro responds in Greek with quick introductions of father and son, godfather and godson from Santa

Barbara and Chicago. Daniel just graduated from high school and Zachary from college and nursing school, Spiro adds. As soon he finds out we hail from America, Father Gabriel switches to English, which he speaks very well.

"She arrived here in 999 AD," explains Father Gabriel, as he shows us Our Lady of Iviron. "This icon has been responsible for many miracles."

The monk points out what appears to be a scar on the Virgin Mary's right cheek. "According to tradition, when the icon was stabbed, blood miraculously flowed out of the wound. You know the story?"

We look at each other and shrug.

"No, we don't," Zach replies, answering for all of us.

Daniel gives me a look that says: *So you aren't the only one who tells crazy stories.*

"The name of this beautiful icon is 'Theotokos Portaitissa' or 'Mary of the Doorway.'" The icon first belonged to a very faithful Christian woman who lived in Nicea (this was part of the Byzantine empire and now it's in Turkey) in the middle of the ninth century. It was a very bad time for icons, for people who had icons in their homes. The emperor mistakenly believed that images of our Lord and the Saints were idols." He pauses and turns to Zach and Daniel. "Iconoclasts—you know who they were?"

Back in school. Zach and Daniel freeze. Are they supposed to raise their hand before answering? Before they can respond, Father Gabriel moves on.

"Iconoclasts were bad people destroying icons throughout the east. This godly woman of Nicea, she was afraid this special icon of the Holy Mother would be taken from her and destroyed. So she and her friends from the city put the icon into the Mediterranean Sea to save it, with the belief that the icon would travel to a place where it would be safe. When she put the icon in the water, it remained upright and traveled that way across the sea."

Father Gabriel has the engaging lecture style of a good teacher. Zach and Daniel pay strict attention, perhaps in fear that they will be called on again.

"Years later, the monks at Iviron saw a flaming shape over the waters near their monastery. Several of the monks got into boats and attempted to reach the icon, but when they got near, the icon retreated out to sea. At the same time, the Mother of God appeared to the monk Gabriel in a dream. Gabriel was an ascetic, who lived in a cave high on the slopes of the Holy Mountain. The Theotokos ordered Gabriel to go to the seashore and wade into the water—some say he walked *on top* of the water—to get the icon.

"When he brought the icon back to shore he set it on a rock. At once a stream of water flowed from the rock; this stream has never stopped and flows past the monastery today. Gabriel brought the icon back to the church. The monks placed the icon near the doorway and then after a few days installed it more permanently in the center of the church. However the icon had a mind of its own and moved itself back to the doorway. Again the monks moved the icon back into the church, and again the icon returned itself to the doorway. This went on several times until finally the Theotokos appeared again to the monk Gabriel and told him: 'Leave me here! I did not come her to be protected, I came here to protect the monks and this monastery.'

"Years later, Iviron was attacked by pirates. Just as a pirate was about to kill a monk, the Holy Mother stepped in front of him. The pirate's dagger pierced her cheek and blood flowed. The icon dripped blood, too, from the cheek of the Theotokos. The astonished pirate repented of his sins and became a monk, Barbaros by name."

We look up at the doorway of the church and wait for Father Gabriel to continue. After a long pause, when it appears we've reached the end of the story, it's Spiro who breaks the silence.

"And Father Gabriel, you got your name from the monk Gabriel?"

He nods very slowly. "Monk Gabriel is a saint now. I chose the name Gabriel when I became a monk."

No surprise Gabriel was canonized, I think. He was an ascetic, he was visited by the Mother of God, and he performed a miracle. Qualifications enough for sainthood.

"I became a monk not so many years ago," the saint's namesake says.

"Because of this icon?" I inquire.

He shakes his head. A monk is modest. He's not sure he wants to tell his story. I think of urging him on—*So tell us what brought you to Iviron*—but let Father Gabriel decide for himself.

Father Gabriel turns to Zach. "Zachary, in your studies to become a nurse you studied biology?"

"Yes. My degree is in biology."

"I, too, studied biology. In England. Bachelor's degree, master's degree, and then a PhD in Developmental Biology. For many years I did research on mice, using animal models for human diseases. When I was nearing thirty years of age, I prayed to God for guidance. I left university life to go to work for a health agency in England, like your Center for Disease Control in the U.S. When I was nearing forty years of age, I again prayed to God for guidance. I realized that I did not want to work until I was sixty-five. I realized that I wanted to do my best work for God. So that is why I left my job to come here."

Zach and Daniel are surprised and intrigued. And what we all want to know but don't know how to ask is: What's a man of modern science doing telling ancient stories full of events that defy the laws of physics?

"Thank you for sharing how you came here," I begin rather lamely. "You were so recently in the busy world we live in...and your English is so good...you tell the stories of the

Theotokos and of the monastery so that the men who come here understand...." I sputter to a stop.

"The stories," Father Gabriel picks up. "They are hard to believe, maybe, exactly like they happened."

Daniel and Spiro nod.

"Yes," says Zach.

"Yes," I say.

"A wise man said God gave science to us so that we would praise him for His miracles. It's my work now, with the help of the Holy Spirit, to share the stories and share the holy traditions."

Our attention is distracted for a moment by the arrival of a dozen Russian pilgrims at the church door.

Father Gabriel edges toward us, looks into our eyes. "It is your work to take the stories into your hearts, to learn from them, to use them in your own way. And then you must ask yourself: 'What is God's plan for me?'"

The art and architecture, monks and monasteries, flora and footpaths are all so memorable; but perhaps what we shall most remember from our hike is the fellowship. We hike together so well, get along so well. Four Americans in a foreign land, united by our American-ness.

And united in our naughtiness. Once we hike out of sight of a monastery, we wriggle out of our long pants and put on walking shorts. Bare legs are strictly forbidden, but we can't stand the heat. When we near the monasteries, we put our long pants back on.

We bond by our style of worship, which is low key and awkward compared to that of the far more fervent Greek and Russian pilgrims, who know the prayers and who venerate the icons far more vigorously than we. At Philotheou, known to be among the strictest monasteries on the mountain, the monks take us to task. One monk criticizes Daniel for the way he makes his cross: his thumb, index, and middle fingers not tightly enough joined in the trinity, giving the effect of a five-fingered *Catholic* cross. The monk asks Daniel (in Greek) if he is Orthodox. I hurriedly assure the monk "My son is Orthodox," and he responds with a Bible verse and a comment that I don't understand but take to mean: *You're not doing a very good job of raising your son as a good Orthodox Christian.*

Daniel is embarrassed, even humiliated by the experience, as am I, though Spiro and Zach make light of it; and we agree that even if at times Daniel's fingers are more splayed than they are supposed to be, this need not have called his faith into question. No doubt Daniel, superbly coordinated and one of the few high school pitchers able to throw a split-fingered fastball, will digitally adjust; but the monk's criticism of his sign-of-the-cross-making stung him.

Zach, older and wiser than Daniel, and with more experience in dealing with uncompromising authority, is better able to handle the remarks of two Philotheou monks directed at him about his earring: the feminine nature of jewelry, the disrespect to tradition. Zach decides to remove it: two years is enough time to sport an earring, it's causing him nothing but grief on the Holy Mountain, and, more pragmatically, he will be applying for jobs in a few weeks.

Zach and Daniel grumble that the Philotheou monks are altogether too uptight. As for earrings, surely he's not the first pilgrim to wear one. "Maybe," Daniel suggests, "with your beard and earring you remind them of a pirate. The monks have a thing about pirates."

True enough. It seems nearly every monastery has a history of raids by pirates, who came ashore and looted the monasteries. Zach and Daniel begin making bad pirate jokes. *How would the monks react if a guy came into a monastery with an eye patch, a hook and a wooden leg?* "Arrrrrr!" they call out, a little too loudly.

The farther from the monasteries we hike, the louder and more boisterous the young men become. The more meaningful the religious experience we have at a monastery, the more sarcastic and gross Zach and Daniel act afterward on the trail. It's as if there were a Reverence-Irreverence Scale, and the sacred and the profane must be balanced.

It's easy to lead a hike with such strong followers, I muse. Zach is as fit as can be. Baseball season and daily workouts just ended for Daniel, a ballplayer in top form. Spiro is a man transformed, the result of a year-long conditioning program, which culminated in his running the Chicago marathon just before departing for Greece. He has transformed from the pudge I knew twenty years ago who struggled along the trail to a totally buff marathon man. Now, at fifty, he looks better than he did at thirty, with lots more muscle tone and core strength.

I make sure my hikers fill their water bottles at the trail-side springs (many of which are accompanied by religious shrines) and stay hydrated. And I insist they stay fueled, too: in Karyes I purchase plenty of dried fruit, nuts, and cookies to replace the meals (lunches and sometimes breakfast) not offered at the monasteries.

While I'm the trail guide, Spiro is our spirit guide and translator. He talks with the monks and translates for us, adding his interpretation of the ancient art and treasures we view, and of the stories we're told.

As we hiked away from Xeropotamou, Zach teased his godfather about his "Spiro-tology"; we all got a good laugh and the term stuck. We continue to joke about his "Spiro-tuality," but readily acknowledge that we would be quite lost in church and in all matters spiritual and ritual without him.

Sometimes we all hike single-file down the trail in companionable silence. More often, though, we pair off and talk as we walk. Spiro and I reminisce about our last trip, plot how we are going to convince the next monastery en route to let us stay the night without reservations, and wonder how it's going to work with Father Daniel. Will we stay with the monk for a few days and have deep discussions? Or will we share some tsipuro, pick up Daniel's icon, receive a quick blessing, and be sent on our way?

As for Zach and Daniel, the hungrier they get, the more they talk about food; likewise, the longer they are in this world of only men, the more their conversation turns to girls.

Daniel brought two pounds of steak strips to the Holy Mountain (possibly the first pilgrim to do so) and shares them with Zach, who loves them too. The jerky seems to bring out their caveman instincts while supplementing our few meatless monastery meals.

Often Spiro and Zach walk together, and it is heartwarming to see godfather and godson getting to know each other again after a long separation. I like hiking with Zach, too: a good hiker and a great kid, with a terrific sense of humor. As it turns out, he's a fellow Eagle Scout, and our trail talk turns to merit badges, backpacking trips, and summer camps. We are a long way from Camp Napowan, Zach observes with a smile.

I want to bottle this camaraderie, take it with me, and share it with hikers everywhere. Let's raise a glass of Camaraderie Red Wine, aged in oak, with a hint of laurel, and a berry aroma. Let's drink a pint of Camaraderie Trail Ale, malty and full-bodied. Let's sip Camaraderie Tsipuro, with the flavor of the Greek mountains and deep-blue sea.

As Daniel and I hike together, it's a special experience for us to visit places that meant so much to me on my first trip to the Holy Mountain: the café where I so *loved* the gigantes; the Church of the Protaton and the amazing over-the-top frescoes of Manuel Panselimos; and the trails themselves—up, down, and all around the Holy Mountain.

After months of waiting, after a week of travel, after three days of hiking, Daniel is about to meet Father Daniel. He is no longer, as he put it to his schoolmates, "going to Europe," "going to Amsterdam to visit our friend Susan," "going to Greece and hiking around monasteries"; he is going to meet

Father Daniel, who has made an icon for him. As the reality of the trip's mission hits him, Daniel grows increasingly on edge.

To his credit he conceals his anxiety very well. For nearly his whole baseball career D-Mac has batted in the cleanup position, number four in the lineup, always under pressure to produce the big hit, to drive the runners home. He's learned how to manage his emotions, breathe, stay loose, smile, and perform.

"He made me an icon." As expressed by Daniel, those five words are alternately a statement and a question. His conflicting feelings of confidence and self-doubt come out little by little during our long hours on the trail.

He made me an icon. *He*, the rare iconographer on the Holy Mountain who works in wood. *He* could be this amazing undiscovered artist, that's what Spiro says, and the icon *he* made for me could be priceless one day. *He*, who told my father to pray to St. Anna for a son. *He* in the old pictures: on the trail, at his house. *He* made my icon in that studio. But how are *he* and I supposed to get along? *He* speaks only Greek and I speak only English. *He* could be a fanatic about things like the monks at Philotheou. What if *he* doesn't like the way I pray or make my cross? What kind of man is *he*, anyway?

He made *me* an icon. How cool is it that he made *me* an icon? A reward for what I have accomplished in life so far. School was a lion's den for me, but I was stronger than the lions. Despite having dyslexia to the max, I graduated from high school with a 3.8 grade point average and earned a college scholarship. Despite having a baseball coach always yelling 'Jesus F---ing Christ' at *me* and so abusive he was fired at the end of school year, I led the team in homeruns and didn't make a single error in the outfield. Wait a minute, this monk doesn't know *me*, he doesn't know anything about *me*. So why would he spend all this time carving an icon for *me*, a kid who disliked Sunday school because it was school, and spent most Sundays traveling around and playing baseball?

Me with the shaky faith. *Me*, who is so over going to these monastery church services that go on forever. *Me*, who doesn't know what to believe anymore.

He made me an *icon*. How cool is that? Who gets their own special *icon*? I've always liked having the Prophet Daniel above my bed. I can replace the painted one with the new wooden *icon*, no problemo. It's going to be great taking this *icon* and the story that goes with it back home. Except that my head is going to explode if I hear another story about another *icon* of another saint. We've seen the *icon* of St. Christopher the Dog Saint, the *icon* of St. Nicholas the Wonderworker, the strange *icon* of John the Baptist that my dad thinks looks like a hiker. And now we're headed for the end of the trail and the *icon* of St. Anna. When Father Daniel hands me the *icon* of Daniel he made, what am I supposed to do? What am I supposed to say?

Spiro's phone rings again. He's received several calls—from Father Daniel, he guesses, but the calls dropped shortly after hello. Finally, as we pause at a bend in the cliff-side trail, he's able to have a half-minute conversation.

Spiro smiles broadly. "It was Father Daniel," he reports. "He said he is looking forward to our visit. I told him where we're walking and he said he will meet us on the trail, about a kilometer past St. Anna's, at two p.m."

"Are we staying with him?" Daniel asks.

"How did he get your number?" Zach asks.

"Did he say anything else?" I ask.

Spiro shrugs. "That was it. Except that if we're going to be late to please call him on his cell."

CHAPTER 22

ON EARTH AS IT IS IN HEAVEN

At Skete St. Anna, the Wi-Fi is weak but the welcome is strong. Zach and Daniel busy themselves with their mobile phones. They say they are trying to access news of The Crisis, but I suspect they really want to connect with friends and tell them: *You'll never believe where I am.*

Not five minutes after we sit at a picnic table in the courtyard outside the church of St. Anna, a tall handsome, mustachioed man of about thirty emerges from the refectory. Carrying a tray, he glides toward us in the practiced way of a waiter.

"Good afternoon and welcome to St. Anna," he greets us.

"Good afternoon," we return, adding thank-yous as he places the traditional hospitality tray on our table. Refreshment for four: four glasses of water, four shots of tsipuro, and four wedges of loukoumi.

After our long hike, with plenty of ups and downs on Monasteries of the Rocks Trail, it's most pleasant and relaxing for us to sit at the edge of the wide terrace of St. Anna's and enjoy the view of sea. The welcome tray is the same as that offered by the large monasteries, but the welcome is altogether different.

"Is this your first time to St. Anna?" our host inquires.

"For the boys," I answer. "My friend Spiro and I came twenty years ago." I surprise Spiro, and myself, too, by speaking for us. All of a sudden it's easier for me to speak and understand Greek.

"You are the four Americans." It is a statement, not a question.

Apparently, our reputation precedes us. Or my American-accented Greek is a dead giveaway.

"Yes, we're from America," I answer. "Spiro and Zachary from Chicago, my son Daniel and I from Santa Barbara, near Los Angeles."

"Shee-ka-go," he pronounces slowly. "Many Greeks there."

Daniel and I look on with mild disgust as Spiro and Zach each devour a piece of loukoumi. Daniel is plainly impatient. He gets up from the table, paces the perimeter of the courtyard, and peers down at the trail that will lead us to Father Daniel.

"You will be staying with us?"

It's barely a question, more like a statement, with the expectation that we will stay with them.

Spiro and I exchange glances. By now we are gun-shy around guest-masters. We managed to talk our way into overnight accommodation at three monasteries—Xeropotamou, Philotheou and Dionysiou—but it was a challenge, and awkward to say the least.

"Are you the guest-master?" asks Spiro.

He shrugs. "I help with the guests," he replies.

"We have no reservations," Spiro says hesitantly.

"That is not a problem," the assistant guest-master answers quickly.

This is too good to be true. I imagine my five-star review posted on Yelp: *At Skete St. Anna, the Director of Guest Services welcomed us with brandy and sweets. He offered lodging for our party of four even though we had made no advance reservations.*

"We might stay with Father Daniel, a monk who lives nearby," Spiro hedges.

At the word *Daniel,* my son returns to the table.

"You are welcome to stay here the night," the assistant guest-master confirms. "If you want to stay, return before five o'clock."

"Thank you," I say for all of us.

"Tomorrow, we will have many, many monks, but not so many guests," he explains.

Spiro and I shake our heads. Say what?

St. Anna's special helper looks surprised when we look clueless, and even more surprised when Zach and Spiro each take *seconds* on loukoumi and Daniel and I make no move toward the hospitality tray.

"The special service," he announces, his voice rising in excitement, "here at St. Anna is for...." He speaks faster, and I lose his Greek...something about how far we Americans have come, how lucky we are to be here. He mentions The Crisis, the people of Greece, and a service tomorrow night. I think I hear *all-night* service, but am sure I misunderstood.

"Thanks for letting us know about this," Spiro says as noncommittally as humanly possible.

Spiro translates: "He says we arrived at a good time. They have room for us. If Father Daniel doesn't put us up, we can stay at St. Anna. And tomorrow there's a big church service, with monks coming here from miles around, with prayers for The Crisis and the suffering of the Greek people. Apparently this service will last all night."

Zach and Daniel are unable to hide their horror at the prospect of an all-night service.

"Are you kidding me?" Daniel mutters under his breath.

"The Crisis must've gotten much worse," Zach adds, still fiddling with his phone and trying to connect with the outside world.

After an all-day hike up the Holy Mountain tomorrow, no way are we going to an all-night service, I think.

The beaming assistant guest-master wishes us safe travels and returns to the refectory.

"To the Holy Mountain," I toast, raising my glass of tsipuro toward the peak.

"To the Holy Mountain," echo my companions. Daniel downs his tsipuro as though drinking whiskey served at a western bar—a shot of courage before heading for the gunfight at the OK Corral.

Soon after we rejoin the trail, it divides. One branch ascends eastward toward the Holy Mountain, while the other descends westward to the sea and the tiny harbor of St. Anna. At the junction is a trilingual trail sign in Greek, Russian, and English reading: To THE TOP OF MT. ATHOS with a red arrow on the bottom and a red Byzantine cross on the top.

I lead us along the trail to the harbor and try to remember where Father Daniel's cottage is located. If memory serves me, it's about a half-mile hike down the main trail to a junction, with a narrow path splitting off toward Father Daniel's cottage.

The mid-afternoon sun blazes brightly onto outcroppings of white stones that line the trail. Our eyes narrow as we squint into the white light; and when we first spot Father Daniel sitting near the trail junction, it is as if he were posed in an old and slightly overexposed black-and-white photograph: white beard, black cassock, white mountain.

As we hike past the white rocks and the worst of the glare, our view dissolves from black and white to color: Father Daniel's well-worn cassock is not black but a faded dark blue, his beard not white but silver.

I look back at Spiro, then Zach, then Daniel, stepping from the white light onto more shaded ground. Father Daniel stands to greet us, and there he is, after twenty long years, right in front of me. The monk's face is a kindly one, long and olive-colored, with a high forehead, a prominent nose, and a strong chin draped with six inches or so of beard.

"Yannis," Father Daniel greets.

"Father Daniel," I manage to squeeze from a throat gone dry. Seconds later the blessing comes back to me. "*Evlogeite*," I hurriedly add.

"*O Kyrios,*" Father Daniel replies.

"Welcome, Spiro," Father Daniel greets.

"Father Daniel, *Evlogeite,*" Spiro offers.

"*O Kyrios,*" blesses the monk.

"Father Daniel." Spiro signals Zach, who lingers with Daniel ten paces or so up the trail. "This is my godson Zachary."

"Zachary," Father Daniel pronounces in warm welcome as Zach joins us.

"I'm pleased to meet you, Father Daniel," Zachary says in English.

I beckon Daniel, but he stands alone, motionless on the trail. "Father Daniel, this is my son...."

Father Daniel and Daniel walk slowly toward each other. First it's their movements that coincide, small steps on a big mountain. Then it's the colors of their clothing that seem coordinated, all blacks and blues, with the monk in a blue-black cassock and the young man in black T-shirt and blue jeans. And then it's their eyes.

Matching blue eyes. Father Daniel's blue eyes and Daniel's blue eyes sparkle, brighter than the Aegean Sea, lighting up as they draw near. With my own blue eyes I witness a meeting that I have tried to imagine since the day the woman who gave birth to my son placed him in my arms.

"Daniel," Father Daniel greets.

"Father Daniel," Daniel returns.

All of a sudden it's completely silent on the trail, on the entire south-facing slope of the Holy Mountain. Zach and Spiro stand and watch, a Greek chorus observing a drama taking place on this rock-strewn stage against a backdrop of cliffs and the green-blue sea.

Were this theater, the characters would have much to say and a long story to tell—of two mothers on earth, of the Holy Mother of God and the Holy Mother of the Holy Mother, and of fathers, too, and about fate on and off a sacred mountain, and of how a boy became a man.

In real life, in real time, there are no words. And the only action is a smile, a slight one by Father Daniel as he gazes into Daniel's eyes. When Daniel smiles back, the monk nods in satisfaction, turns, and speaks to all of us with a voice that seems to come from the mountain itself: "Follow me home."

I fall in line after Father Daniel, with Spiro at my heels and Zach and Daniel trailing. He leads us up stone steps to join another path. Now I remember the way.

After seeing the Daniels connect, I am profoundly relieved. My backpack feels many pounds lighter than it did this morning when I was hiking Monasteries of the Rocks Trail and watching my son grow ever more anxious with each step we took closer to St. Anna.

"How was your walk?" Father Daniel asks, directing his question over his shoulder at me.

"The path is beautiful," I answer. "The mountain above, the sea below. Spiro and Zachary and Daniel and I—we walk together…very well."

"Very good," says Father Daniel. "And where did you stay?"

"Xeropotamou, Philotheou, and Dionysiou."

Spiro joins in and the three of us gab about the poor cell phone coverage on the Holy Mountain and about the large number of Russian pilgrims, our conversation punctuated by the slap of Father Daniel's sandals and the scruff of our shoes on the stony path.

Compared to the last time I saw it, Father Daniel's livestock pen is much improved, with stronger fencing and a sturdy gate. The enclosure holds two mules, and I wonder what became of the monk's donkey.

Before I can inquire about the fate of the donkey, we reach the back gate of Father Daniel's cottage. The monk unlatches the gate and ushers us onto the veranda.

When Zach and Daniel take in Father Daniel's home and garden, they are all smiles.

"Nice," Daniel comments to Zach.

"This is great!" Zach agrees.

For reasons unknown, Zach and Daniel were unwilling to believe me and Spiro when we assured them that Father Daniel lived alone in a tidy hillside cottage. Really. Instead the two awful-ized, imagining Father Daniel as semi-crazy ascetic in a windowless stone hut, or dwelling in a garret on the grounds of a giant monastery full of stern monks, strict rules, and soul-sapping regimentation.

Instead we have come to the kind of old home still found throughout the Greek countryside, a modest dwelling of stone walls topped with a slate roof and a brick chimney. But the house has its uniquely Athos touches, too, with the round dome of a small chapel rising from the middle of the roof.

On closer inspection, I note a modest addition constructed of cedar and featuring large wood-framed windows. Curiously, the add-on is crowned by the kind of Spanish-style red roof tiles commonly used in Santa Barbara.

"Follow me *home*," Father Daniel said.

And home it is. Green towels and gray T-shirts hang from a clothesline. A half-dozen cats scurry across the deck to greet Father Daniel.

A few neighboring cottages are scattered on the hillside below the monk's garden, but mostly the view from the flagstone patio is of the Aegean Sea extending all he way to the western horizon.

Father Daniel motions to a low wall near his back door. "Please, put your things there."

A funny word, *pragmata*, the Greek word for *things*. Commonly it refers to things such as our backpacks, which we slip off our shoulders and lean against the stone wall. Pragmata also means concrete reality. Leave it to the Greeks to remind us the things we see and touch are only part of the world around us.

Before veering into his kitchen, Father Daniel directs us to a table in the shade.

When he opens the backdoor we see a large pot simmering on the stove, and a savory aroma wafts toward us.

We each select a rickety seat from the mismatched collection of chairs made of wood, metal, and canvas; and Father Daniel soon joins us with a welcome tray: five glasses of water and five of tsipuro.

And no loukoumi.

Daniel and I exchange knowing smiles.

We start with the water, cool and refreshing. Our conversation begins with water, too. With Spiro translating when needed, I explain, in Greek and English, that during our first days of travel on the Holy Mountain I ordered my companions to drink-drink-drink and insisted they fill their water bottles at every opportunity. I then realized that water is available along the trail from springs and fountains, often at shrines that remember saints with pictures and with words chiseled into stone.

Father Daniel nods. "Men have walked here for a thousand years—long before we had plastic bottles."

That gets a smile out of us, as Spiro goes on to describe some of our more memorable water stops—at a little fountain opposite the grocery store in Karyes, one near the church at Philotheou, and another at a seaside shrine to the Holy Mother located outside the walls of Iviron.

We turn to the tsipuro and, following Father Daniel's lead, we sip it slowly—as opposed to tossing it down the hatch as we have before.

This tsipuro is simply delicious.

Zach, Daniel and I look at one another in such wonder that even the usually abstaining Spiro is compelled to pick up a glass.

"Good," I pronounce after the first sip.

This has to be an altogether different brand of tsipuro from the one served at the big monasteries. Every variety we've sampled before this one tasted like medicine in comparison.

Daniel sees Father Daniel watching him drink and my son adds, "Very good."

Spiro takes a sip and smiles as Zach contributes his own review: "Nothing beats this."

As for my palate, I don't know what's on it, but as the tsipuro passes by it leaves behind hints of berries and mysterious Greek herbs. Fennel? Saffron?

"This is the best tsipuro on the Holy Mountain," I proclaim to Father Daniel.

Father Daniel pauses. "It's...good," he agrees, almost reluctantly.

"Who makes this?" Spiro asks.

There is another pause. "This tsipuro...I make it," Father Daniel admits.

A monk is humble.

This tsipuro is a monk in a bottle, prayers in a glass, truly a distilled spirit.

Even a little praise is too much for Father Daniel, and when the four of us begin complimenting his tsipuro, he abruptly stands and asks: "Do you like figs?"

"Yes," I answer for all of us, with perhaps more enthusiasm than my fellows might muster.

"Come, Daniel," the monk beckons, and the two Daniels step into the kitchen. A few minutes later Daniel alone emerges, carrying a tray of fresh figs.

"He's cooking up a big meal," Daniel reports. "Two pots on the stove, vegetables all over the counter, and the table is set for five."

Daniel rests the tray full of halved figs in the middle of the table. We get right to work on the fruit, which proves to be lusciously sweet.

Why not substitute figs for loukoumi on the welcome tray? I muse. Surely figs are mentioned somewhere in the Bible. In season fresh figs are abundant, and dried figs are available all year.

Good Greek boy that he is, Spiro savors every bite, and Zach and Daniel feast away, with fig juice running down Zach's beard and the two of them enjoying some private joke that causes them to act sillier and sillier.

Who decided loukoumi had to be part of the monks' welcome to pilgrims anyway? As the story goes, a sultan demanded that his cooks come up with a candy to appease his many wives, who were always squabbling amongst themselves. The cooks concocted Turkish delight, which quieted the quarreling women and pleased the Sultan. So a treat that soothed Turkish wives in a harem is now served to male travelers by Greek monks? I can't even pretend to understand this.

"Why not serve figs instead of loukoumi?" I propose.

Almost as soon as I pose the question, I realize why fresh figs might not be the best choice of treats in a man's world.

"A week without women and look what happens," Spiro says, covering his eyes with his hands in mock shock, and regarding his godson and Daniel trying and failing to suppress their laughter.

I take another look at the last fig on the plate. Hollow, pear-shaped...red, split at the seams...could there be a fruit more *vaginal* than a fig?

"Never mind the figs," I say, as laughter explodes from around the table.

We manage to compose ourselves by the time Father Daniel rejoins us.

"The figs are delicious," I tell him. "My mother's family is from the Peloponnesus, from a village named Sykea."

Sykea means "fig," Spiro explains to the boys, before turning to the monk. "Father Daniel, where's your family from?"

"I was raised on Zakynthos," Father Daniel replies.

"A beautiful island," I attest.

"You've been there?" he asks.

I nod.

"To walk?"

I nod again. "The Blue Cave, Mt. Skopos. The island is very green."

"Zakynthos is green because so many springs come up from underground," Father Daniel explains. "Perhaps the water comes to the surface because so many earthquakes shake the island and make cracks in the earth."

At this point in the narrative, most monks would tell us about a saint who called forth the waters from the earth after a visit from the Holy Mother, but Father Daniel leaves the waters of Zakynthos as a natural phenomena.

"My mother lived her whole life—ninety-two years—on Zakynthos," Father Daniel continues. "She was a woman of strong faith. On her last day, a Sunday, she was sick, but wanted to go to church anyway. She received communion from the priest, then died. They took her in an ambulance to the hospital, but she had already passed away. I was sad, but at the same time happy for her that the Lord called her from the place where she was most at peace. Imagine: spending your last moments in church."

I can't imagine. And judging from the looks around the table, neither can Zach, Daniel, or Spiro.

"Do your mothers worry about you?" Father Daniel asks.

Now *that* we can imagine.

"My mother always worried about me," he continues. "Did I get enough to eat? Was I warm enough at night during the cold winter? Could she send me a blanket or a coat?"

I think of my own mother, Helen, the good Greek Orthodox Christian who died four years ago on Good Friday. She always worried about me hiking alone on the trail. And I think of Cheri, a fiercely protective Mother Bear of a mom, who I am sure worries about Daniel.

Father Daniel continues. "I wrote her: 'Mother, I am on the Holy Mountain. God provides.' Along with my mother, I was blessed to have teachers of strong faith, and learned much from Bishop Daniel on Zakynthos, a very wise man, who helped my spiritual growth. When I became a monk, I took the name Daniel."

What? Spiro and I look at each other. Twenty years ago, at this very cottage, didn't Father Daniel tell us a long crazy story about Father Daniel the Wilderness Monk? Maybe something got lost in translation. Perhaps he was merely telling us a story and we just assumed Father Daniel took the name Daniel from *that* strange Daniel.

"Daniel," Father Daniel repeats, beaming at Daniel. "Daniel."

My son can't help smiling back.

Father Daniel wants to know all about young Daniel, about school and sports, about his life in Santa Barbara. He asks Daniel in the most gentle way, "Daniel, tell me...."

Daniel, however, is nearly as reluctant as Father Daniel to talk about his accomplishments, and Spiro and I must supplement my son's responses to the monk's inquiries. Father Daniel seems particularly intrigued when Daniel explains that he will be taking a gap year, working and traveling for a year before he goes to college. And the monk is fascinated when Daniel loosens up and describes his next travel experience—a hike along the John Muir Trail through Yosemite National Park and over the peaks and passes of the High Sierra. Father Daniel marvels at a path so long (350 kilometers) and peaks so high (more than 4,000 meters). He has long thought California was like Greece and is surprised to learn part of California is like Switzerland. Daniel promises to send pictures of his journey.

The largest of the cats rubs up against Father Daniel's foot. He bends down, picks her up, and introduces her. "This is Melina." She is an odd-looking creature, all white except for a few brown spots on her back. The top of her head is orange-brown; she looks like she's wearing a wig. Melina purrs contentedly as the monk pets her and she looks at us with half-closed eyes as we tell Father Daniel of our lives and work.

Both Zach and Spiro conclude their accounts with the immediate task of looking for jobs—Zach his first position as a nurse, and Spiro another position in the Far East airline industry. With Father Daniel smiling, godson and godfather tease one another with the suggestion that should his job search fail, he should become a monk.

As for my work, Father Daniel learns all he needs to know with one question: "Yannis, are you still walking in the wilderness and writing books?"

"Yes," I reply.

Father Daniel places Melina back on the deck with the suggestion that she rejoin the other cats, and asks Zach and Daniel to follow him into his garden. In no time, Zach has a basket in his hands and is picking something and Daniel is pulling a hose and opening a spigot.

Spiro and I watch from the veranda as the three tend the garden and to our surprise seem to be *talking*. How can they converse? Father Daniel speaks little English and the boys no Greek.

As Spiro and I sit at the table and ponder this, I have a flash that we've suddenly become the old Greek guys trying to make sense of the modern world at the village kaffenion, where men gather to talk and down cups of coffee and shots of ouzo.

After the garden is watered, Father Daniel leads us upstairs to the guest quarters.

Spiro and Zach are assigned tiny rooms, each furnished with a single bed and a lamp stand with no lamp. Father Daniel gives Daniel and me a slightly larger room under the eaves, with room enough for two single beds placed end to end, and a chest of drawers.

After he checks us in, Father Daniel heads back downstairs, with Daniel following closely. An hour passes and I worry. It seems it's not just mothers who worry. *Are they getting along? What could they possibly be talking about?* For a time

I hear them in the kitchen, then it's silent. I step softly down the stairs. They're not in the kitchen, but I see them out the kitchen window on the veranda, seated close together at the table. Daniel shows Father Daniel pictures on his iPhone. He has a lot of pictures to show, and videos, too, of him playing baseball and riding crazy fast downhill on his mountain bike. There is something about this connection without words between Father Daniel and Daniel that brings a lump in my throat and a tear to my eye, and I quickly turn away from the window and head back upstairs.

After what seems another hour, but is only another few minutes, Father Daniel and Daniel ascend the stairs, and the monk announces that vespers will start in five minutes.

Five men and Father Daniel's prayers fill a church smaller than the monk's kitchen. Zach, Daniel, Spiro, and I stand at four prayer stalls, Father Daniel at a lectern.

The only really large thing in the church is the monk's prayer book, a worn volume with tattered pages yellow-brown with age. Father Daniel reads prayers that praise the Lord and ask mercy for us all. He stands so close, which makes me feel the monk is praying not only for us, but *with* us.

We are not crowded; we are close. Close to the icons on the walls, close to the Holy Mother and Jesus on the small dome just above our heads, close to one another.

Spiro is in deep prayer, and Zach and Daniel are feeling it, too. We follow Spiro's lead and cross ourselves with vigor.

Around us are rows of small icons—a few familiar faces and many that are obscure to us, including St. Artemius, to whom this chapel is dedicated. Artemius helps those suffering from hernias, Father Daniel told us when we entered the church. As he prepared for vespers, he provided a brief bio of the saint: A general under Constantine the Great, Artemius was sent to Egypt to bring the faith and destroy pagan idols and temples. This Artemius did well over the years, but unfortunately a regime change occurred in Constantinople. The evil emperor Julian the Apostate (the one who infamously destroyed the monastic capital of Karyes) took the throne, and the pagan ruler had Artemius beheaded.

Father Daniel fades into silhouette. The chapel's only window faces east and is positioned to receive the first light of day, not the last. As I watch the monk pray, I too fade, into another time, into another place, and I slip from inside a church to just outside of one, from a worshiper to a warrior.

To Captain Yannis, triumphant. On this day, on this hill, near this church, his band of Christian soldiers defeated the Romans. Between tending the wounded and caring for the women and children, his soldiers stride over to thank him for his leadership, for his strategy, for his belief in them. But he knows who is really responsible for their victory.

"Thank the Lord, not me," Captain Yannis tells Tashi the Impaler and his other brave men.

Captain Yannis looks up at the church to find the Saint looking out the window. There he is again, the Saint without a name, the one who comes to him when he is most needed. Many of the men and women pause in their labors and look up at the church, and Captain Yannis wonders if they see what he sees, if they are as fortunate as he to have a Saint, named or unnamed, to guide them.

"Our Father who art in Heaven."

The words thunder across the battlefield from a hundred soldiers praying together.

"Hallowed be thy name."

And continue with one strong voice, Father Daniel's.

"Thy Kingdom come."

Then two voices in Greek as Spiro recites the Lord's Prayer with Father Daniel.

"Thy will be done."

I nod to Zach and Daniel and pray in English.

"On earth as it is in Heaven."

As Spiro nods his approval, Zach and Daniel join me in reciting the rest of the prayer in English, our voices just above a whisper. As we finish the prayer, I see faint smiles cross the faces of Zach and Daniel, and I know what they're thinking: it feels great to participate, to say this most familiar of prayers in this strangest of settings, in a church, at a service unlike any they've ever known or could even imagine.

A few moments later, to our surprise and delight, Father Daniel repeats the Lord's Prayer, and we have the opportunity to pray again in English, this time with increased volume and feeling.

"Lead us not unto temptation, but deliver us from evil."
Amen.

Father Daniel's studio has more windows and far more light than his chapel, we observe as he leads us into the narrow enclosed balcony where he does his work. A row of windows let the light in, and offer us views to the east of the Holy Mountain. The monk's workshop has the pleasant smell of an old-time carpentry shop, of sawdust and shellac.

We converge near the few samples of his work that hang on the wall above his workbench. "These are the saints of the monasteries near St. Anna," explains Father Daniel, pointing to two wooden icons. "St. Paul and St. Dionysios."

Just this morning we hiked from Dionysiou to Pavlou (Paul) to St. Anna along Monasteries of the Rocks Trail. Father Daniel's St. Paul is as plain as plain can be, whereas his St. Dionysiou is a complex character, with wrinkled face and furrowed brow and wearing a cassock made in an intricate checkerboard pattern featuring dozens of tiny crosses.

"And the Panagia," Father Daniel adds, directing our attention to his showpiece. The Holy Mother holds her child close, cheek to cheek, the little arms of young Jesus wrapped around her neck.

We marvel at Mary's eyes, which simultaneously gaze lovingly down at her son and out at all of us. *I'm here for Him, and for you, too*, her eyes seem to say. She is resolute in her purpose and in her faith, but one of her eyes is slightly narrowed in worry, as if to suggest that the Holy Mother, like every mother, can't help worrying about her little ones.

"My mother always worried about me," Father Daniel told us of his mother. The monk has managed to capture a small measure of that maternal worry in his art.

"The eyes are…beautiful," Spiro says.

Daniel is speechless. His excitement is palpable. *He made me an icon.*

"The detail in the wood is amazing," Zach says quietly.

As if to duck any more compliments, Father Daniel suddenly sits at his workbench, busies himself arranging his tools, and beckons Daniel to sit down beside him.

He shows us the basic tools of his trade—a half-dozen finely made chisels with wooden handles that he special-orders from Austria—laid out neatly on his workbench alongside smaller sets of chisels, a sharpening stone, fine-grade sandpaper, and a set of silver-framed spectacles with large lenses, which I gather serve as Father Daniel's safety glasses.

I wonder how Father Daniel learned his craft, and how he learned it so well. "Father Daniel, how did you learn to work in wood?" I ask.

"About forty years ago, after I took my vows, I lived at Simonopetra," he began, with Spiro translating. "I welcomed guests and worked in the garden." Father Daniel pauses, as if considering how much of this story to tell. When he sees that the four of us are looking on with great interest, he continues. "An old monk there worked in wood. His work was beautiful. I had never seen icons carved from wood, and I started helping him. He taught me how to draw an icon with a pencil and how to use the tools. At first I helped him with the backgrounds; and then the clothing, the halo, and the words; and finally, the hardest part—the faces."

He pauses again. "I felt...called to do this. The Lord blesses my hands. When I moved to St. Anna, I began making icons on my own."

"How many monks are iconographers with wood?" I ask.

"I am the only one on the mountain who works in wood," Father Daniel answers quietly.

I am surprised, Spiro shocked, but he quickly translates for the boys. The instant it registers with Daniel that Father Daniel is the *only* maker of wooden icons on the Holy Mountain, the monk stands, reaches alongside his workbench and picks up an icon. Instantly Daniel stands to meet him, their blue eyes meet, and Father Daniel places the icon in my son's hand.

"Daniel," Father Daniel says.

My son warms to the icon instantly. Smiling, he holds it up to the window light. He likes the look of it, and the feel of it, too, as he runs a finger ever-so-lightly over the Prophet Daniel's face and around his halo. The icon is powerful in its simplicity. Prophet Daniel appears more youthful carved in wood than in most of the painted depictions of him, including the one hanging on the wall in his room.

"Thank you," Daniel replies. For a moment, Daniel and Father Daniel stand as still as icons. The monk who makes icons, the young man who holds his latest work, and Prophet Daniel appear to have the same look.

No one is smiling but everyone is happy.

I, too, am happy—for my son, and for the monk who all-of-a-sudden feels like part of our family. I *must* get a better look at the icon, and I step closer, Spiro and Zach right with me.

Carved Daniel is young, but wise looking, too, with dreamy, half-closed eyes and a firm grip on a scroll. From the expression on his face, the tight lips and firm jaw, his faith is as solid as the wood of the icon. And yet there is something altogether mystical about him, too. This is very much the Prophet Daniel, sharing dreams and visions no one quite understood in the seventh century BC, and are still debated to this day.

Father Daniel has signed his work in small letters finely chiseled at the very bottom of the icon: *Monk Daniel, St. Anna Skete.*

I take a few photos of Father Daniel and Daniel with the icon, and then, at the monk's suggestion, we head downstairs and out onto the veranda for more pictures.

In the late-afternoon light, with the sun setting slowly over the Aegean, the icon glows golden and illuminates a Prophet Daniel who appears so very young. He has a mop of unruly hair that seems stuffed under his halo and has little more beard than the young man who holds him.

The three Daniels line up for a photo: Father Daniel on the right, Daniel in the center, and the icon of Prophet Daniel on the left, held in Daniel's right hand. Father Daniel and Daniel are locked in warm embrace, arms around each other shoulders. Even after I finish taking pictures, the two continue to stand close together, their arms around each other, talking together in low voices.

The only word from their conversation that I can make out is "Daniel."

We sit around the monk's kitchen table and feel right at home. After offering a blessing, Father Daniel fills our bowls with soup and we begin to eat and *talk.*

How quickly we have grown accustomed to eating supper quickly and in silence in large dining halls. And how easy it is to return to what for us is normal—conversation around the dinner table.

The monk's country kitchen is equipped with a small sink, small stove, modest refrigerator, cupboards, and a long shelf filled with jars of spices. Father Daniel and Daniel sit at one side of the table, Zach and I at the other, with Spiro, heroically eating and translating at the same time, at the end nearest the back door.

Father Daniel's fish soup is delicious, and after a few spoonfuls Daniel knows the reason why. "Father Daniel likes to fish," he announces, pointing to photos affixed to a kitchen cabinet.

"Yes, yes," Father Daniel says, oddly before Spiro has a chance to translate.

I turn and look over my shoulder at two photos of Father Daniel the fisherman. In one photo, the monk sits dockside and holds up a modest-sized fish on a hook. It's a fish any fisherman would be satisfied to take home and fry–or put in a soup. Father Daniel wears a worn blue-black cassock and has a Thank-You-Lord expression that is neither sad nor happy. In the other photo, Father Daniel is one joyful angler. Clad in crisp black cassock, he stands near the back of a boat, holding a big fish—a whopper—by the tail. With the Greek flag flying behind him, the happy fisherman sports a big smile.

Father Daniel is pleased when Daniel tells him he likes to fish and is positively delighted when Daniel finds a photo of a prize catch on his iPhone and shows it to the monk. In the photo, which I took of him in San Juan del Sur, Nicaragua last summer, he holds up a three-foot-long black-fin tuna that he reeled in between playing baseball games.

Much to our amusement, the two Daniels joke about whose fish is the bigger one, and then Father Daniel asks Zach if he likes to fish.

"Yes," Zach replies.

"Excellent," Father Daniel responds quickly. "Then Zachary and Daniel and the monk will go fishing Sunday after church. We will fish in the waters near the harbor."

"We're in!" Daniel affirms after Spiro translates the invitation for them.

"Spiro, Yannis, I can only take the boys fishing with me," Father Daniel apologizes. "There is only room for three in my boat."

Boat. Father Daniel has a *boat?* Daniel wants to know all about the boat, its size and engine, but before Spiro can translate his questions Father Daniel has a story about his boat that he rushes to tell.

Just as I was starting to sail slowly along with Father Daniel's Greek, the monk jumps into a high-powered speedboat, leaving me in his wake. He will be taking St. Anna in his boat. No, that makes no sense at all. He will be taking the Abbot of St. Anna...out to sea from the port of St. Anna. That can't be right either.

I look to Spiro for help, but he, too, is lost. "Yannis, he's saying something about his boat and St. Anna—I'll try to get the story later."

We enjoy every bit of our soup and I am pleased to note that Zach and Daniel have learned to eat Greek-style and use bread as a utensil to mop up the bottom of their soup bowls. Father Daniel is pleased that the boys take him up on his offer of a second bowl of soup.

Father Daniel is a wonder, a one-man mission, I muse. He catches fish from the sea, grows vegetables in his garden, makes tsipuro in the still in his basement. And he still has time to make extraordinary icons and hold down a full-time job.

"I remember our last visit," he tells me, after our soup bowls and wine glasses are refilled. "I remember meeting you and Spiro the day after you climbed the Holy Mountain. Now here you are, twenty years later, on the day before you climb the Holy Mountain again.

"I remember our talk about the name Daniel. I remember telling you to believe in St. Anna and how she can help those who believe. What I don't remember is receiving a letter from you back then about baby Daniel."

"I am so sorry," I reply, not knowing a better word in Greek to express my feelings. "I sent a short thank-you to St. Anna and a photo of baby Daniel, to you, care of Skete St. Anna. Perhaps the post office...."

Father Daniel dismisses my chagrin with a smile. "The important thing is that St. Anna receives your thanks."

Spiro translates the bare minimum, just enough to keep me on track but likely not enough for the boys to follow; we'll need to fill them in later.

"When you return tomorrow evening from your walk to the top of the Holy Mountain," Father Daniel continues, "I will have a dinner for you, and then we will all go together to St. Anna. Eighty monks will be there, and we will pray all night for God to help fix The Crisis and to help the Greek people."

Spiro shakes his head. Yes, we did hear right: it's an *all-night* service. Wisely, he does not translate for the boys.

Smiling, Father Daniel leans over in his chair and puts an arm around Daniel. "Tomorrow night we will visit St. Anna and thank her," the monk tells my son. "And when morning comes, we will go fishing."

CHAPTER 23

HIKE ALL DAY, PRAY ALL NIGHT

G od never forgets.

The sun rises every day.

But until daybreak, we need a little light to find our way. Adjusting my hiker's headlamp to its lowest setting, I lead us out the gate of Father Daniel's cottage to the trail to St. Anna's. As we file past the corral, the monk's mules snort a farewell.

We carry the last of our food: every dried apricot, cookie, and power bar. And plenty to drink: a water bottle each, plus two two-liter bottles that Father Daniel froze for us and insisted we take.

Today is the Fourth of July, a special day for Americans: Independence Day, the day back in 1776 when America declared its independence from England and its intention to create a new nation. Allowing for the time difference, we will return from our climb of the Holy Mountain at just about the time our friends and relatives back in the U.S. begin to celebrate.

A week ago, it dawned on me that our schedule might be such that we would hike the Holy Mountain on the Fourth of July. With that in mind, Daniel and I located and purchased a small American flag from a souvenir store in Amsterdam.

Just exactly what the only U.S. citizens on Mt. Athos will do with an American flag on our national day remains to be seen, but last night Zach and Spiro were delighted to learn we would be carrying the Stars and Stripes to the summit.

With thoughts of home to the west, we hike east into the gray dawn. By the time we reach St. Anna and the sign marking the trail to the Holy Mountain, our eyes have adjusted to the faintest of daylight, and I turn off my headlamp.

I lead us along a pathway that ascends steeply past outlying settlements. Part mule track, part concrete stairway, the first mile of rocky trail seems designed to test the resolve of the pilgrim and cause him to question himself: *Do I really want to endure sixteen miles of this?*

My eager companions, close at my heels, have no such question. In fact, they are close at my heels, so close I have no doubt what they're thinking: The Trailmaster, the *old* Trailmaster, is setting too slow a pace.

I pause at a bend in the trail and address the troops. "Guys, I use a really low gear and slow pace on a mountain like this. With this pace, we'll make the summit between twelve and one. But enjoy at your own speed. Feel free to go ahead."

"Yannis, you're doing fine," Spiro assures me.

"We're cool," Zach adds.

"You're not *that* slow," Daniel adds.

At my insistence, Zach and Spiro surge ahead at their more rapid pace. I give Daniel permission to do likewise but he says he'll stick with me. "Anyway, we'll catch them."

I smile. My son has been paying attention on all these hikes with me, and now he's thinking like a true hiker: Spiro is in splendid condition, a distance runner, and Zach fit and trim, but neither is used to hiking, with each step a slightly different length and pulling on the muscles in a slightly different way. Daniel and I are *hikers*, as opposed to walkers and runners. And then there is the matter of footwear. We wear lightweight hiking boots, Zach and Spiro running shoes; their feet are going to take a beating on the rocks, and this will eventually slow them.

"I promised Mom I'd keep an eye on you," Daniel adds.

"Mom…you miss her?" I ask.

"I miss her *sandwiches*," he replies. "Soon as we get back I'll have her make a big, bad-ass sandwich. Wish I had one right now."

Sandwiches. Cheri makes great sandwiches for Daniel. She buys the best meats and cheeses and piles them high on fresh bread or rolls. "Make me a sandwich," Daniel orders his Mom. "Make me a sandwich, *please*," Cheri answers. And so their banter begins, often followed by more elevated conversation. Mother and son are closely connected. Love and sandwiches.

"I miss her, too," I say. We reach a little vista point with a cross, and my voice seems to drift out over the Aegean. Cheri has been so supportive of this father-son adventure. I purchased incense and a Mt. Athos cookbook (!) as gifts for her, but I want to bring her back so much more from this place she—and every other woman on the planet—will never see.

And yet I know what Cheri feels, know what she would say. *You already brought me the best gift ever from the Holy Mountain. A son named Daniel. Born on my birthday.*

We hike on for another half-hour or so, then step off the trail for a quick clothing change: from long pants to hiking shorts. I roll up the sleeves of my shirt while Daniel removes his and elects to wear only a bright blue T-shirt. Resting on this background of blue, his silver cross and chain sparkle with the rising sun.

Watching the sun rise over the water is something different for us, we agree. We live and hike on the shore of the sundown sea and associate sun and saltwater with the end of the day, not the beginning. For another mile or so, before the trail turns more northward, it's the sea, not the land, that fills most of the panoramic view.

Up and up and up we go. "Does this trail go anywhere except straight up?" Daniel asks as we ascend out of the Mediterranean zone and out onto open rock-strewn slopes.

"Not much. The monks put this trail in a thousand years ago. Before the invention of the switchback."

Daniel groans.

"It's good practice for your hike up Mt. Whitney," I tell him.

"Yeah, right."

One year I was lucky enough to win a hiker lottery—that is to say I became one of the fortunate few hikers to get a permit from the U.S. Forest Service for a July 4 hike up Mt. Whitney. So popular is the Mt. Whitney Trail that reservations must be made six months in advance.

Hiking to the top of Mt. Whitney, at 14,505 feet the highest peak in the U.S. (outside of Alaska), is a once-in-a-lifetime hike.

And so is the hike to the top of the Holy Mountain.

To pass the time, I tell Daniel about the two mountains. From the trailhead to the top of Whitney is a hike of about eleven miles with an elevation gain of six thousand feet. We will gain six thousand feet in elevation as well to reach the top of Mt. Athos and do so in fewer miles than the climb to the summit of Whitney. The high-elevation ascent of Mt. Whitney is a challenge to the lungs; the ascent of the Holy Mountain a challenge to the legs.

Mt. Whitney Trail, with one hundred switchbacks hewn out of granite slopes, is one of the finest examples of the trail-builder's art in the entire world. And Mt. Athos Trail? Well, let's just say the workmanship of the Byzantine trail crew was not the best.

We catch up with Spiro and Zach and continue the climb in good fellowship that takes our minds off the stiff climb and rocky trail. We discuss how we can possibly stay awake during the all-night prayer service at St. Anna's and the reaction of our friends and family when we relay a photo of the four of us standing atop the Holy Mountain with an American flag.

We can't say enough about Father Daniel, "a totally chill guy," in the words of the boys: our conversations around his kitchen table, vespers in his chapel, work in his garden. And his *boat*. Zach and Daniel get to go fishing tomorrow with a monk!

The natural beauty of the mountain enchants us. Spiro, especially, is taken by the many varieties of wildflowers that flourish at every elevation. I'm able to identify purple anemone, pink and white cyclamen, and a few more for him, and wish I could tell him the names of the many other blooms we see.

Daniel really likes a mile-long section of trail that leads into gentle woodland of chestnut, oak, and beech. Zach's magical moment in nature comes when a butterfly with a blue streak and gossamer wings lands on the ring finger of his left hand. He holds it up, chest-high to take a closer look. Surprisingly, the beautiful creature doesn't fly away, and Zach continues hiking with the butterfly for a few more minutes before it takes flight.

Heal us O Lord in Your Nature.

Daniel and I surge ahead as Spiro and Zach fall behind to talk, and by the time we spot the cross atop a high promontory near the Panagia Chapel I estimate we are at least a half-hour ahead of them.

"Hey, Saints grow on trees up here," I call out, pointing to the trunk of a tall black pine. On closer inspection they're not saints but baseball-card-sized photos of elder monks wedged in the wide fissures of the bark. I particularly like the photo of a fellow with a white beard and black cassock, posed with his walking stick on a mountain trail. I don't know who he is, but he appears to be a happy hiker.

Daniel peers over my shoulder at the photo. "A couple more years on the trail, and you'll look just like him."

"Hey, look who's out in front."

"Zach and Spiro—they got tired of following—you walk so slow. Or they have a lot to talk about."

"Your dad's secret, The Trailmaster advantage: he can walk and talk at the same time."

"Mom says that's your only talent."

"She's right."

Panagia Chapel has undergone a major makeover since last I visited. It's Panagia Refuge now, a Euro-style hiker's hut offering a dorm room with iron bunks and mattresses, a community room with a fireplace, and a well with clear cool water.

After paying our respects to the Holy Mother in the adjacent chapel, we exit to the stone courtyard.

We decide to wait for Zach and Spiro, drop our packs, and take a seat on the low wall on the south side of the courtyard. To our right is an oh-my-God vista of the Holy Mountain and the clouds floating above it, and to our left a commanding view over the blue-green Aegean.

If ever there was a place for a Big Talk, this is it. The setting makes me think of the courtyard of St. Anna and of Gerontas, the elder monk who preferred to take pilgrims outside for a view of Holy Mountain when he offered his spiritual counsel.

During our travels together, I have purposefully avoided having a Big Talk with Daniel, especially one beginning with: *So kid, now that you graduated from high school, what are you going to do with the rest of your life?* Instead, we talk about cars, trucks, and baseball, and why we like Dutch beer and dislike Turkish delight.

I feel no need to have a Big Talk with my son about faith. The way Daniel connects with Father Daniel, the way he held the icon, the eagerness with which he looks forward to fishing with Father Daniel…he has a spiritual father now. Apparently, they have Big Talks without speaking.

Anyway, when it comes to fathers and sons, why have a Big Talk together when you can have a Big Walk together?

Panagia Chapel is the latest in a long series of encounters with the memory of the Holy Mother, I muse. "I was just thinking, here we are on this mountain without women, and the monks make so much of Mary."

"That's for sure."

"She came to St. Athanasius when the whole monastery thing was just getting started here. Then we saw the icon of Panagia Sweet Kiss at Philotheou—"

"Where the monks told me I was crossing myself wrong," he interjects.

Wow. That was just about our only prickly encounter with the monks, but it's going to take Daniel a while to get over it.

"And then there was the icon of Theotokos Portaitissa (Mary of the Doorway) at Iviron that Father Gabriel told us about."

Daniel grimaces slightly and points to the chapel. "And let me guess there's a story about this Mary."

I nod and try to keep a straight face. "As a matter of fact there is. And it's a long story." I gesture down the mountain. "But it looks like we have plenty of time before Spiro and Zach catch up to us."

We can see more than a half-mile of trail leading up to Panagia Refuge and the Deligiannis contingent is nowhere in sight.

"It was about a thousand years ago when a monk climbed the mountain to this very spot…"

"Really?" Daniel interrupts, rising to his feet in exasperation.

"Not really," I say with a grin.

Daniel realizes he's been fooled.

"There probably is a long story, but I don't know it," I confess, unable to keep the laughter out of my voice.

"Ha-ha." He grins back and pretends to push me off the wall. "You sit here and wait, I'm going to check out that hill."

Daniel strides toward the base of the distinct promontory nearby. Minutes later, he's ascending the pathway to the cross.

That's my boy.

A young man, really.

This growing up, it happens so fast. Every parent must feel this way. All of a sudden our sons and daughters have minds of their own, lives of their own.

Story time is over.

For a moment my heart beats faster and my breath grows short, as if I were hiking hard at high altitude near the top of Mt. Whitney.

It was just yesterday when I read my son *The Lion, the Witch and the Wardrobe*, a story about four children and their adventures in Narnia, a land of talking animals and mythical creatures, the White Witch and Aslan, the great lion. And then time passes, all too quickly, and we have to read things differently: Aslan is a king mocked and scorned, who sacrifices himself to save the kingdom, who dies for our salvation, and his body is discovered to be missing from where it had lain.

I remember fondly the first time I read the story to Daniel and miss that innocent time when Turkish delight was just a candy, the witch just a witch, and the lion just a lion.

Daniel does not linger long on the summit of the promontory, and almost as soon as I take his picture, he is back to Panagia Refuge. Zach and Spiro rejoin us, and all together we head for the top of Mt. Athos.

I set a slow and steady pace for my companions along the ancient stone path. We ascend past great blocks of cracked marble—not the ruins of a kingdom long gone but the raw materials of a city never built. What we now call Classical Civilization never reached here, thank God. The Byzantines preserved this mountain for prayer, and pagans stayed away. Other faiths and factions made their history elsewhere in Europe. This place remained an Empire of Rock. Only ascetics lived on Athos, taking nothing from the Holy Mountain but rocks for pillows, clouds for blankets.

Lord Jesus Christ
Have mercy on me.

The Jesus Prayer gets shorter with my breath.

Our fellowship is a quiet one, limited to a few observations shared when we stop to drink water and catch our breath: appreciation for the yellow flowers surviving in the fields of rock, for the quiet beauty of the mountain, and how great it is to be an American hiking the Holy Mountain on the Fourth of July.

No visions for me this time on the mountain. Captain Yannis does not return.

Lord Jesus Christ
Have mercy on me.

I try to synch the Jesus Prayer with my steps along the trail. But I cannot. My mind wanders to my companions, drifts to my loved ones back home, and travels along the trail as it climbs relentlessly over the rocks.

I cannot walk like a monk with unconditional surrender to the grace of God.

My poor thoughts are interrupted by the sound of machine-gun fire coming from the top of the mountain. For an instant I imagine I've walked into a World War II movie, American marines charging a Nazi machine gun nest at the top of a hill. But no, it's not my imagination. Zach and Spiro and Daniel hear the sound too.

We see no signs of warfare, but hear a very loud and rapid rat-a-tat-tat coming from near the cross at the peak. When we reach the summit ridge, we still can't see the source of the unholy racket. Only when we reach the very top of the Holy Mountain and the Church of the Transfiguration do we see who's making the noise and how.

A monk with a jackhammer.

We burst into laughter, certain that the monk and two lay workers laboring with him can't hear us.

We draw closer and discover the Church of the Trans-figuration is closed and a new church is under construction. Fortunately for us, it's lunchtime, and after a few more minutes of chiseling away at old cement, the monk shuts down his jackhammer, and he and the workers adjourn to the far side of the construction site.

We spread our feast under the cross: lemon cookies, choc-olate cookies, cashews, dried apricots, power bars and steak

strips. We wash it down with iced coffee, which Daniel prepares with a package of instant coffee and Father Daniel's still
almost freezing bottles of water.

Then it's picture time: Holding to the big iron cross,
Spiro and Yannis, posed just as they were in the pictures from
twenty years ago. And then father and son, godfather and
godson. Finally the four of us, with the camera on Daniel's
phone set on time delay—time enough for him to leap back
over a big rock to join us in the group picture.

We can't help taking pictures of the view, even though
we can't possibly capture what we see—the entire Mt. Athos
Peninsula extending to the mainland, roads and monasteries,
fields and forests. We raise the American flag and take more
photos of each other. Happy Fourth of July from the Holy
Mountain.

When the monk resumes his jack-hammering, we depart
the summit. Shouldering our packs, we spontaneously make
the sign of the cross and head down the mountain.

It occurs to me that, allowing for the time difference, it
is now just about the time our friends and relatives back in
the U.S. are waking up to celebrate the holiday with lots of
noise: baseball games, barbecues, hometown parades, and
fire-crackers. We have had a loud Fourth of July too, with
noise provided courtesy of a monk and his jack-hammer. *How
would the 1812 Overture sound with jackhammers substituted
for cannon?* And for the millions of Americans who like to
hike, Independence Day is a day to enjoy a trek into America the Beautiful. We Americans abroad have enjoyed a hike
today too—a hike we'll never forget.

The heavens are aglow with stars, and we have little need for
my hiker's headlamp as we follow Father Daniel along the
trail from his cottage to the church of St. Anna. In the western sky the two brightest planets, Venus and Jupiter, appear so
close to each other that they seem to be touching.

Sirius shines so brightly it appears to illuminate the church courtyard, where a dozen monks warmly greet one another. There is a buzz in the air, like that around eager concert-goers awaiting the start of a performance.

A service like this one directed to The Crisis is special, Father Daniel explained. On the Holy Mountain, each day of the liturgical calendar is full, even crowded, with remembrances of saints, martyrs, and miracles. In a place where tradition is everything, a service held in response to *current* events is unusual to say the least.

"At the end of the service we will celebrate with a meal," Father Daniel tells us as we spot two workers lugging boxes of string beans across the courtyard and into the dining room.

I wonder: What are we *celebrating?* People all over Europe, including the monks, refer to the dire situation in Greece as The Crisis.

The buzz follows us into the narthex but does not light the way. It's darker than night inside the church of St. Anna. We can see only the distant glow of oil lamps and the icons they illuminate. Spiro, Zach, Daniel, and I stumble after Father Daniel, pause to venerate icons of saints we don't recognize, then trail after him to four empty prayer stalls. Father Daniel greets a brother monk and the two fade into the darkness.

After we stand awhile, our eyes adjust and we can make out more detail. First, the saints' faces; what little light there is in the church spotlights the icons of the saints—particularly concentrating on their faces. A few moments later, we are able to see more saints looking back at us from the frescoes painted on the walls and pillars and gazing down at us from the icons on the altar screen. Lastly we see the men in black (Father Daniel's estimate of about eighty monks in attendance appears quite accurate) and fellow civilians—perhaps a combined total of twenty pilgrims and workers.

Vision restored, I scan the interior for the monks praying and chanting. I finally locate the voices when I see a lamp lowered via a pulley and come to rest just above a tight circle of monks. The reading lamp has a cone-shaped shade so the light is directed downward, not outward.

No light is wasted.

The reading lamp is lowered close to the prayer books when needed and raised and dimmed when not.

Over and over again.

As the monks pray and pray and pray.

We are rubber-legged, exhausted from our hike. I wonder how—or if—I can snooze for a while in the prayer stall, a solid oak piece with high sides and back and a low narrow seat. We took Father Daniel up on his offer of Nescafé before we hit the trail for St. Anna, but the coffee has no stimulating effect on us, and by the end of the first hour of the service, we are fighting a losing battle to stay awake.

Especially during this most wordy of worship services.

Is there a simple way to express the sacred? Can extra adjectives and adverbs be removed? Can a generalized prayer be made for "all the peoples of the world" rather than so many specialized ones for government and church leaders, for so many poor souls with such a variety of afflictions—not to mention protection from evil in a dozen guises and perils to travelers on land and sea?

If the answer is "Yes," then this is *not* Orthodox prayer. In worship, more is always more and never less.

The original liturgy is said to have been five to six hours. We must be using the original prayer book for that liturgy, I decide.

Near us, occupying another row of prayer stalls, are half a dozen Russians. A Russian lad about the same age as Daniel is fast asleep, as are his older brother and father.

Zach is the first of our party to doze. Standing, then slumping, then half-sitting in the prayer stall to my left is Spiro. Behind his glasses, his eyes narrow to slits, then close.

I suspect Spiro has succumbed to sleep, but knowing my devout friend, he could also be, like the monks around us, in a state of deep prayer.

Daniel stands firm in a prayer stall built for a skinny, elderly monk, not a broad-shouldered young man like him. As if resenting its confinement, he stands in front of it. Daniel understands none of the service, but you wouldn't know it from looking at him. His eyes follow the dozen priest-monks conducting the service and he makes the sign of the cross, at the appropriate times, in unison with the monks.

I point to Zach and the sleeping Russian pilgrims and whisper to Daniel that it would be okay for him to close his eyes and rest for awhile, but he shakes his head. Daniel keeps an eye on Father Daniel, who is difficult to distinguish in the darkness amidst the other monks.

And apparently Father Daniel is watching over Daniel.

Lord Jesus Christ
Son of God
Have Mercy on me.

The Jesus Prayer sent and delivered. I feel it, vibrating through the armrests of the prayer stall, traveling from my elbows to my heart, even as I am about to fall asleep. Judging by the way Daniel stands so strong, he must be receiving the transmission, too.

Every hour or so the good shepherd Father Daniel returns to check on his flock of four. Especially on Daniel. Father Daniel and Daniel. A connection without words. A connection beyond words. Unconditional love.

With Father Daniel standing watch over my son, I can rest easy now. Nevertheless, I fight sleep, listening with little comprehension to the prayers and the long readings of wisdom from the elders. On and on it goes. I wonder, half seriously, if the monks are going to pray for each and every one of the eleven million Greek people by name.

Eyes all but closed, I see in poor focus a familiar-looking monk in the faint light: Gerontas, the elder monk who greeted Spiro and me at St. Anna's twenty years ago. It can't be him, I argue with myself. He would be more than a hundred years old. It must be another Gerontas. It must be.

The old monk stops before the flickering candles at the altar. He crosses himself before each icon. Increasingly, the younger monks and the novices have been taking over the work, just as he assumed the duties of the old monks when he first came to the Holy Mountain as a young man.

He came to Agion Oros so long ago, back when the world was at war. It seemed the world was still at war. Every month or so when he picked up a Greek newspaper a pilgrim had left behind, he read the report of yet another war.

When he was a young man, few pilgrims managed the arduous journey to the far end of the peninsula to St. Anna. He and the other brothers always sent the pilgrims to the old one, the wise elder, Gerontas, for spiritual counsel and to share the stories of the saints. Nowadays the younger monks sent the pilgrims to talk to him.

He was the Gerontas now.

He lingered before the icon of St. Anna, that wise woman who held her daughter Mary close.

St. Anna's was not a monastery but a skete, a dependency of the Holy Monastery of Great Lavra, he explained to the pilgrims. It was founded in order to preserve the left foot of St. Anna, the mother of the Virgin, brought to the Holy Mountain by monks in 1686. The church was built in 1754 and dedicated to St. Anna.

When he stepped out of St. Anna's into the bright morning, two men intercepted him in the middle of the church courtyard.

"Your blessing," the two men said in unison.

"The Lord blesses you," he returned.

"We've come to St. Anna's because..." one of them began before his voice faded away.

Few could admit why they came here. Sometimes it took days for a man to admit why he came to St. Anna's. Sometimes men came and went without knowing why they came.

When he told the story of St. Anna, he liked to seat the pilgrims on a bench at the edge of the courtyard. He liked to stand as he spoke and look up at the Holy Mountain. Always, even when it was nearly obscured by clouds, the mountain inspired him.

The mother of Mary was born in Bethlehem. Anna was married in Galilee to Joaquim, a shepherd from Nazareth. They loved each other very much and prospered when they moved to Jerusalem. Joaquim owned a large flock of sheep. When Joaquim was chosen to supply the temple in Jerusalem with sheep from his flock for its sacrifices, his business increased greatly.

Over the years, the love between Joaquim and Anna grew stronger and deeper. In so many ways, their lives were blessed. Except something was missing.

A child.

After twenty years of marriage, they had no children. They prayed long and hard. Day after day, year after year. When they entered the temple, each pleaded with God for help. But no help came. No child came.

Once, when Joaquim came out of the temple, some men laughed at him for not being able to father a child. "What kind of man are you?" they ridiculed.

Hurt, his pride shattered, Joaquim walked into the hills, past his flocks of sheep, past the most remote pasture, into a hidden mountain meadow. He cried out to God, told the Heavenly Father of his unbearable pain, of the emptiness in his heart.

After he had spent many days alone in the wilderness, fasting and praying, an angel appeared. The angel came in a burst of light so dazzling, so bright, that it frightened Joaquim.

"Don't be afraid," the angel told Joaquim. "The Lord sent me to tell you that God has heard your prayer. He knows you are a good man and your wife, Anna, is a good woman; and He knows of your years of sorrow for having no child to raise. God gave a child to Abraham and Sarah, who were so very old, so much older than you and your wife."

Joaquim stopped trembling. He stared bravely back at the burning light of the angel.

"You will have a daughter. And she will be named Mary. And Mary will be filled with the Holy Spirit from Anna's womb and will devote her life to the Lord. Go now. Walk back to Jerusalem and meet your wife at the city gates. Soon your heartbreak will become joy."

Meanwhile, Anna was very worried about her husband, who had disappeared in the hills and had been gone for many days. Lost in thought, she walked to the edge of the city, where trees grew along a river. It was springtime and flowers were in bloom. She looked up to see two sparrows building a nest for their young. The birds making a nest for their babies reminded her of her deep sorrow at being unable to bear a child. God's punishment, she thought. But she had so struggled to be a righteous woman. Why would God punish her in this way?

"O Lord, birds make nests for their young and are blessed with baby birds. All the animals of the earth and the fish of the sea are blessed with more of their kind to care for. And yet the years pass, twenty of them, and I cannot conceive, I have no baby to hold in my arms, no child to raise."

Quite suddenly, an angel appeared before her, the same angel that had appeared to Joaquim. The riverbanks and the willows seemed to be on fire. She shielded her eyes and fell to the ground in fear.

"Rise Anna. Do not be afraid," the angel said. Then he told her what he had just related to Joaquim. "Return now and meet your husband at the Gates of Jerusalem."

Just as the angel promised, Anna and Joaquin had a daughter and they named her Mary.

"Of course you know the story of Mary," Gerontas concluded.

"Yannis," Spiro whispers.

The pilgrims of today aren't like the people who lived at the time of the Savior. Men today ask for God's help last, not first. "Begin by trusting in God to help you." He gestured toward the church door. "And by praying for St. Anna's help."

With a grin, Spiro nudges me with his right elbow. "Yannis, you might want to wake up and hear this. The Crisis talk."

"Good morning, Sunshine," cracks Daniel, nudging me with his left elbow. Zach hears Daniel's salutation and wakes up.

From where could Daniel possibly have gotten his sarcasm? Blinking away my dream, I listen to the monk speaking from somewhere in the front of the church. It's hard to locate The Crisis speaker in the dim light.

Cranky upon waking, I have the ridiculous and blasphemous urge to take the hiker's headlamp out of my pocket and use it to locate the sermonizer. On high-beam mode, the headlamp can reach seventy meters. Three tiny AAA batteries produce the same intensity as two hundred candles in this church. I could really light up this place.

The monk's sermon about The Crisis, delivered at modest volume and in rapid Greek, is impossible for me to follow. I catch only the occasional word: *God, Greece, sin, mercy, St. Anna, crisis, St. Gregory, money, light, Theotokos, evil, Jesus.*

After fifteen minutes, the sermon ends and the prayers resume. We happily agree to Spiro's suggestion that we step outside.

"Halftime," Spiro announces as we sit at picnic table in the courtyard under a canopy of stars.

We groan in response. It's one-thirty in the morning. So maybe we really are only halfway through the service.

"Daniel, good job staying awake," Spiro says. "I don't know how you do it."

Daniel nods, but says nothing.

"No service," Zach announces.

At first we think he's referring to The Crisis Service but soon realize he is referring to the No Service indicator on his smart phone. We are but ten feet from St. Anna's Wi-Fi hot spot, which is clearly spelled out in English letters on a sign affixed to a courtyard wall. Apparently it's not working this evening. Or it's turned off for festal services.

"I was hoping to get news of The Crisis," Zach explains.

"How do the monks see The Crisis?" I ask Spiro. "I didn't understand much of the sermon."

"In the sermon, if you could call it that, there were readings from St. Gregory Palamas," Spiro answers. "You know he's big deal on the Holy Mountain."

The boys are baffled.

"Fourteenth century," I fill in. "Left behind a wealthy family in Constantinople to become a monk. Big time promoter of silence, meditation, the Jesus Prayer."

"So St. Gregory is all about sin and repenting for your sins." Spiro pauses. "Guys, I'm not sure I got this right."

"Just give us your own Spiro-tuality," Zach teases.

We all laugh, Spiro included.

"St. Gregory says, 'Hate sin and love virtue. Godliness is not in our words but in our actions.'"

Isn't that what every monk says? I muse.

"Maybe we should just pray for the Germans to have a little heart and call it a night," Zach suggests.

Amen to that idea, we all agree with a laugh. Pray for the German bankers to forgive the Greeks their debts. In exchange, the Greeks could offer free drinks and free beach chair rental for all German travelers to the Greek isles.

"No surprise, there was a lot of discussion about sin," Spiro goes on. "The monks go all the way back to Adam. Because of Adam's disobedience, we got all these issues passed down to us—sin being the big one."

Zach frowns. "So we're supposed to feel guilty because—"

"No guilt," Spiro says quickly. "Don't confuse us with the Catholics. It's not about beating up on yourself over Original Sin."

Spiro pauses to gather his thoughts and continues, much to our appreciation, to share his Spiro-tuality. "The monks, and the Greeks, too, have a different way of looking at sin. The Greek word is *hamartano*. I sin. But it's not capital S kind of Sin. The ancient Greeks used *hamartano* to describe an archer missing the target. When we sin, we miss the mark. We miss the mark, do wrong, sin against others. And we miss the mark with God."

After Spiro's homily about *hamartano*, we stand, stretch, and return to our prayer stalls. We are too tired to think about any more theology, even Spiro's simply put Spirotology.

I'm too tired to contemplate any secular issues either, but I can't help wondering: how can The Crisis be resolved when the disputing parties don't even share a common definition of crisis? *Krisis* is a Greek word. To the Greeks, The Crisis is an intolerable situation, an extremely difficult, even desperate time of great disagreement, uncertainty, and suffering. From the perspective of European Union political leaders, The Crisis is all about money: bankruptcy and banking panics, disorderly functioning of the marketplace, interest rates, currency collapses, debt servicing, and defaults.

Here on The Holy Mountain, even as we pray for the resolution of the bitter dispute between Greece and the European Union and relief for the suffering of the Greek people, it seems The Crisis is really about our estrangement from God, dating back to Adam's fall.

I am far too tired to contemplate anything like this. I watch Zach's eyes close. Back inside the church, Spiro leans back in the prayer stall, asleep or in a deep meditative state. Daniel is defiantly awake. He moves his feet, stepping forward and back. This comes from his many years as a ballplayer. An outfielder must always be ready to make a play, and that means taking a few steps on the grass before every pitch, never standing flat-footed.

The Orthodox athlete and his dad stare out at the lights. Suddenly, as if on cue, as if the monks know it's time to wake up those sleeping pilgrims, the light show begins. Star of the show is the *horos*, a beautiful Byzantine chandelier that hangs by eight chains from the perimeter of the dome. It's like an ornate circular picture frame, and when you look up, you get a clear, candle-framed view through the horos to the dome and its many icons.

A young monk carries a long pole, with what appears to be an ancient socket wrench at the end of it, over to the horos. He inserts the tool in the base of the chandelier and gives it a swing. The candle-laden horos twists back and forth on the chain.

The effect is hypnotic. A river of light.

Daniel's eyes are so glassy they reflect the light. He sways, just a little, holds to the armrest of the prayer stall to steady himself. The slightest of smiles crosses his face when he sees Father Daniel approach. The monk beckons Daniel to follow him, and the rest of us to follow Daniel.

We walk around a pillar and there she is: St. Anna. I know the icon, and Spiro does, too. And we exchange a look: *Here it is. A moment we've been waiting for.* But Daniel's attention is focused on Father Daniel, and besides, a large Russian pilgrim, a bear of a man, steps in front of us and partially screens St. Anna from our view.

Father Daniel gestures to the icon and, Daniel turns to it. My son looks baffled, turns to me for help. I get in line behind the big Russian, leaving a space for Daniel and gesture for him to get in front of me. The Russian completes making his cross and walks away, giving Daniel an unobstructed view of the icon. Daniel looks up to see a mother and child, lit by the warm glow of an oil lamp. Only this isn't the usual mother and child, not the Holy Mother and Jesus icon that he has seen so many times, not one of those Holy Mother icons that work wonders. In the icon, where Jesus is supposed to be…is a girl. He takes it all in, hesitates until he sees the pictures of babies arranged near the icon. And then Daniel knows, just knows, who's in this icon. Instantly after this realization, he takes off, as if at the crack of a bat meeting a baseball. Daniel strides forward quickly, charges St. Anna, makes a quick sign of the cross, kisses the icon and steps away. He stands close to Father Daniel and looks back at me.

I can't help hurrying my veneration of St. Anna. Spiro and Zach move quickly to and from St. Anna as well. We want to see the three of them together.

Father Daniel, Daniel, and St. Anna, her eyes shining in the flickering light.

With Daniel trailing him closely, Father Daniel takes the long way back to our prayer stalls. After so many hours in the darkness, we stumble no more. Now, as Father Daniel takes us on a circle tour, there seems to be plenty of light inside the church. Light reflects off polished brass and silver, and off the gold halos of the saints. A living light it is, with a hundred flickering candles, flames fanned by a hundred men making crosses.

Near daybreak, we pilgrims file past a row of portable icons and a table displaying relics, including an ornate silver case with St. Anna's foot. Spiro, Zach, Daniel, and I pay our respects quickly. Perhaps it's the promise of a meal or the realization that the service is over, finally over, that prompts our haste, but at any rate we rush our venerations and head for the exit.

From the church courtyard we watch the sun rise over the Holy Mountain and the stars fade away.

CHAPTER 24

WE NEVER HIKE ALONE

Sitting sidesaddle on one mule and pulling the other along with a rope, Father Daniel leads the way down the steep path to St. Anna Harbor. "Cowboy monk," Father Daniel jokes to us in English.

The cowboy monk wears a cassock the color of faded denim, black pants, brown sandals, and a wide straw hat with blue band and trim. Contemporary cowpoke accessories include sunglasses and a cell phone.

Reins in one hand, mobile phone in the other, Father Daniel takes a call. "Yes, half past nine," he confirms. "St. Anna. We're on our way."

On youthful legs and with the prospect of a fun fishing trip, Zach and Daniel bounce down the trail close behind the monk and his mules. Spiro and I follow more slowly, though thanks to liberal doses of the hiker's good friends—strong coffee and Vitamin I (ibuprofen)—we manage to keep the others in sight.

I am too tired to be tired. This happens to me after a particularly long and glorious hike; I feel buzzed rather than beat. Yesterday's hike to the top of the Holy Mountain was truly a challenge to body, mind, and spirit; and it was followed by a sleepless night—except for the catnaps guiltily taken in a cramped and uncomfortable prayer stall surely designed to *prevent* poor Christians like me from falling asleep. And yet for all of that hiking and praying, my eyes are clear, my heart beats strongly, and my feet are light upon the trail.

When Daniel and I, father and son, stood triumphant next to the cross atop Mt. Athos, I felt certain we had completed our journey. As easy as one-two-three. 1) Meet Spiro and Zach and hike to Skete St. Anna; 2) Visit with Father Daniel and pick up the icon; 3) Climb the Holy Mountain. Check, check, check. Mission accomplished.

However, as an experienced hiker like me should remember, a trail leading down a mountain makes for an altogether different experience than that same trail ascending it. And so it was with the Holy Mountain's ancient trail, which on descent provided us with views much different from those offered on our summit climb. As we hiked down through rocky ravines and gentle woods, we gazed upon the Aegean Sea, so blue-green, so beautiful, shimmering in the soft light.

And the light changed, too, as we hiked east in the morning and west in the afternoon. Sunrise and sunset views of Skete St. Anna—monks' quarters, church, and brick bell tower—were nearly as unalike as day and night. Furthermore, our trek up and down the Holy Mountain proved to be the end of a hike, but not the end of the journey, which continued when Father Daniel led us along the starlit trail back to Skete St. Anna.

A map is flat, and so is the floor of a church. Not so the geography of God, which is full of mountains.

St. Anna shines always. Whenever they are close together, Father Daniel and Daniel glow, as though the vigil lamp that lights the icon of St. Anna illuminates them as well. On his left wrist Daniel wears a thin prayer rope with tiny knots—a gift from Father Daniel.

"I know we should all be exhausted," I tell Spiro, "but just look at Zach and Daniel hiking along, and you're looking happy as can be, and I've got to tell you I'm feeling pretty good myself this morning."

"Well, it might be from the amazing hike," he suggests. "Or from what took place in the church." He pauses, and then a big smile spreads over his face. "Yannis, it was the power breakfast!"

We can't help laughing. Another odd breakfast in Byzantium.

As the new day dawned over Skete St. Anna, we followed the monks from the church to the refectory and sat down to breakfast. To our surprise, this was no after-church coffee-hour gathering, but a sit-down meal, a five-course feast beginning with bowlfuls of vegetable soup, followed by a main course of fish in a delicious sauce, which was accompanied by rice and string beans. *Pass the wine, please.*

Once we got over the idea of eating fish at five-thirty in the morning, Zach, Daniel, Spiro, and I enjoyed the meal nearly as much as the monks, who ate with great gusto, polishing their plates with slices of bread fresh from the oven. Looking at the joyful faces of the monks, we at last understood what Father Daniel meant when he said we would "celebrate" this night at Skete St. Anna.

A country in peril, the suffering of the Greek people, the machinations of world bankers—these are causes for alarm, not celebration. What the monks, and we, celebrated is a Lord who listens to our prayers, blesses us with His wisdom, and helps us survive—and sometimes even thrive—during our time on earth.

God provides.

Dessert, even.

I can't keep from laughing when I think of the grand finale to our morning meal. "Did you ever see a group of grown men take such pleasure in dessert?"

"The monks were so happy!" Spiro agrees. What was it anyway, caramel pudding? They were like little boys eating that sweet stuff."

As we continue our descent to the waterfront, our conversation moves from breakfast to a discussion of the day's itinerary. We understand one purpose of our journey to the harbor and why Father Daniel brought the extra mule:

supplies for his incense-making enterprise are stacked on the dock and must be carried back uphill to his cottage. Earlier in the morning the monk showed us the dust-caked, primitive machine that assists him in the manufacturing of incense—a business that supplements his icon-making income. I began sneezing ten feet away from this cottage industry as Spiro reflected on the sad state of the Greek economy that requires even a monk to work multiple jobs to make ends meet.

Of course the day's highlight is the fishing trip. Zach, and especially Daniel, are excited about fishing with Father Daniel, though both worry about going to sea in what they imagine to be a leaky tub or a boat similar to the one used by the apostles of Jesus to fish the Sea of Galilee. *What kind of a boat can a monk afford anyway?*

A third purpose for Father Daniel's trip to the harbor (and his need to arrive by nine-thirty) confuses me. "Spiro, you ever figure out what the deal is with Father Daniel and his boat?" I ask.

"Not really," Spiro answers. "Before he and the boys go fishing, he's taking the Abbot of St. Anna somewhere."

Where could he possibly be taking the Abbot? If the Abbot wishes to boat up-coast to one of the monasteries, he could take the ferry. Down-coast is the peninsula's wilderness shore and little habitation. Perhaps the Abbot wishes to land on a remote beach and scramble up the cliffs to visit a hermit.

We'll find out soon enough, I muse, as St. Anna Harbor comes into view. Storage buildings and a handful of dwellings cluster around the unpretentious little port. A long quay extends to a few boat slips and to the ferry landing.

It's going to be a hot day, we all agree, as Father Daniel ties the mules under the shade of a tree. The monk, joined by Daniel, removes rods and reels from a shed and the two are soon talking about fishing, apparently in a language that requires no translation.

When a cruise ship stops a mile offshore and the Abbot's mule train arrives at the harbor, I start to get the picture:

Father Daniel will take the Abbot to the cruise ship—perhaps to give the passengers a blessing or to conduct a short service.

We walk along the quay with Father Daniel. Zach and Daniel look relieved when they see the monk's boat—a well-kept craft of modest size, about an eighteen-footer I guess, white with a black Yamaha outboard and a Greek flag flying from the stern. A white canopy shades the cockpit and a single bench seat with room enough for the captain and two passengers.

"Nice!" Daniel calls out when Father Daniel steps aboard his boat.

A flash of light from the Abbot's mule train catches our eyes. We can barely see him in the gap between two animals. A second flash of light causes us to wonder: is he signaling us? After the third flash we detect its origin: the sun reflecting off a large silver cross affixed to the pack frame atop one of the animals.

As if on cue, the Abbot emerges from behind the mules and steps onto the quay. Carrying a small black attaché case, he walks slowly and deliberately toward us.

"This is right out of a spy movie," I whisper to Spiro.

"James Bond," he replies in a hushed tone.

It's easy to imagine this scene taking place on a remote and backward Greek island, far off the tourist track. The elusive Dimitri (*is the Greek a good guy or a bad guy?*), disguised as a monk and carrying a briefcase, walks along the quay of the quaint harbor. From the balcony of a little building on the hillside above the waterfront, a swarthy and suspicious-looking fellow smoking a cigarette watches the monk.

The boat's captain, also dressed like a monk, checks the fuel gauge and untangles the vessel's yellow and black Byzantine flag. The double-headed eagle on the flag looks left to the monk approaching with his attaché case and to the right, where a sleek ship waits a mile offshore.

A black cat skitters over the top of wooden crates with Russian lettering. With an angry cry, a gull swoops low over the harbor.

What's in that little black attaché case the monk holds so tightly? As he get closer to the little boat, he appears to have a kindly face—at least that part of it not covered by his silver beard. A thick cascade of silver hair is tied in a braid that rests on the back of his crisp black cassock.

"Yannis?" Spiro says softly. "The Abbot's got the relic."

My film fades out and reality fades in. "The what?"

"St. Anna's left foot."

The Abbot boards the boat, the outboard motor roars to life, and, with a wave at us, Father Daniel steers his boat out of the harbor.

The four of us sit in the shade near the mules and look out to sea at the waiting ship.

Although smaller than those luxury liners that resemble floating hotels, the handsome, modern ship is plenty big and much larger than the ferries and "Mt. Athos Tour Boats" that ply these waters. In comparison, Father Daniel's boat looks ever so tiny when it ties up on the ship's port side.

"Yannis, we were thinking this is like a movie scene," Spiro begins, "but while Father Daniel was getting his boat ready, he gave me the real story."

Zach and Daniel give Spiro their full attention. Unlike the monks who can take forever to tell a story about some obscure saint, Spiro is always short and to the point, and he shares his Spiro-tuality in a way that engages the young men.

The ship's passengers are good Greek Orthodox Christians from Cyprus, Spiro explains. The Cypriots very much want to venerate the relic of St. Anna. However, a ship of this size cannot land on Athos shores, and neither can half the passengers—the women aboard the vessel—so the ship had to anchor offshore from St. Anna Harbor. Because the faithful cannot come ashore to see St. Anna, the abbot of Skete St. Anna agreed to bring St. Anna to them. A water taxi is required to transport relic and abbot from shore to ship, which is where Father Daniel comes in: the right monk with the right boat for the job.

"A boat full of believers," Spiro concludes. "And they all get the chance to experience St. Anna."

A half-hour passes. We pace the waterfront. Zach and Daniel are particularly impatient for Father Daniel's return.

"Do you think everyone on that ship is…" Daniel starts to question.

"…are they *all* going to venerate St. Anna?" Zach finishes the question.

Clearly Daniel and Zach want to start fishing, and if every Cypriot on board pays his or her respects….

Spiro shrugs. "My guess is yes."

After another half-hour of waiting and pacing, we spot Father Daniel's boat returning to port, as the cruise ship, sounding a loud farewell with its foghorn, heads out to sea. We're joined dockside by a clean-shaven young man wearing dark sunglasses and a green military cap. He looks more like an off-duty soldier than the Abbot's assistant.

Father Daniel eases his boat into the slip, cuts the engine, and ties up. The boat has taken on cargo. The Abbot and his assistant unload three large cardboard boxes onto the dock. The boxes are sealed all around except for a thin letter-sized slot at the top. "NAMES FOR PRAYERS" reads the Greek lettering in capitals. By this I assume that the boxes contain slips of paper filled with the names of friends and family members of the Cypriot faithful. The monks of St. Anna will read the names and pray for these people.

Twenty years ago, when Spiro and I arrived at Skete St. Anna, we, too, made lists of names of friends and family members; and the old monk on duty prayed for all our loved ones by name. And he prayed for the Greek pilgrims, and the *hundreds of names* on their lists, I remember with a smile.

I hear the Abbot thanking Father Daniel and then talking further about something I don't comprehend. Father Daniel explains something to Spiro.

With a nod and a wide smile, Spiro turns to us. "Father Daniel says the Abbot is asking if we want to venerate St. Anna."

"Here?" I ask, gesturing to the dock.

"Yes, right here, right now," Spiro answers.

"Okay," I agree, struggling to keep the surprise out of my voice.

Speechless, Zach and Daniel manage to nod.

Seemingly in one quick practiced motion, the Abbot opens his attaché case, unfolds the red cloth wrapped around the silver display case holding the left foot of St. Anna, and beckons us forward. I wait to follow our Orthodox leader, but Spiro defers, insisting with a gesture that I make the first veneration.

I look at Daniel, his eyes wide in wonder. With a slight nod at my son, I surge forward toward the Abbot, making a quick sign of the cross and placing an even quicker kiss on the silver case. As I stand back, a pleasant warmth travels from my lips to my chest as if I have swallowed fine tsipuro.

With more deliberate veneration, Spiro pays his respects to St. Anna. Zach rapidly follows his godfather.

Daniel looks to Father Daniel. That glow they have when they look at one another, as warm as the Greek sun on this summer day, it's so difficult to describe.

I realize I have no words to describe this moment, and have the sudden fear I shall never find any, and in an instant my iPhone is in my hand and I'm touching the red start button and recording video. My son looms large on the screen of my phone and appears larger still when he approaches the modest-sized Abbot. With his big right hand, Daniel makes a big sign of the cross before St. Anna, plants a kiss on the silver case, then withdraws with a skip in his step and a slight smile on his face.

I pocket the iPhone and stand by my son.

The Abbot wraps the relic in red cloth and gently closes his attaché case. He looks a bit miffed and talks to Father Daniel. About us. I don't fully understand, but he seems to be saying, complaining really, about the Americans and St. Anna, about our *stavro* (cross) and our *filí* (kiss).

Spiro moves in to translate for me. "The Abbot is telling Father Daniel that he understands that we're Americans and do things quickly and might have a different way to venerate icons and relics." He adds in a voice just above a whisper: "Maybe he was expecting full prostrations or something, and thinks we should have shown more respect to St. Anna."

"It's all right," Father Daniel assures the Abbot in Greek I can understand. "The boy—his name is Daniel—and his father Yannis, they believe in St. Anna and know of her miracles."

Satisfied, the Abbot nods. "Good fishing," he wishes them, as he walks along the quay to his mule train.

Father Daniel motions Zach and Daniel to step aboard his boat and hands them fishing poles. Moments later, the monk starts the engine.

From the dock, Spiro and I wave at Zach and Daniel, who wave back as the monk pilots his craft out of the harbor. Just beyond the breakwater, Father Daniel hits the throttle. With the flags of Greece and the Byzantine Empire flying, the boat speeds along the coast, rounds a rocky point, and disappears from our sight.

It's time to go, but we don't want to leave the Holy Mountain. Spiro and I come to this conclusion as we ascend the steep trail back to Skete St. Anna—or more precisely the courtyard of St. Anna, where we've decided to relax in the shade while waiting for Father Daniel and the young fishermen to return.

Our reasons for needing to leave are highly practical ones. We've overstayed our pilgrim's permit by four days and fear we'll be chastised—or worse—when we pass through "customs" in Karyes and again in Ouranoupolis. And then there's The Crisis. Who knows how long the buses and trains will continue to run in a country without money?

But we love it here on this side of the Holy Mountain, and we want to extend our time with Father Daniel, with the young men in our charge, and with each other. Our time with Father Daniel in particular is flying by much too fast. Tonight, vespers for the last time in the monk's tiny chapel. Then our last dinner together—hopefully of fresh-caught fish.

I think of tomorrow morning when Spiro, Zach, Daniel, and I will gather our *pragmata*, our things, and say goodbye to Father Daniel. How hard that will be.

I see our four backpacks lined up in a row at the edge of the monk's little courtyard. And Daniel's backpack, with the Prophet Daniel inside. *He made me an icon.*

When I envision Father Daniel giving Daniel a big hug goodbye....

"There's no crying in baseball" and "There's no crying in hiking," that's what Daniel and I always say; and yet, when I think of Father Daniel hugging Daniel goodbye, a lump forms in my throat and tears come to my eyes.

Lord Jesus Christ,

Have mercy on me.

Quickly I wipe away the tears, and look behind me at Spiro. My friend looks lost in thought. Or prayer.

In silence, we hike a length of trail with no habitation in sight, and all that is visible is the summit of Mt. Athos high in the clouds above us and the Aegean far below us. At the end of our journey here we are, hikers six thousand miles away from home, by ourselves on the western slope of the Holy Mountain.

No, not all by ourselves.

Nearby is St. Nicholas, St. Constantine, and St. Anna. And St. Athanasius, St. Barbara, and St. Gabriel, too. And everywhere on the mountain is the Holy Mother Mary.

We can find the Holy Spirit in a prayer, at the top of a mountain, or at the center of an icon. The Holy Spirit leads us, and we follow, on the trail between earth and heaven. The saints, the holy men and women in the icons, are our trail companions, our friends who help us along the way. They show us that we never hike alone.

Glossary

Agia Saint (female)
Agios Saint (male)
Akathist hymn to Holy Mother
Acheiropoieta "made without hands"
archondaris guest-master
Avaton doctrine prohibiting women
avga eggs

diamonitirion visitor's permit

eremia desert, wilderness
Evlogeite Bless me

Geronta Older monks, "Elder"
gigantes beans
gynaika woman, wife

Halkidiki, region of Greece
Hieromonk, monk ordained to
     priesthood
horiatiki a village salad

Koinotita Holy Community
Igoumenos Abbot
Ikonographos Icon writer
Iconostasis, altar screen

kalderimi ancient stone pathway
Kalimera, Good morning
kalyva hut
karoulia pulleys, severe monks,
     hermits
kathismata settlements
keftedes Greek meatballs
kellia monks' cells
koulourakia, Greek cookies

Kyrie Eleison Lord have Mercy
Kyrios the Lord

loukoumi Turkish delight
lykeio Greek high school
metrio "medium" (sweetness for
     Greek coffee)
mezedes hors d'oeuvres
monopati footpath

ochi no

pastichio macaroni casserole
philotimo Greek male pride
prosforo altar bread
Protaton, church at Karyes
psomi bread
rasophoros "cassock wearer" (nov-
     ice monk)

stavro sign of the cross
semandron bar of wood struck by
     mallet as call to prayer
skete monastic community, not
     strictly a monastery

tipota nothing
thavma miracle
Theós God
Theotokos Mary, Mother of God
trapeza refectory

xenodoheio hotel

Yasou a greeting
Yi-ya grandmother

ABOUT THE AUTHOR

John McKinney is the author of 30 books about hiking, parklands and nature, including *The Hiker's Way* and *Hiking on the Edge: Dreams, Schemes, and 1600 Miles on the California Coastal Trail*, a lively narrative of his solo hike from Mexico to Oregon while pioneering the California Coastal Trail.

For 18 years, he wrote a weekly hiking column for the *Los Angeles Times*, and has hiked and enthusiastically described more then ten thousand miles of trail across California and around the U.S. John, aka The Trailmaster, has written more than a thousand articles and stories about hiking, as well as numerous regional bestselling guidebooks, and created the popular Trailmaster Pocket Guide Series.

A passionate advocate for hiking and our need to reconnect with nature, John McKinney shares his expertise on radio, TV, online, and as a public speaker. To learn more about the author and his work, visit TheTrailmaster.com.